Visual Journalism

Visual Journalism

A Guide for New Media Professionals

Christopher R. Harris

Middle Tennessee State University

Paul Martin Lester

California State University, Fullerton

Allyn and Bacon

Boston ■ London ■ Toronto ■ Sydney ■ Tokyo ■ Singapore

Series Editor: Molly Taylor
Editor in Chief, Social Science: Karen Hanson
Editorial Assistant: Michael Kish
Marketing Manager: Mandee Eckersley
Composition and Prepress Buyer: Linda Cox
Manufacturing Buyer: Julie McNeill
Cover Administrator: Linda Knowles
Editorial Production Administrator: Deborah Brown
Editorial-Production Service: Susan McNally
Design and Composition: Denise Hoffman

Copyright ©2002 by Allyn and Bacon
A Pearson Education Company
75 Arlington Street
Boston, Massachusetts 02116

Internet: www.ablongman.com

Library of Congress Cataloging-in-Publication Data

Harris, Christopher R.
    Visual journalism : a guide for new media professionals / Christopher R. Harris, Paul Martin Lester.
        p. cm.
    Includes bibliographical references and index.
    ISBN 0–205–32259–X
    1. Journalism—Data processing.   2. Reporters and reporting.
3. Photojournalism.   4. Newspaper layout and typography.   I. Lester, Paul Martin.

PN4784.ES H364 2001
070.4'3'0285—dc21   2001053377

Printed in the United States of America
10 9 8 7 6 5 4 3 2 1   RRDV   04 03 02 01

Credits: Page 1, Pashe, courtesy of Art Crimes (www.graffiti.org), artwork © 1995 by Hatch.D2R of San Diego; pages 4, 27, 117, 131, 152, 284, © Will Crocker, Will Crocker Studios; pages 2, 48, 49, 69, 71, 73, 74, 81, 95, 96, 97, 98, 99, 100, 102, 103, 110, 111, 112, 113, 115, 116, 118, 119, 120, 124, 126, 127, 128, 129, 234, 239, 267. 268, 270, 300, 321, ©Christopher R. Harris; page 88, © Christopher R. Harris, page from *Illustrated American*, 1890s; pages 13, 15, 206, 214, 316, courtesy of the Library of Congress; page 20, New York *World-Telegram*, courtesy of the Library of Congress; page 99, photo by Dorothea Lange, courtesy of the Library of Congress; page 208 (bottom), Currier & Ives, 1865, courtesy of the Library of Congress; page14, courtesy of Guanping Zheng; page 16, courtesy of the Photography Collection, Harry Ransom Humanities Research Center, The University of Texas, at Austin; page 19, courtesy of Archive Photos; page 21, courtesy of Nikon, USA Inc.; pages 31, 33, © Jean Trumbo; page 37, Courtesy of Carmichael Lynch Advertising, Minneapolis, MN; pages 46, 47, 209, AP/WideWorld Photo; page 60, Steven E. Frisching/Corbis Sygma; page 66, courtesy of Hasselblad, USA; page 67, courtesy of Leica Camera Inc., USA; page 76. courtesy of LumiQuest; page 80 from the U.S. Customs Travelers Information Web site (http://www.customs.ustreas.gov/top/sitemap.htm); page 114, ©Louis Sahuc. Courtesy of PhotoWorks Gallery, New Orleans; page 122, courtesy of Nikon USA, Inc. ; pages 167, 168, 169, 170, 172, 173, 181, 183, 186, 188, 189, 190, 191, 192, illustrations by Steve Masiclat; page 208 (top), courtesy of Edward R. Tufte, *The Visual Display of Quantitative Information* (Cheshire, Connecticut: Graphics Press, 1983); page 210, courtesy of The Weather Channel; pages 211, 212, 215, artwork courtesy of Litigation Visuals, Inc., Cleveland, Ohio (www.litvis.com); pages 226, 227, 228, courtesy of "The Silents Majority" On-line Journal of Silent Film; and pages 241, 244, 249, Tom Jimison, courtesy Dept. of Radio-TV/Photography, Middle Tennessee State University.

CONTENTS

Section One   Using Visuals

CHAPTER 1

Visual Journalism: Past, Present, and Future   11

by Paul Martin Lester

CHAPTER 2

A Visual Literacy Primer   27
by Paul Martin Lester

CHAPTER 3

An Ethical Approach   45
by Paul Martin Lester

Section Two   Using Photography

CHAPTER 4

Technical Considerations   63

by Christopher R. Harris

Color Plates 1–10

CHAPTER 5

Documentary Assignments   87
by Christopher R. Harris

CHAPTER 6

Manipulated Assignments 109
by Christopher R. Harris

Color Plates 11–21

Section Three   Using Words

CHAPTER 7

Reporting   135

by Steve Doig

CHAPTER 10

Graphic Design   179
by Jean Trumbo

CHAPTER 11

Informational Graphics   205
by Paul Martin Lester

Section Five   Using Motion

CHAPTER 12

Visual Motion   225

by Douglas Mitchell

Section Five   Using Computers

Internet Research   283

by Robert Spires

CHAPTER 16

Computer Applications   299

by Larry Burriss

Conclusion: Visual Journalism Awaits You   321

Bibliography   327

Index   335

PREFACE

Visual Journalism: A Guide for New Media Professionals is the first textbook to examine in depth the field of visual journalism. The discipline of visual journalism evolved through combining photojournalism with reporting, writing, and graphic design. The merging of these components has been the result of continual changes and advances in technology and interaction with other media.

Putting text and audio together including still and moving images, informational graphics, and graphic design for print and interactive multimedia presentations for the World Wide Web is the direction of mass communication. With new technology and practices, storytelling has never been so complex nor has offered the potential for such a visual and complete rendering of a story.

Visual Journalism is a textbook not only for journalism educators, professionals, and students but for anyone engaged in the field of mass communication. But, more important, it is a guide for creating and maximizing media convergence successfully. Practitioners in advertising, film, public relations, television, multimedia production will benefit from learning how to develop and produce visual messages that communicate as well as how to work with professionals within the field itself. It is vital that photojournalists know how to work with reporters and graphic designers, that reporters know how to communicate with photojournalists and designers, and that those who produce presentations for print and screen media know how to talk with photojournalists and reporters.

Features of the Book

- Each chapter and sidebar (called Visual Perspectives) written by recognized educators and professionals from various media
- A clear, concise writing style explaining visual reporting practices and procedures

- Over 100 photographs and illustrations that are both practical and aesthetic
- High quality typographical and graphic design presentation techniques
- Two 4-page, 4-color inserts which highlight the importance of the use of color, shape, and form to enhance visual messages.
- Ideas and assignments for further study at the end of each chapter
- A Website (http://commfaculty.fullerton.edu/lester/abacon) including syllabi, additional articles, assignments, web links, new images to be updated on a regular basis
- Detailed bibliography

Organization of the Book

Visual Journalism is divided into six sections that cover visual history, visual literacy, and ethics; photojournalism, reporting, and writing; typography and graphic design; informational graphics, audio and video production; and multimedia production and presentation. No other textbook combines this number of concepts and practices required for mass communications professionals.

The color plates in the inserts illustrate techniques explained in the text. Bringing attention to these particular images in the insert format gives the viewer an opportunity to study them on their own and to understand why they work. The first insert includes material from Chapters 1–5 and 11. The second insert includes material from Chapter 6.

Introduction: Digital and Convergence and the Age of the Visual Journalist

Visual Perspectives: Dirck Halstead, Senior White House Photographer, *Time*

Comment: Combining words and images honestly and respectfully is vital for telling stories—from a flyer to a presentation on the Web. Storytelling has in a sense become complicated but at the same time filled with potential and usefulness for a large range of viewers and readers.

Section One: Using Visuals

Comment: What are the historical links of the visual journalism field? Why is it necessary to have technical expertise? What are the most important skills in visual journalism? How do ethics impact the field?

Chapter 1: Visual Journalism: Past, Present, and Future
by Paul Martin Lester

>   **Visual Perspectives:** Paul Martin Lester

>   **Comment:** A tour of how visual journalism evolved from telling stories in caves to telling stories via virtual reality.

Chapter 2: **Visual Literacy** by Paul Martin Lester

>   **Visual Perspectives:** Gregory Veen, University of Washington

>   **Comment:** Color, form, depth, and movement are all visual cues that we utilize to perceive the world and that visual journalists utilize in various combinations to make presentations. How those cues can be used to educate, entertain, and persuade are detailed.

Chapter 3: **An Ethical Approach** by Paul Martin Lester

>   **Visual Perspectives:** Deni Elliott, Director, Practical Ethics Center, University of Montana and Paul Martin Lester

>   **Comment:** New media tools require ethical behavior.

Section Two: Using Photography

Comment: Review of production of still images including technical requirements and assignments that range from non-manipulated (documentary) to manipulated.

Chapter 4: **Technical Considerations** by Christopher R. Harris

>   **Visual Perspectives:** Sherri LaRose, Staff Photographer, Columbus (GA) Ledger-Enquirer

>   **Comment:** Instructions in using cameras, lenses, lighting, and film.

Chapter 5: **Documentary Assignments** by Christopher R. Harris

>   **Visual Perspectives:** James K. Colton, Former Director of Photography, *Newsweek*

>   **Comment:** News and picture story assignments, emphasizing documentary style.

Chapter 6: **Manipulated Assignments** by Christopher R. Harris

>   **Visual Perspectives:** Will Crocker, Photo Illustrator

>   **Comment:** Manipulation of people and pictures to create an aesthetic image.

Section Three: Using Words

Comment: A visual journalist needs to know how to find stories, interview subjects, and write a compelling narrative about a complex world in simple everyday language.

Chapter 7: **Reporting** by Steve Doig, Arizona State University
>   **Visual Perspectives:** Alan Schwarz, Senior Writer, *Baseball America*
>   Comment: How to focus on stories that will interest viewers and how to collect the facts.

Chapter 8: **Writing** by Gerald Grow, Florida A&M University
>   **Visual Perspectives:** Bryan Grigsby, Photo Editor,
>   *The Philadelphia Inquirer*
>   Comment: Telling a story with words that complement the images.

Section Four: Using Design

Comment: How to combine words and images for print and screen presentations and how to use informational graphics and other visual messages when images take precedence over words.

Chapter 9: **Typography** by Jean Trumbo, University of Missouri
>   **Visual Perspectives:** Julia Ptasznik, Editor, Visual Arts Trends
>   Comment: How typography enhances not only appearance but meaning and a reader's understanding.

Chapter 10: **Graphic Design** by Jean Trumbo, University of Missouri
>   **Visual Perspectives:** Brian Callahan, Web Graphic Designer,
>   Clocktower Books
>   Comment: Detailing designs through graphic principles of contrast, balance, unity, and rhythm.

Chapter 11: **Informational Graphics** by Paul Martin Lester
>   **Visual Perspectives:** Dennis Cripe, Franklin College
>   Comment: Infographics explain and illustrate complex data visually, thereby enhancing text and pictures.

Section Five: Using Motion

Comment: Media convergence: How to use motion, sound, and interactivity to tell stories.

Chapter 12: Visual Motion by Douglas Mitchell,
Middle Tennessee State University

> **Visual Perspectives:** Larry Burriss, Middle Tennessee State University
>
> **Comment:** How to control the medium of motion.

Chapter 13: Audio and Motion by Douglas Mitchell,
Middle Tennessee State University

> **Visual Perspectives:** Lisa Horan, Freelance Writer
>
> **Comment:** How to develop high quality sound to enhance and not distract from the message being communicated.

Chapter 14: Interactive Multimedia by Marc J. Barr,
Middle Tennessee State University

> **Visual Perspectives:** Paul Martin Lester
>
> **Comment:** How to produce interactive presentations that give users control over how they want to read a story.

Section Six: Using Computers

Comment: How to use the World Wide Web as a research tool from initial conception to final presentation.

Chapter 15: Internet Research by Robert Spires,
Middle Tennessee State University

> **Visual Perspectives:** Robert Spires
>
> **Comment:** How and why to use the World Wide Web for credible research.

Chapter 16: Computer Applications by Larry Burriss

> **Visual Perspectives:** Larry Burriss
>
> **Comment:** Proficiency in computer programs and media convergence is mandatory for visual journalists.

Conclusion: Visual Journalism Awaits You

    Visual Perspectives: Tom Kennedy, The Washington Post-Newsweek
Interactive Web site

    Comment: Applications of the disciplines that a visual journalist needs to
produce stories filled with content and compassion.

Acknowledgments

When I first met Chris Harris in New Orleans way back in 1976, I never thought he
would amount to much of anything. I was as green a photographer as you can get,
fresh out of journalism school at the University of Texas and he was a seasoned, but
slightly seedy-looking, internationally known photographer. Think of the photojournalist played by Dennis Hopper in *Apocalypse Now Redux*, but with a Southern
accent, and you know what I mean. Although a brilliant photographer (as you can
tell by his many wonderful photographs included in this book), he pushed himself
so hard that I thought he was on a fast track to being the subject—and not the
recorder—of a second-line New Orleans funeral march. We lost track of each other
for several years. But amazingly we both ended up in academia. What a country!
And then Chris came to me with this wacky idea: Let's write a textbook about what
we know deep in our bones is absolutely vital to teach in this age of new media convergence—visual journalism. And so, with the help of many, many friends and
strangers, here it is in your hands.

    I'd like to thank all the folks at Allyn & Bacon, the reviewers who believed
early on that this book was necessary, all of the collaborators on chapters and side-
bars, and my friends and family in such diverse places as California, Hawaii, Montana, and Texas—Cindy, Coral, and Tony, Tom and Evie, Glenn, Mike, and Johnny,
and my mom and family. And as always, my heart always sings because of Denison
and Allison—the two suns in my life.

    And one more quick thing: working with Chris in any capacity is a joy and a
life-long learning experience. Chris—let's do this again.

Paul Martin Lester
lester@fullerton.edu

After twenty-five years as a photojournalist I returned to university to get an advanced degree in order to teach photojournalism on the college level. Doing research for my thesis, which involved ethics and law, I came across the name of an
old friend, and fellow photographer. But, instead of articles about him, these were

articles authored *by* him. They were about research into stereotypes and ethics, and the new concept of Visual Communication. They had a bright new approach to the emerging new media and the concerns they created. They were academic, yet written for someone to read. And they were important to me. We soon made contact, and renewed our friendship brought about from working in the same town, covering the same news subjects. Paul Lester, the "shooter" for the New Orleans *Times-Picayune* newspaper was an academic of the first order. He was the leading author of new and bold initiatives in the staid old profession of journalism. And he let me come along on one of the finest experiences of my life. He became my author mentor. This book is about Paul. It is about thoughts of applying oneself to the many channels of visual communication that have come about in this modern age. Not since the invention of movable type, followed several hundred years later by the ability to reproduce photographs utilizing the halftone, has such a quantum leap in visual communication come about. I take great pride in my personal and working relationship with Paul Lester; it's not often we can stand with those who have led the awareness of new communication methods. And he has been kind to this neophyte. Paul, Les, yes even Carlos, these are all names I know him by . . . but I often just resort to an old New Orleans name and phrase that sums up my feelings. Bro, you're 'da best!!

The folks at Allyn & Bacon have worked their miracles massaging our words through wonderful copyediting, designing an easy to read layout, and searching out the marketing information to make this whole endeavor work. Kudos to all. But it is to Karon Bowers, my initial editor, and editor Molly Taylor to whom I owe the most thanks. In spite of harried e-mails from me, often seeking obscure information, or seeking some kind of reassurance, they have kept a cheerful attitude. They have done everything possible to lessen the burden felt by this novice textbook author. They have always been gracious, and thoroughly professional. I have no doubt that we worked with the "A" team.

While the above mentioned guided this book to its fruition, there are countless others that helped in other ways. The guidance provided by Julian Feibelman, along with the support and assistance of Bob Spires, Doug Mitchell, Marc Barr, and Larry Burriss from Middle Tennessee State University, allowed me to concentrate on what was important to me, writing and researching. Our thanks go to reviewers: Robert Heller, University of Tennessee, Knoxville; Andrew Mendelson, Southern Illinois University, Edwardsville; C. Zoe Smith, Missouri School of Journalism; and Susan Zavoina, University of North Texas. It was John Vivian who unselfishly introduced me to Karon Bowers, and thus started this whole process. Thanks my friends...I hope I can some day be as important to you. Louis and Will, thanks for letting me show your fine work. And Deni, thanks for making Carlos so happy. My family has always been there for me. To Anne, I dedicate this book to Ed's memory. He always supported my desire to be a photographer, as did you. My eternal thanks for letting me get into this always exciting field. To my wife and son, Kathy and Stephen, thanks for letting me talk, often to myself, about the work—and not reporting me to the authorities. And thanks for giving me the time to work on this project. Yes, I owe you big-time.

Lester, you are a delight to work with . . . and to have as a friend. Hey, I've got an idea . . .

Christopher R. Harris
crharris@mtsu.edu

Visual Journalism

Digital Convergence and the Age of the Visual Journalist

We live in a visually intensive society. Bombarded daily by an unrelenting stream of visual stimulation from all manner of media, we seek understanding from pictures when we are largely taught to understand only words. But we see mediated images (those pictures that come from print and screen: motion pictures, television, and computer displays) more than we read words. Some have warned that if the trend continues, civilization will regress to illiteracy and lawlessness. More optimistic observers predict that technological advances will merge words and pictures in new ways that will create innovative educational, entertainment, and commercial possibilities.

Most people, it is estimated, see about five thousand mediated messages every day. For example:

Graffiti-splattered billboards advertise the next roadside attractions: *Folk art turns commercial.*

A modern-day example of graffiti.

Jump-cut editing techniques have invaded music videos, adding pictures to Dick Clark's music appreciation rating: *"I couldn't understand the lyrics. I really can't dance to it. But the pictures were awesome. I give it a 95."*

Snapshot amateurs with still and video cameras must use images to legitimize and confirm their vacations: *Do Kodak "Picture Spots" count as a real experience?*

A tourist confronts a "Kodak moment" in front of a mansion in South Louisiana.

Christopher R. Harris

Television news producers anxiously await video images shot by an amateur videographer of a police beating that would later burn down a city: *Would we have known about the Rodney King beating if a video recording never existed?*

Colorful pictures, graphic elements, charts, and maps jam newspaper front pages in an effort to attract more readers: *Shouldn't we call them "viewers"?*

Computers are cited as the reason for the image explosion. Computers, the software programs that run them, and the publishing networks that present them offer quick and inexpensive remedies for visual artists.

Introduction

Nevertheless, for hundreds of years technology has kept words and pictures separate and unequal. Before Johannes Gutenberg's printing press, less than 10 percent of the people could read. Seventy years after his invention, 80 percent of the entire population of Europe could read. Seventy years after Louis Daguerre's announcement of the first practical photographic process, almost everyone had a Kodak camera and could see pictures published in their local newspapers. But producers of images did not develop a visual grammar in the same way as producers of words did after Gutenberg. People learned to read words but were never taught how to read pictures.

Consequently, writers, photographers, and graphic designers have been kept apart by separate production facilities, job descriptions, educational backgrounds, and working class biases. Editors have traditionally excluded photojournalists from their decisions about story selection, completion, and display, and newspaper photojournalists have unwittingly contributed to their own exclusion from those decisions by working in separate spaces—studios and darkrooms—that isolate them from the rest of the newsroom. Although this "photographers' club" has been comforting as a special place where equally talented colleagues gather, such isolation deepens the rift between word and image producers.

Computers are changing everything and the reason is simple—only a photographer can use a photographic enlarger. Everyone involved with word, picture, and design production can use a computer. Darkrooms are now lightrooms as computers invade newsrooms. Innovative technology and thinking cause the merger between words and images and the people who produce them.

A New Role for Journalism— the Visual Journalist

As words and pictures become further merged, the combined role of writer, photographer, infographics creator, researcher, and graphic designer demands a new job description—the visual journalist. The ease with which reporters, photographers, and graphic artists can work more closely together calls for a new definition and approach.

Visual reporting calls for a new mindset and a new mission. Yale University's William Zinsser once reminded editors that they were not in the news business or even the information business. They were, he said, in the meaning business. Visual reporting is the marriage of words, images, and designs to convey information. The mission of the visual journalist is to tell readers what the information means.

A conceptual digital illustration of the skills involved in problem solving. (See CP-1.)

Will Crocker

In this new technological age when it is easier and faster to produce and distribute words and images than ever before in the history of communications, a journalist cannot afford to know only how to report, write, and edit words, to know only how to find, take, and crop a picture, or to know only how to create a layout for print and screen media. Today's visual journalists understand that words and pictures form an equal partnership that can deliver the meaning of complex issues to readers and viewers.

Consequently, journalists must be part of a team. Even before the reporting begins, visual journalists and graphic designers must be involved in discussions about how a story might be covered. In most cases, they should be involved in the reporting and be encouraged to ask questions. Reporters, on the other hand, must become visually astute and should be encouraged to collect graphic information at an assignment.

Journalists must not only know how to gather information and write stories and cutlines, but they must also have the confidence to work with pictures and layouts. Consequently, every journalism graduate must know the fundamentals of visual literacy—how to sense, select, and perceive a visual message—*and* how to work a camera, a computer and software, how to research a database, how to create informational graphics, how to combine words with stories, and how to make layouts and designs for print and screen media.

Journalism is at a crossroads in its history just as in other eras when new tools created new methods that inspired new uses for the medium. We are all fortunate to be able to witness the rise of a new form of communication in which words, both written and heard, and pictures, both still and moving, combine to make interactive multimedia presentations that can access informational links on a global scale. But the journalism profession simply cannot afford, in its preparation or practice, to be lured into this pixelated reality.

For although the tools change and are certainly needed, the ability to notice, capture, and use meaningful moments with words, pictures, and designs is the fundamental concern of journalists for this century.

This textbook will start you on a journey toward communicating successfully with words *and* images. An intelligent and thoughtful synthesis of the two media may help encourage people to read more, see more, and become more informed citizens. Such are the challenge and the hope of visual journalism.

IDEAS FOR FURTHER STUDY

- Take pictures of wall murals and graffiti. Discuss the art versus social concerns argument. Is graffiti art or vandalism? Why would someone classify it one way or the other?

- Imagine a future in which a reporter must be responsible for every visual within a presentation. Is that possible? Is that desired?

- Spend a day in a newsroom and observe how photographers and reporters interact. Do you notice close working relationships, or do photographers remain in their own secluded areas?

- When visiting a newsroom, talk with an "old-timer" to find out how the profession has changed.

- How were you taught to appreciate visual messages? Do you think that education has changed? Are educators more sensitive to visual literacy issues?

Revisiting the Death of Photojournalism

by Dirck Halstead, Senior White House Photographer, *Time* Magazine

A few weeks ago, I received an e-mail from a young photojournalist. She was distressed about some of the columns and editorials that we have written in the past months about "the death of photojournalism."

The same bug that has drawn blood from us all had bitten her—the desire to tell stories visually. She had graduated from journalism school, learned her basic photography, and was dismayed to see us here on The Digital Journalist saying that her dreams could not be fulfilled.

I have heard this question raised countless times by audiences I have spoken to in the past few years. I say in my lectures that "photojournalism *as we know it* is dead." What I mean is that a generation of photographers who grew up in the days when *Life* and *Look* were still publishing weekly editions aspired to be part of a culture that would allow them to follow the stories of the day to the far-flung regions of the world, their expenses paid by a huge publication that would then help them to display their images over page after page of editorial space. Someone recently said that I came "from the Wild West of photojournalism," and they were right. I worked in a time when shooters like David Douglas Duncan, W. Eugene Smith, Ralph Morse, and Douglas Kirkland were roaming the visual terrain. Budgets were not a concern. All that mattered was that the photojournalist came back with meaningful and wonderful images.

We still have photographers of this incredible talent working today. David and Peter Turnley, David Hume Kennerly, Ken Jarecke, Sebastiao Salgado, Christopher Morris, James Nachtwey, Tony Suau, and David Brauchli are just a few. But any one of them would readily tell you that the publishing world they work in now is a far cry from the one they started in. Space constraints, budget constraints, and the rise of celebrity journalism have all contributed to a very difficult work arena.

At the entry level of photojournalism, there are far more photographers pursuing fewer jobs than ever before. The result is that salaries and fees are held at bare subsistence levels. The picture gets gloomier as the would-be photojournalist tries to climb to the next level. Those lucky few that hold full-time jobs in photojournalism are clinging to them. Younger photographers are being shuttled from publication to publication without any appreciable increase in earning power. It is the time of the eternal intern.

On the higher level of magazine photojournalism, powerful forces have been arrayed against the photographer. Editorial departments no longer have final say over budgets, but must bend to the will of the publishers and lawyers. Rights grabs are commonplace. Fear and dissatisfaction stalks the halls of formerly proud editorial institutions.

So, there is the case for "the end of photojournalism as we know it." But that is only the

Dirck Halstead is the creator of The Digital Journalist website (www.digitaljournalist.org).

headline of the story. Changes are occurring at blinding speed, and these changes far outshine these negative developments. With the arrival of the World Wide Web, we are only beginning to comprehend the implications for visual storytellers. Empowerment is at hand, and it will allow the photojournalist to transcend the current marketplace, whether it is in newspapers, magazines, or even television networks.

The history of photojournalism is a remarkably short story. If we consider Matthew Brady the first "photojournalist," photojournalism has only been around for some 140 years. It is a short time indeed when compared to art, poetry, music, and writing. If you talk about "modern" photojournalism, you have to start with Dr. Erich Solomon in the 1930s and his invention of the Ermanox. The glory days of *Life*, spanning only some forty-five years,

are long gone. If you think in terms of visual storytellers, however, you go back to the stone age and the artists who drew images on the walls of caves. The tradition has been around far longer than we can ascribe to modern means of picture capturing.

When I say photojournalism is dead, I am talking only about capturing a single image on a nitrate film plane, for publication in mass media. Visual stories will soon be told primarily through moving images and sound on both television and the Web, which will increasingly replace printed media. The role of the storyteller who can capture the events and people of our time, and place them in perspective for our history, however, will only be enhanced.

Happy New Millennium! ∎

Using Visuals

The three chapters in this section describe the fundamental building blocks that every visual journalist should know. The first chapter discusses the historical developments that have led to the concept of visual journalism. The second chapter explains how light affects the eye and brain and how to analyze visual messages that you produce and see within print and screen media. The third chapter identifies the chief ethical concerns for all visual journalists. With an understanding of history, visual literacy, and ethics you will be able to produce more meaningful messages because you will be sensitive to the work that has gone on before, the work that you currently witness, and the work that is in progress for the future.

C H A P T E R 1

Visual Journalism
Past, Present, and Future

by Paul Martin Lester

Visual journalism, or the telling of stories with words, pictures, and designs, has evolved from the individual histories of typography, graphic design, informational graphics, photojournalism, motion pictures, television, and computers coming together within various print and screen media.

Visual Journalism: 30,000 B.C.E.–0

It may be hard to imagine, but the roots of visual journalism begin with prehistoric cave drawings and carvings, which suggests that even the earliest humans needed to communicate ideas beyond their immediate tribes.

Although researchers are not certain about what motivated the drawings, it was surely more than just making caves more hospitable. Some have argued that rock carvings and paintings might have given the artists a sense of power over the animals they wanted to slaughter. The eloquent images are important to study because they are our earliest links to the fields of graphic design and perhaps informational graphics and motion pictures. When studied closely, cave paintings are a collection of words in the form of ideographs, or abstract concepts and ideas rendered usually as simple lines, and images as pictographs, or much more highly detailed representations of actually viewed objects and animals. From the time humans first tried to communicate in a medium beyond their own bodies, words and pictures shared the same space. These efforts mark the beginning of graphic design.

These early artists even had a concept of design. Ideographs and pictographs were carefully rendered on the dark, fire-lit walls so as not to overlap each other. The size of the animals was usually governed by the available space on the walls. If a blank space were open, an artist would be free to fill it with a picture. And, remarkably, as early humans visited these caves for thousands of years, the design principle of not overlapping previous images was largely obeyed.

Another explanation for the purpose of cave pictures may lie within the field of informational graphics. Animals might have been drawn in exquisite detail as a guide for others to study, just like a modern-day diagram. In some of the vital areas of the drawn beasts chips in the rock have been found, indicating that after a painting was finished others in the cave used the picture to practice their spear-throwing techniques.

The history of moving images may also reach back to early cave drawings. It has been discovered in recently found caves that, when illuminated with a lighted torch, pictures of overlapping antlers on several animals appear to move as if they were running. Perhaps these early cave artists were simulating motion with their designs.

Writing during this era advanced from line drawing ideograph images on cave walls to an organized system of characters because of the Sumerians, one of the first civilizations to cease a nomadic lifestyle and live in one place. With their complicated and growing city, in an area now known as Iraq, the Sumerians invented a writing style (3500 B.C.E.) that included numbers and words in order to record business transactions and significant events. Over hundreds of years Sumerian writing eventually became more and more symbolic in order to reduce the number of individual pictures that had to be written. Cuneiform or wedge-shaped writing was invented about 2800 B.C.E. and aided by a stylus. The scribe would press the pen into soft clay to make the writing. When it hardened, there was a permanent record.

The Phoenicians revolutionized writing and thus typography around 2000 B.C.E. by inventing a symbol system with only twenty-two characters. Each picture or word in the alphabet corresponded to a sound a person made when speaking. Using simple line drawings to convert sounds to pictures proved to be a great boon for the Phoenicians, who traded with diverse clients who spoke several different languages and used varied and complex writing systems. Over hundreds of years,

*Fragment of Assyrian kinglist
with cuneiform inscription.*

mostly Western countries and especially the Greeks adopted the Phoenician system
of writing and gradually transformed the alphabet into one that can be recognized
today. By this time writing, for most cultures, had lost its pictographic roots and
had became completely ideographic. As with the words used in this textbook, the
lines formed to make the individual letters have no pictorial equivalent but are
instead highly symbolic line drawings representing complex concepts.

Visual Journalism: 1–1000 C.E.

The Chinese invented paper around the year 105. By 325 C.E. they were stitching the
papers together and binding them within leather covers to form books. Chinese,
Japanese, Korean, and Greek, Italian, and other European scribes used this book
format to combine words and colorful and illustrative pictures in designs. Words,
however, dominated most pages, since images were expensive to create. By 950 C.E.
scriptoriums in Europe, mostly financed and run by religious organizations,
became common.

  The history of photography may trace to this era when, in 1000 C.E., the
scientist Alhazen first described viewing a solar eclipse from inside a tent by using
the principle of the *camera obscura*. This "dark chamber" was much later employed
by those who invented photography when they recorded images from nature with
light-sensitive emulsion.

Visual Journalism: 1001–1500

The Chinese advanced the field of informational graphics with detailed maps about 1050, while in the area of typography and graphic design a major development occurred that would prove to be one of the most important advances in the field of communication—printing with replaceable type.

Although the Koreans had invented printing in about 1397 by creating clay versions of their characters, dipping them in ink, and transferring them to paper, it was not a practical system because of the enormous number of characters used for their writing. It was far easier to simply write the characters by hand. Consequently, calligraphy in Asian cultures is an established and enormously respected art form. But European languages with their simple alphabet were perfect for some type of removable letter printing system.

And so a German, Johannes Gutenberg, invented the first printing press that employed interchangeable metal typefaces (1455). His Bible was a beautiful and elegant composition of words and pictures. He left space for enlarged graphic letters to begin a passage and at the bottom of many pages so that artists could draw finely detailed and colorful letters and pictures that corresponded to the stories told in words.

By the end of the fifteenth century there were more than one thousand printers in Europe alone using the press that Gutenberg invented. The birth of literacy, humanism, state over religious power, and the decline of the importance of oral communication were key issues of this era sparked by the invention of the printing press.

Visual Journalism: 1501–1800

During this time in the history of visual journalism typeface artists invented additional designs that aided the readability and legibility of the text printed in all manner of media—books, newspapers, pamphlets, and posters. Graphic designers also combined words and images on the pages. Such type designers as Robert Granjon (1557), William Caslon (1722), John Baskerville (1750), and Giambattista Bodoni

Chinese lettering for visual journalism.

视 像 新 闻 学

Mural in the Library of Congress, Jefferson Building, depicting a man working a press and Gutenberg and another craftsman examining a proof.

(1768) created elegant typefaces still used today. The American printer Benjamin Franklin used his printing press in Philadelphia (1768) to further the cause of the American Revolution against British rule. Aloys Senefelder invented lithography (1796), which allowed the printing of simple pictures during the same press run as text. No longer did a graphic designer have to leave open space in some copy for another artist to fill in a picture. With lithography the designer had more control. The Rosetta Stone, originally a tablet created in 196 B.C.E. to commemorate the arrival of Ptolemy V in Egypt in hieroglyphic and Greek languages, was deciphered by Jean-François Champollion (1799). His translation resulted in greatly furthering the understanding of the Egyptian peoples' early history and culture because researchers could read their words.

The fields of informational graphics and computers were also advanced during this time. Edmund Halley, best known for his discovery of a comet that visits the Earth about once every seventy-six years, created the first published weather map in 1686, using temperature and wind data superimposed on a map of England. The British economist William Playfair (1786) made a vital advance in the field of informational graphics when he invented the line and bar charts. Blaise Pascal advanced computer technology when he invented the first adding machine (1642) that could find answers to addition and subtraction problems using mechanical gears.

Visual Journalism: 1801-1850

The boldface type attribute (1803) and the square serif typeface family (1815) along with the first steam-powered printing press (1828) with a much improved Richard Hoe press (1847) were invented during this time to contribute to advertising displays in newspapers designed to draw attention to themselves rather than to be aesthetically pleasing. Color lithography (1837) further improved printing methods for advertisements by easily combining words and now colored pictures for posters.

The field of informational graphics was furthered by the publication in the London newspaper *The Times* of one of the first diagrams. The infographic showed the floor plan of a house where a murder had taken place (1806). When the telegraph was invented (1848), weather information superimposed on maps could be drawn more quickly and accurately and came into popular use.

In 1820 Thomas de Colmar introduced his Arithometer, the first commercially successful calculator. More importantly, Charles Babbage of London is credited with inventing the world's first computer (1833), though lacking proper funding he could take his machine only to the design stage.

The first half of the nineteenth century is best known for advances in photography. In 1826 Joseph Niépce, a French inventor, created the first photograph, which can still be seen today. Soon another French inventor, Louis Daguerre, teamed up with Niépce and his son to invent the first practical and popular photographic process, modestly named the daguerreotype (1839). Coincidentally, the

Joseph Nicephéore Niépce,
View from My Window at Gras.
The first photograph. 1826.

same year a British doctor, Henry Fox Talbot, announced his independently discovered process, the calotype, which introduced the modern photographic concept of the negative and positive image.

Visual Journalism: 1851–1900

An English physician, Frederick Archer, published his unique process (1851) using wet collodian as a base for a photographic emulsion on a glass plate. Archer's discovery soon replaced the awkward daguerreotype and fuzzy calotype processes for serious photographers around the world. England's Queen Victoria's Crystal Palace exhibition (1851) heralded (among other technologies) the fields of informational graphics and photography, with weather maps and photographic exhibits for the entire world to admire. Informational graphics improved during the latter half of the century: British physician Robert Snow's data map showed the source of a cholera breakout in London (1854), Charles Minard's map displayed the march and deadly retreat of Napoleon's forces to Moscow (1869), and Stephen Horgan's first regular weather map appeared in New York's *Daily Graphic* (1879). Photography also improved greatly during this time, with stylistic leaps from such photographic artists as Oscar Rejlander (1857); Gaspard Felix "Nadar" Tournachon (1860); Mathew Brady, renowned for his American Civil War photographs (1864); Timothy O'Sullivan (1873); and Jacob Riis, whose photographs documented New York tenement slums (1890).

There were also important technical improvements to photography, with the color slide process of Scottish physicist James Clerk Maxwell (1861), the gelatin-bromide dry plate photographic process (1871) of Dr. Richard Maddox that gave George Eastman the means to invent the Kodak amateur camera (1888), and the first halftone printing process for photographs by Stephen Horgan of the *Daily Graphic* newspaper (1880).

Graphic design made gains by Hoe's improved printing press (1868), postcards were invented (1869), Frederick Ives improved on Horgan's halftone process (1885), and the art nouveau movement (1890) by artists such as Henri de Toulouse-Lautrec showed how words and pictures could be combined for advertising purposes in aesthetically pleasing ways.

This era also marks the invention of the motion picture and television media. With the gelatin dry plate photographic process and Eastman's use of it in roll film cameras, American Thomas Edison invented the first motion picture camera he named the Kinetograph (1891). The French brothers Auguste and Louis Lumiére used their own improvement on Edison's device to project a film before an audience in 1895, marking the birth of modern motion pictures. Meanwhile, Paul Nipkow advocated a mechanical television process (1884) ahead of its time, while Guglielmo Marconi successfully demonstrated that voices could be transmitted over part of the electromagnetic spectrum now known as radio waves (1899). Using radio waves to send pictures became the basis for the television medium.

In the history of computers, this time period saw Herman Hollerith, an American inventor, sell his data punch computer to the U.S. government to process the growing census data (1890). His machine proved to owners of large banks and insurance companies that it was a valuable business tool.

Visual Journalism: 1901–1950

There were major contributions in all the areas of visual journalism during the first half of the twentieth century. In typography and graphic design the art movements of Dada (1916), De Stijl (1917), Bauhaus (1919), and art deco (1925) further strengthened the aesthetic link between words and pictures in all printed media. And informational graphics became seen not simply as a way to explain the weather, but an important means for telling complicated stories involving both world wars (1917 and 1941).

Photography advanced both technically and aesthetically. Autochrome color film from the Lumière brothers (1903), the small hand-held Leica camera (1924), high quality color slide film (1935) and amateur color print film (1942) from the Kodak Company, and the inventions of holography (1947) and instant photography from Edwin Land (1948) were introduced. Photography advanced aesthetically through the child labor photographs of Lewis Hine (1911), the art photography and writings of Alfred Steiglitz (1930), the documentary photography of Farm Security Administration photographers (1935) and *Life* (1936) and *Look* (1937) magazines, and the foundings of the first photojournalism major at the University of Missouri (1942) and the National Press Photographers Association (1945).

During this era the motion picture medium introduced the first feature-length blockbuster, D.W. Griffith's *The Birth of a Nation* (1915), formed United Artists (1919) and MGM (1924) movie studios, established the Academy Awards (1929), developed sound (1929) and wide screens (1930), and produced such classics as *Frankenstein* (1931), *The Wizard of Oz* (1939), *Citizen Kane* (1941), *Bambi* (1942), and *Casablanca* (1943).

Television gained with advances in the vacuum tube that allowed sound (1906), experiments by high school inventor Philo Farnsworth that allowed sound and pictures (1927), and the forming of the radio networks—NBC (1926), CBS

Scene from Citizen Kane.

(1927), and ABC (1943) to help with programming. The New York World's Fair (1939) organizers introduced most of the public to the invention of television by showing baseball's World Series (1949). In the computer field, IBM (1924) emerged from Hollerith's earlier computer company, and the ENIAC computer (1946) and the UNIVAC computer (1950) were developed, along with the transistor (1948), which paved the way for smaller computers.

Visual Journalism: 1951–1983

In this last era before the introduction of the low-cost, desktop computer, many advances in technology and style were recorded. As in earlier times, the graphic design field was enhanced by the introduction of several artistic movements. Most notably, the pop art (1956), optical art (1965), and punk art (1978) movements drastically changed the way mass communications content was delivered for commercial, entertainment, and editorial uses. For newspaper designers, modular design (1966), a variation of the grid pattern influenced from the earlier De Stijl art movement, served to modernize front-page formats.

Informational graphics improved with the launching of the TIROS-1 weather satellite (1960), the work of infographics designer Nigel Holmes (1978), and the introduction of *USA Today* (1982), which featured informational graphics on its front page sections and a much admired and copied national weather map.

Crowds from the 1939 World's Fair surround the first exhibit of television at the RCA exhibit.

Photographers such as W. Eugene Smith (1951), Henri Cartier-Bresson (1952), Edward Steichen (1955), Robert Frank (1959), and Mary Ellen Mark (1979) served photojournalism well. Rick Smolan's first *Day in the Life* books started with Australia (1981) to mark a resurgence of photojournalism. Conversely, however, *National Geographic* magazine published a cover image of Egyptian pyramids (1982) that were manipulated using a computer. The controversy that followed introduced many to the ethical issue of computer manipulation and the dangers to a publication's credibility. The first digital camera, the Mavica, from the Sony Corporation (1981) introduced photographers to the concept of the filmless, computer-based camera.

The motion picture and television industries began competing in earnest for the attention of the public. This rivalry continues to this day. Movie moguls used a variety of gimmicks to attract audiences—screens grew larger with CinemaScope (1953), three-dimensional films were introduced (1954), drive-in shows became popular (1955), and multiplexes at suburban locations were begun (1975).

Television after World War II enjoyed an immediate "golden age" with high-quality programming and increased viewership. Cable, as a way to transmit programs without the need of large broadcast networks, also got its start (1952). Videotape (1956) allowed the taping of news programs for West Coast audiences and special effects for sports presentations. Small portable cameras became popular (1965) while home video equipment (1976) and video rentals of movies (1979) began. But this was also a time for controversies in the television industry, with

Senator Joseph McCarthy's hunt for Communists (1954), quiz show scandals (1958), and concerns about television violence (1975).

The computer field saw many important events during this period. The U.S. government began its ARPANET computer communications network (1969) that would become known as the Internet. Video games started with Atari's *Pong* (1972) and expanded into a worldwide entertainment business. Computer equipment, always quite large, difficult to use, and enormously expensive, was now designed for the average person, with such machines as the Altair (1975), the first personal computer, the Apple II (1977), and the IBM PC (1981).

Visual Journalism: 1984 and Beyond

It was a low-cost personal computer, the Macintosh (1984), that began to break down the walls between the various media. The desktop computer allowed typographical designers to create their own typefaces and begin a controversial era of typeface design known as garbage or grunge fonts (1992) in which typography was to be seen, but not necessarily read. The new wave (1986) and hip-hop (1992) graphic design movements were enhanced by the ease of computer software operations. With the success of *USA Today* and the press restrictions during the Gulf War (1991), informational graphics created with a desktop computer became a standard part of the telling of stories in print and on television. Photojournalists virtually quit using their darkrooms to process film and to make prints because newspaper publishers invested in still video (1984) and still digital (1993) cameras in which traditional film was replaced by images recorded on disks. Television and motion picture production, especially in the area of special effects following the success of the computer-generated images of the 1989 film *The Abyss,* were greatly aided by the computer. And finally, the World Wide Web (1992) transformed the Internet into a graphical showcase filled with text, audio, and colorful still and moving images with interactive hypertext links to global sources of information, making it

The Nikon 990 still digital camera.

Ideas for Further Study

accessible to anyone with the equipment and software and a basic understanding of the medium.

Computer processing took another giant step forward when Intel scientists announced completion of a mainframe computer that could perform one trillion calculations in a second (1996). The original ENIAC computer (1946), largely used by the U.S. government to calculate missile trajectories, could process at a snail's pace of only five thousand calculations a second. In a wonderful example of unintentional irony the government announced that the new family of supercomputers would be used to simulate on computer monitors DNA permutations and nuclear explosions.

CONCLUSION

The culmination of the history of visual journalism is the convergence of technical, operational, and social functions for mass communications purposes. Words and pictures can now be combined in traditional and interactive formats with extraordinary ease using the hardware and software breakthroughs of computer technology. Consequently, photojournalists, writers, and graphic designers who used to be separated from each other must now learn to work together as smoothly as the computers available to them. It is clear that traditional journalists must become visual journalists or they simply won't be able to keep up with the changes all around them.

IDEAS FOR FURTHER STUDY

- Imagine seeing a particular visual medium for the first time. How would you respond to it? How would you describe it to another person who hadn't seen it?

- Rent an early (pre-1920) motion picture. Why is the pace so different from today's movies? Have movies changed or have people?

- Take a look at an early (1930s-era) newspaper front page and compare it with a modern front page. What are the similarities and the differences?

- Pick any specific medium. Write out the significant events including the year in a table format. What social event or trend was happening at each time period? How do you think world events influence technical and aesthetic advances?

Virtual Photojournalism—A Fictional Look at a Possible Future

by Paul Martin Lester

It's thirty minutes before Dr. Mark Premack's advanced photojournalism class. Premack, a tenured professor at a California liberal arts commuter school with about twenty-five thousand students, walks through what was once the photographic darkroom. It is now a computer lab.

As he makes his daily inspection of the computer facilities, he thinks about the advances and changes that have occurred in the darkroom since he started at the school about ten years ago.

All the enlargers are gone. Premack smiles to himself—he still misses the smell of fixer. "If they could only come up with a spray that could be piped into the computer room," he thinks, "I would finally accept this new technology."

The dark is out of the darkroom now. The area is still called a darkroom perhaps out of respect for the old technology. Where the safe lights, running water, chemical trays, and enlargers used to be is a brightly lit room with fifty desktop publishing computer workstations with fiber optic links throughout the world. Since all print and screen communication is now digital, the computers are shared with typography, graphic design, motion picture, and television students. In addition, graduate students design educational lessons for commercial applications using the latest Web technology.

Each workstation costs about $10,000. But each software program costs only about $100. The manufacturer saw tremendous success in the entertainment operation of its virtual reality machines at arcades and at homes and wanted to establish educational benefits for the technology, and so it provided similarly equipped virtual reality workstations at drastically reduced prices for five universities.

Located at Premack's school and in Missouri, Texas, New York (Rochester), and New Jersey, the five colleges are linked through optical fibers that keep all of the instructors up-to-date on successes and problems with the systems. Every year, the manufacturer sponsors a weeklong conference that attracts international attendance where research papers about the new technology are read and the latest software programs are demonstrated.

When virtual reality technology was first introduced, companies produced war-type games for computer arcades in shopping malls in which players thought they were shooting at a computer-generated foe. Although initially engaging—the helmet and gloves that a user wears gave the illusion of real-time movement within a simulated computer environment—most players were disappointed with the crude, stick-figure cartoon characters and the brightly colored, chalk-like backgrounds. The programs of today, packed in a cassette about the size of a VCR tape, are much more realistic because they can use preexisting films and videotape combined with holographic effects for true, three-dimensional realism. There is lifelike, real-time movement with no delays as in the earlier models. Interactions between the players and computer-generated characters and objects seem much more real because of the highly detailed graphics. There are even sensory detectors built into the gloves and leg wrappings so that a player has the sensation of actually holding and feeling the weight of an object. There are also complex morphing effects, common in computer animation films for years, which enhance fantasy games—the player can become and interact with any character stored within the computer's memory.

Premack turns on the light for the classroom and sees the eleven VR-2000 players. Each student workstation contains a circular railing that the student stands within and a computer with a color monitor resting on a table near the railing. For every station there is a helmet, two gloves and two leg wrappings with wire connections linking them with the computer. The separate student workstations look like the individual booths used for language instruction when Premack was a student.

At the front of the room sits his workstation. It is almost exactly like the students' stations except for a bigger monitor and an expanded keyboard. He turns on his computer workstation. It takes a few minutes to boot up, which gives him time to select a program for today's viewing. He sees the titles of the VR-2000 educational programs available to him behind a locked cabinet. Since this virtual reality classroom is used by all of the sequence instructors for their students, there is a wide variety of software programs on the shelves.

Among his teaching choices there is a lesson on sports photography based on Super Bowl L, where a dramatic come-from-behind win gave the Dallas Cowboys football team their third straight Super Bowl win. Another lesson represents the recent Cuban War and lets students experience the difficulties involved with taking pictures during war conditions. There is a lesson on shooting a rock concert, favored by most students because they enjoy the loud music, a lesson that takes students to a remote area of Alaska to complete a picture story on Native American fishermen, and the lesson Premack selects for today's class: the Budd Dwyer press conference and suicide. Although the event happened several years ago, Premack thinks it is an excellent example of a general news assignment, a press conference, suddenly turned into a horrifying spot news assignment. It tells students they must be prepared for any eventuality. And since this week the students are learning about spot news coverage, it is an excellent program choice. He takes it off the shelf, locks the cabinet, and slips the cassette into his VR-2000 player.

At the top of the hour, Premack's students file into the classroom and sit at the workstations. This class is filled with serious photojournalism students: Of the ten students in the class, eight have worked on newspapers as interning staff photographers. It is Premack's favorite class because the students are professional in their command of the technology and also are caring individuals who are concerned about the people they photograph. Though they receive a healthy dose of ethics throughout the curriculum, in this class they are particularly challenged.

After a few general announcements and the students have settled down, Premack explains what they are about to experience. A detailed description is needed because of the problems in the technology when it was first introduced—some students were disturbed by its realism. Besides, the Dwyer episode is an intense viewing experience that may easily upset the unprepared.

Pennsylvania State Treasurer Budd Dwyer had just been convicted of bribery. Journalists from several newspapers, news services, and television stations gathered around a small podium that sat on a table expecting to hear Dwyer announce his resignation from state government. What they heard was the long, rambling final monologue of a seriously troubled man. Dwyer pulled out a .357 magnum long barrel pistol, waved back reporters, stuck the revolver in his mouth, pulled the trigger, and ended his torment before a stunned audience.

Premack explains that if it gets a little too real, they can stop the lesson at any time or look the other way. They can try to prevent what is happening or use their cameras to record images of what they are witnessing. Each student's computer will record every picture taken. After the lesson ends, the students can review the images on their computer monitors, pick their favorite, manipulate it, crop it, use it in a layout, print it out, and turn it in.

Premack starts the program. The students walk into the press conference scene as if it were a stage play. Dwyer is in the middle of his speech at the front of the room behind a podium with many microphones attached to it. The room is crowded with reporters and photographers so to get any good pictures his students must weave their way between the computer-generated figures. All of the stu-

dents have digital cameras around their necks and shoulder bags that contain an assortment of lenses supplied by the computer program.

The lesson continues with Dwyer talking about his career as a public servant. Most of the students are now close to the podium along with the computer-generated still photographers and videographers. Suddenly Dwyer pulls out his gun. Even though Premack has seen this lesson several times, it is still a bit of a shock. There is some yelling and chaos among the spectators. One of his students tries to rush Dwyer and take the gun from him. Dwyer points the gun in his direction and waves him back. Premack makes a mental note to caution the student about trying that action in the real world. Suddenly there is a huge explosion as Dwyer shoots himself.

And then there is another, somewhat muffled voice, "Daddy. Daddy. Dinner's ready."

He knows the voice is not from any of his students.

"Daddy. Dinner's ready."

It's his thirteen-year-old daughter, Allison.

"Okay, honey. I'll be right there," Premack answers.

Premack touches the quit button on his keyboard and stops the program. A graphics display superimposes the words, "You have elected to quit. Do you want to save up to this point?" Premack presses the "OK" button on the keyboard. "Program saved under the previously named file: Premack3." Then the last words from the program that always gives Premack a chuckle are projected: "Thank you for playing the VR-2000: Photojournalism Adventure Game. Have a real day."

Visual Perspectives

The screen goes blank. Premack slowly takes off his helmet, gloves, and leg wrappings and steps out of the circular railing. He sets the equipment on his desk and turns on the lamp in his office. He sits down at his chair and rubs his eyes for a few moments, turns off the computer and walks downstairs.

His wife and daughter are already sitting at the dinner table.

"Did you win a Pulitzer Prize yet?" his wife, Deni, asks with a smile.

"No," Premack laughs.

"Daddy," Allison explains, "you were really gone. I had to call out to you three times."

"Sorry, sweetie. Those games are fun to play. I'm glad dinner didn't get cold."

Deni asks, "Mark, after dinner can we play that Sherlock Holmes mystery game together? I love to walk those streets of London."

"Sure thing, my dear. Pass the peas, please." ■

CHAPTER 2

A Visual Literacy Primer

by Paul Martin Lester

This chapter discusses the basics of visual literacy: the nature of light, how the eyes and brain respond to it, the visual cues of color, form, depth, and movement, and the visual literacy approaches of gestalt, semiotics, and cognition. A visual journalist who understands the fundamentals of the physics of light, knows how the eyes capture and how the brain processes light, and understands the theories that have been advanced to explain the sociological effects of light and the objects it illuminates is better able to notice how light shapes a scene, grabs our attention, and communicates moods.

A digital illustration of the concept "insight to completion" . . . painting a picture, if you will. (See CP-2.)

Will Crocker

Light

Light's importance in society is clearly evident after a simple search for the keyword "light" in the Yahoo database search engine on the World Wide Web (http://www.yahoo.com). Below is a partial list of light references:

Different Light Bookstore
Electric Light Orchestra
Gordon Lightfoot
Guiding Light
Household lighting
Light bulb jokes
Lighters
Lighthouses
Lightning protection
Lightwave graphics
Northern Lights
Northern Lights College
Power and light companies
Stage lighting
Tampa Bay Lightning

From the dawn of human existence light has been a powerful fascination. Religious leaders, scientists, and the general public have sought explanations for all the light they noticed around them—from the sun, moon, and stars that awed them, from the fire of logs that cooked their meals, and from the eyes of others that communicated inner feelings. It might be assumed that early scientists believed that light came from the sun, but that wasn't necessarily so. In fact, an early Greek writer, Empedocles, made a strong case in 500 B.C.E. that light came from the eyes. He argued that the eyes acted like tiny searchlights that illuminated the world when we opened our eyelids. Of course his idea didn't explain why it became dark at night or inside a cave or house.

It was several hundred years later that a scientist of any stature made pronouncements about the nature of light. From an area of the world known as Iraq today, Alhazen, a scientist most noted for being the first to use a camera obscura device to view a solar eclipse advanced the simple argument in 1000 C.E. that light came from the sun and other such sources.

Nevertheless, it took some convincing because later in the history of light it was a mistaken belief, held even by the great Leonardo de Vinci, that color, an attribute of light as a function of the workings of our eyes and brain, came from colored objects. Da Vinci reasoned about 1485 that mixing six pigments of paint could produce all the colors we see. But paint and light are two entirely separate entities and mix in vastly different ways. In fact, colored pigments will mix to form black paint, while colored lights mix to form white light. Sir Isaac Newton, in a simple experiment using two prisms in 1666, demonstrated that colored light comes from the sun and other light sources and not from paints or other colored objects. About 150 years later, in 1801, Thomas Young and Hermann von Helmholtz independently announced that only three colors were necessary to produce all of the colors that we see—red, green, and blue. Not surprisingly, those three colors are the ones the photosensitive cells in the retinas of our eyes respond to and are used in color photography and television and computer monitors.

A year before Young and Helmholtz published their papers, British scientist William Herschel discovered that each color band projected from a prism had a distinct temperature. Furthermore, when he moved his thermometer to each side of the color spectrum but where no light was visible he was able to record other temperatures. When Scottish physicist James Maxwell in 1861 discovered another key to understanding the nature of light—that electricity and magnetism are actually the same type of force known as electromagnetic energy—the discoveries of Herschel and Maxwell sparked scientists such as Heinrich Hertz and Albert Einstein to explore this mysterious world of unseen energy. Hertz discovered radio waves and Einstein won the Nobel Prize for discovering ultraviolet waves.

What we call light is actually a narrow band of wavelength frequencies along that electromagnetic spectrum that includes extremely fast-moving cosmic, gamma, and X-rays, visible light in the form of colors, and slower-moving waves such as micro and radio. The color red is often used for emergency purposes because it has the longest wavelength of any of the colors, and so red stays in our eyes and brain for a longer time so that we notice and are warned by the color. Knowing that light is a collection of wavelength frequencies along a broad spectrum of energy levels allows us to appreciate how light can be used in a variety of communicative messages to attract our attention.

Eyes and Brain

Eyes have been called windows to the soul because they can reveal much about the inner emotions and thoughts of their owners. A visual journalist with an understanding of how the eyes work learns to decipher the differences when a subject of a still or moving image has direct eye contact with a camera's lens, looks away from the camera, or shuts her eyes completely. Such gestures often indicate the mental state of the subject—deliberate, deceitful, or depressed.

Physiology of the Eye

The study of eyes to a visual journalist is important because cameras were constructed to mimic their actions. The major parts of the eye with corresponding photographic camera functions are the eyelids/shutter to allow light to enter the eye or camera, pupil/aperture opening to restrict the amount of light that enters the eye and lens/camera lens to focus the image on the retina or film plane, and the retina/film to convert electromagnetic light energy into chemical energy for further processing by the visual cortex of the brain—or a one-hour photo processor at your local shopping mall.

The retina is a small area in the back of the eye in which the focused light is converted to chemical energy by the photosensitive nerve cells called rods and cones. Named after their individual shapes, rods are used for seeing under low-light conditions while cones, sensitive to the electromagnetic wavelengths associated with the colors red, green, and blue, are used to see colors.

Physiology of the Brain

Once the images are converted to chemical energy by the photosensitive cells in the retina, the pictures travel the length of the optic nerve at the back of each eye through the thalamus of the brain and to the back of the head in an area of the brain responsible for sight known as the visual cortex. It is in the visual cortex that three types of nerve cells—simple, complex, and hypercomplex combine to form the four visual cues discussed next. The images in the visual cortex are stored in short-term memory and compared with other images in a person's long-term memory storage. Scientists believe that the hippocampus, a Greek word meaning seahorse because of its shape, is the part of the brain where comparisons are made between what is a new image and one that has been seen before. It is still unknown where long-term visual messages are stored in the brain—it may be the hippocampus or it might be some other part of the brain yet to be identified.

The Visual Cues: Color, Form, Depth, and Movement

Nobel Prize–winning neurophysiologists David Hubel and Torsten Wiesel in 1962 discovered that nerve cells in the visual cortex work in conjunction to deliver four basic visual cues—color, form, depth, and movement. It is not surprising that graphic artists use the four cues alone and in combinations in their designs—

whether for print or computer—to draw attention and to forward the design's message. By studying each visual cue, you, too, will have a better understanding of how to make designs that combine impact with memorability.

Color

We can talk about color objectively, comparatively, or subjectively. When scientists or photographers discuss the actual temperature of a specific color, they are using the objective method. Colors fall on the electromagnetic spectrum at discrete and separate locations. Each color has its own wavelength on the spectrum and temperature on a scale. In this way scientists can discuss specific colors with definitely measurable attributes. Although accurate, this method leaves out much of the mystery and emotional quality that colors often evoke.

Most of us use the comparative method. When you look up a specific color in the dictionary, for example, the color will be described not by its specific location on the electromagnetic scale but in relation to another known and agreed-upon entity. The comparative method is less accurate than the objective method. A

A Web design emphasizing color. (See CP-4.)

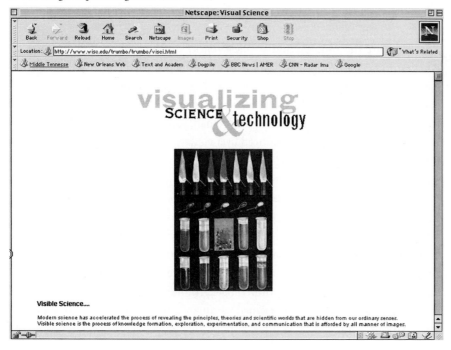

dictionary may define the color blue as the color of a clear sky. But depending where you live, of course, a blue sky may have many slight variations, and a dark blue is a much different color than a light blue. Nevertheless, we learn to identify the general hue of blue by comparing a specific color to a whole class of colors we call blue. More exotic colors may give you more problems. A color known as salmon is a slight pink color resembling the meat of the popular fish. But if you have had no experience of a salmon you will have no idea what color is being discussed.

The third method for describing color—subjective—is the least accurate but the most interesting for graphic designers because it makes use of emotions evoked from a specific color for its meaning. A color's meaning is highly dependent on a viewer's experiences and cultural heritage. The color blood red may evoke numerous memories of emergency situations for a viewer or the color yellow may remind a viewer of a religious figure familiar in his country. Consequently, visual journalists must be careful when selecting colors for a design because meaning is so subjective.

Form

As with color, forms also convey specific meaning for viewers based on their experience or cultural heritage. Visual journalists need, then, to be aware of the message being conveyed by a simple form. There are three basic forms—dots, lines, and shapes.

Dots are the simplest and smallest mark you can make within a substrate. Whether a mark from a pen's point or a single picture element (pixel) on a computer screen, the impact of a dot when standing alone within a frame can be enormous. Humans are naturally drawn to round objects particularly if separated from other elements on the page. A company's small, round logo set in the bottom corner of a page will be sure to be noticed by a viewer.

Lines have dynamic qualities because they are considered a series of dots drawn so close to together that there is no space between them. Consequently, lines are always attention grabbers that direct a viewer's eyes away or toward another graphic element. A line moving diagonally upward is seen as being optimistic while the reverse is true for a downward-leading line. A horizontal line along the top of a frame sends a message of compactness, while the same line set near the bottom of a frame gives a sense of expansion. Again, these are emotional messages that are learned by viewers and vary by cultural backgrounds.

Shapes can either be represented as squares, rectangles, circles, triangles, or combinations. And as with all other graphic elements, cultures assign meaning to

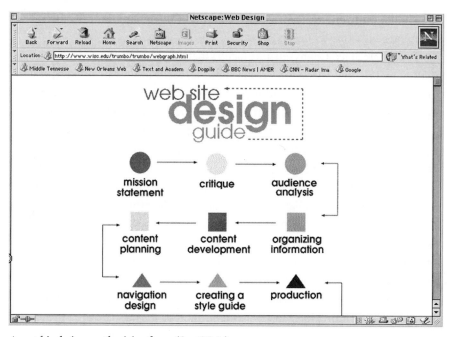

A graphic design emphasizing form. (See CP-5.)

each shape. Squares are boring, yet reserved and stable. Rectangles are more dynamic. Circles evoke comforting emotions because they can express the cycles of the sun and moon or the familiar face of another person. An equilateral triangle, for example, an Egyptian pyramid, has stability while an isosceles triangle, for example, the Washington Monument, conveys a dynamic but less stable mood. Visual journalists need to be aware that a viewer may subconsciously label a design as boring if the graphic elements cause a person's eyes to travel in a square or circle. Likewise, a design will be viewed as dynamic and more modern if a viewer's eyes are directed by graphic elements that include direct lines. The decision to make a square or rectangular design is based on the audience's cultural identity.

Depth

Depth is probably the most complex visual cue because there are so many factors that create the illusion of three-dimensional depth within a two-dimensional substrate such as a piece of paper or a computer screen. But visual journalists should study how depth is conveyed because viewers strongly respond to the visual cue.

This attraction to 3-D images is the reason motion pictures and virtual reality systems are constantly being improved.

There are at least eight separate factors that help give a viewer a sense of depth to a graphic design: space, size, color, lighting, textural gradients, interposition, time, and perspective. Space refers to the size of the frame and the objects within its edges. When a viewer senses a great expanse, there is also a feeling of great depth. Size is the actual size of the graphic elements within a frame. Size as a depth factor depends on our knowledge of a particular object. An image of a person's hand that fills a frame gives viewers little in the way of depth cues while a hand pictured small within a frame does. The darker colors used by an artist to convey depth are viewed as being farther away than lighter colors. Studio backlighting in photographic portraits or television studios helps separate the subject from the background for an illusion of depth. The ripples caused by the wind on sand dunes are examples of textural gradients. The wind waves seem to be more closely aligned the more distant they are from a viewer. Interposition simply means that one object is in front of another. By carefully placing objects in a scene a visual journalist can enhance the illusion of depth. An individual viewer's specific interests may also be a depth factor. If a viewer's interest is drawn to a specific visual message, the viewer looks at that graphic element longer, causing it to appear to be in the foreground rather than the background.

Finally, the most complicated depth factor is perspective because it is probably the most dependent on the cultural heritage of the viewer. There are three major forms of perspective—illusionary, geometrical, and conceptual. Illusionary perspective as a way to add depth to two-dimensional paintings had to be learned by artists beginning in the sixteenth century when devices were developed to aid artists in this quest. Before this era, painters simply drew with a geometrical or flat perspective, placing people and objects in the frame in specific regions to signify importance and to convey depth. A building, for example, often appeared in the lower part of a frame with all the subjects illustrated higher up to denote that the house was the most important element in the picture. The third form of perspective, conceptual, involves two types—multiview and social. Whenever various views of a person are displayed within the same frame, as in much of the work by Pablo Picasso, the multiview conceptual form is evoked. Depth of meaning comes from the layering of the different views. Social conceptual perspective helps identify the important subject of a group photograph. Usually a photographer will place the head of a corporation in the center of a group. Depth is conveyed as attention is directed to that person while all the other subjects are grouped around him/her and farther back in the frame.

Movement

Start to notice how often you react to someone walking past you while you sit reading and you will become aware of how important the visual cue of movement is to your total visual array. In fact, movement is so important to visual journalists as a way to interest viewers and tell stories that you cannot afford to be unaware of its impact, whether for print or more dynamic display media. There are four types of movement—real, apparent, graphic, and implied. Real movement is what we notice directly with our eyes. Virtual reality computer systems with their helmets and body gloves try to simulate real movement to give its users a heightened sense of reality. The best example of apparent movement is motion picture film. Each frame does not have movement in itself, but when sped through a projector at twenty-four frames per second, each still frame appears to move. Graphic movement is the way a viewer's eyes travel throughout a design noticing or ignoring the graphic elements within a frame. Through careful placement of text and pictures, a visual journalist can make sure a viewer notices every element in a frame in order to achieve the maximum meaning from the piece. Implied movement is a kind of motion brought about by the careful combinations of colors or lines in a design so that the piece seems to have an internal, pulsating engine. Pop and hallucinogenic art of the 1960s and the hip-hop art of the 1990s often have this motion quality to their designs.

Theories of Visual Literacy

It is not enough to recognize the power of light and color, to understand the physiology of the eyes and the brain, and to know how the four visual cues can combine to create messages with impact and meaning for the study of visual literacy. You also need to understand the approaches that have been devised over the years to help explain why we see and process pictures the way we do. These three major approaches to visual literacy theory are labeled gestalt, semiotics, and cognitive.

Gestalt

The word *gestalt* comes from the German noun meaning form or shape. It is an approach to visual literacy theory that looks at an entire visual array rather than its individual parts. In fact, the most famous phrase to come out of the gestalt approach makes that point: "The whole is different from the sum of its parts." The sentence has come to mean that individual graphic elements that make up either a printed or screen presentation have less importance than their total effect has upon the viewer. A newspaper front page is usually composed of headlines, subheads, body copy, pictures, captions, cutlines, and various graphic elements such as rules and spot colors. But a graphic designer knows that a reader will get the most meaning from the page if those elements work together rather than if each element competes for the attention of the reader. For this reason, headlines usually are designed with the same typeface with only variations in size, attributes, and placement. Pictures on the page are almost always either all in color or all in black and white. The page, then, has a stylistic whole that has greater impact as a complete entity than do the individual parts that make up the whole.

Gestalt researchers have also recognized several laws that help visual journalists understand how viewers respond to various graphic elements on a page or screen. Four of these laws—similarity, proximity, continuation, and common fate—are most commonly used in graphic design settings.

The law of similarity states that our minds group things that we see when we judge them as being alike. Photographs and text are obviously different elements used in a design and are thus easily differentiated by viewers. But if a designer places text over part of a picture, the meaning of the image and the words may not be understood.

The law of proximity says we tend to group graphic elements that are near each other. In graphic design a cutline is almost always directly under the picture it explains. The closeness of the words and picture makes their connection obvious to the reader. But if a designer sets a cutline off to the side and separates it by too much white space, the reader might not understand that the copy block is meant to accompany the picture.

The law of continuance states that our minds naturally follow a line of objects to their destination. If you stretch out your arm to point in a particular direction, you will stimulate those around you to follow your gaze. Following that principle, it is considered an error in graphic design to place a photograph on the edge if its content points toward the frame. It is better for a picture's direction to point toward the inside of the frame where a viewer will be drawn to more information within the page or screen.

Finally, the law of common fate states that graphic elements will be linked if they draw the viewer's eyes in a similar direction. Conversely, a viewer can be distracted by an element headed away from the main group of elements. In an advertising design a company logo is best set apart from the main grouping of elements so that it gets noticed. But for most editorial graphic designs an unusually sized picture, a color rule that does not complement the other colors in the layout, or headlines composed of vastly different typestyles will distract viewers and so the message may be lost.

A Trex ad illustrating the concept of continuance.

Semiotics

Semiotics is the study of signs. A sign is defined as anything in a visual array that has meaning for the viewer. From the color of a shirt worn by a subject in a visual message to the type of chair she sits in, all individual elements have meaning to someone and are signs to be studied. Consequently, semiotics is more concerned with what graphic elements actually represent than how they may be grouped in the mind. A sign's meaning is highly dependent on the viewer's experience level and cultural heritage. Just as with colors and forms, signs have more or less meaning depending on the viewer observing them. Visual journalists must be aware of how a graphic design's impact can be enhanced or diminished because of the various meanings a sign might have for all possible viewers within a mass communications context.

Signs may be iconic, indexical, or symbolic. An iconic sign has almost a one-to-one relationship with the pictorial representation and what it is supposed to represent. For example, a photograph of a chair is an iconic sign because it is undeniably a chair for all viewers who happen to see the image. Indexical signs are a bit more complicated because their meaning must be inferred more than with iconic signs. For example, smoke coming out of a chimney is an indexical sign that there's a fire in the fireplace. Consider an image of a chair with a thick, velvet cushion that showed an indentation. The chair itself is an iconic image, but the dent in the cushion is an indexical sign that someone recently sat on the chair. A symbolic sign is the most abstract type of sign and thus requires experience, cultural awareness, and practice to accurately decipher its meaning. Since a chair can be anything from a smooth rock to a king's throne, the type of chair pictured in the last example would significantly contribute to the meaning of the image.

Visual journalists must be aware that the three types of signs always act together. For example, a photograph of an accident involving a car and a train may be initially seen as a simple iconic picture detailing the wreck of two modes of transportation. But with a closer look, indexical signs are obvious: steam and fire erupt from the engines, indicating the power of the wreck, and the warning lights are not flashing, indicating they may not have been working just before the accident. Symbolic signs are also a part of the picture: the uniforms of medical workers are different from police personnel; the license plate on the car, indicating it came from a rental agency, symbolically shows that the driver might not have been familiar with this part of the road. To make visual messages have meaning for a viewer, a visual journalist must understand that every image is a complex set of designs.

Cognitive

Besides the brain's natural tendency to group like and unlike picture elements and to discern meaning in those elements, there are several mental activities that also greatly affect a person's ability to understand an image. Those inner brain and highly personal activities include culture, environmental factors, expectation, dissonance, habituation, memory, mental state, projection, salience, and words.

Where a person comes from and what she has learned from parents, friends, and other acquaintances make up that person's cultural orientation. Consequently, if you are not of that person's culture you may be insensitive to the harmful effect an image might have. For example, the name of the popular NFL football team in America's capital, the Washington Redskins, may seem inoffensive to some, but to a Native American "redskin" is a derogatory word that brands his or her culture as inferior to the dominant culture. Visual journalists must be constantly on the lookout for terms and images that have injurious effect upon those from other cultures.

Environmental factors in a room can be harmful to a visual message. If the room is too hot, the sound system not loud enough, or the lights too dim, a viewer will be distracted and not concentrate on your presentation.

Expectation is the mental activity that defines a set of rules of what to expect when opening a magazine, starting a computer program, or walking into a room. If viewers come across a visual message that is totally unexpected, they may be intrigued and want to see more or they may be put off and not proceed further through the piece. A visual journalist must always match the message with the potential audience.

Dissonance is a condition in which two or more modes of communication compete for a viewer's attention. For most viewers, having moving pictures narrated by a news anchorperson does not cause distractions. But if multiple and quickly edited pictures, narration, music, and a line of text along the bottom of the frame are included, that may be too many communications channels of information at one time for the viewer to comfortably process, and the viewers will likely stop watching.

Habituation is a mental activity in which a viewer becomes used to her surroundings so that even unusual occurrences are overlooked. Habituation is most obvious when searching for typographical errors in a body of copy. The writer of the piece often overlooks misspelled words because he or she is familiar with the words. An editor with more objectivity is better at finding typos. And because standard sites lose their special quality after familiarity, or habituation, photographers and videographers often travel to unfamiliar sections of a city to find unusual feature pictures and moments.

Memory is one of the most powerful determinants of a person's willingness to look at your visual message. A viewer with previous experience of a situation or picture will be immediately interested. An unusual image will also initially spark interest. But a visual journalist must be careful that an image is not so confusing that a viewer won't take the time to figure out its message.

Ideas for Further Study

A viewer's mental state also significantly determines whether an image receives all the attention it deserves or needs. The viewer may be experiencing personal problems or the image may trigger memories that place the viewer in an emotional state beyond the control of the visual journalist.

Projection is a mental activity in which the viewer turns iconic images into highly symbolic signs. Finding familiar forms in cloud patterns or tree trunks are popular examples. To avoid this possibility a visual journalist must carefully scan an image to make sure there are no distracting elements that will dilute its message.

Salience is a condition in which a viewer recognizes an element within a visual array because it has personal meaning. When looking in a crowded theatre, all the faces of strangers will not be salient, but the instant you recognize a friend your eyes focus immediately on his or her face. Visual journalists must take care to explain with carefully crafted words any picture that might not be recognizable to most of the audience.

Finally, the words accompanying a visual message within any medium are vital to a reader's or viewer's understanding the total message. A visual journalist in a mass communication context cannot assume that every person understands a visual message in the same way. When words are included—either as accompanying text or off-camera audio—the limitations imposed by the other mental activities just described are reduced.

CONCLUSION

The key to the study of visual literacy is learning to take the time to really look at a visual message. With so many pictures, both still and moving, whizzing past our eyes, the meaning is largely lost because we can't spend the time to analyze each one. By knowing how light illuminates a scene, how the eyes and the brain process those light images, and how picture elements are grouped, defined, and explained, we learn to produce memorable images that educate, entertain, and persuade.

IDEAS FOR FURTHER STUDY

■ Find examples in print and/or screen media in which light communicates special meaning to the viewer. What do color, intensity, and direction of the light communicate?

■ Find examples in print and/or screen media in which the eye contact of the subject has special meaning for the viewer. What is the meaning of a subject who looks right into the camera, looks away, or has eyes covered or closed?

■ Find an advertisement or commercial that demonstrates one or more of the gestalt laws. Deconstruct the piece in order to analyze it completely.

■ Find a symbolic advertisement in a magazine that is an example of the semiotic approach to picture analysis. What is the literal meaning of the ad and what is its symbolic meaning? Who will likely understand the symbolic meaning?

■ Think of all the ways you can be distracted from really seeing a visual message. Which ones are distractions in your mind and which ones are environmental factors?

Ideas for Further Study

Digital Images and the "New" Visual Literacy

by Gregory Veen, Department of English, University of Washington
(www.veen.com/veen/greg)

The way images are used and understood in today's dominant forms of communication is strikingly different from the way they were most often used and understood when printed text was the preferred site of public discourse in the West. As Gunther Kress, head of culture, communications, and societies, London Institute of Education, and Theo van Leeuwen, a professor for the Centre for Language Communication, Cardiff University observe,[1] from sometime during the early modern period until relatively recently, images in publicly disseminated texts tended to be viewed either as individualized artistic expression or as uncoded replicas of reality—as objective snapshots that faithfully represented the world of objects. Readers during this period, in other words, approached images with a particular kind of visual literacy, one in which images were for the most part viewed not as meaningful in themselves, but instead as mere virtual pointers to the meaning of the real world or as illustrations of the text that surrounded them and directed their meaning. Because meaning was to be found primarily in text, the ways that the characteristics of images might both reveal perspectives and be used to produce meaning—say, through specific arrangements of an image's visual elements—received little attention. Images in this "old" visual literacy, to put it simply, did little meaning-making work.

As forms of communication have become increasingly visually saturated, approaches to images have begun to change. As Steven Johnson, named one of the most influential people in cyberspace by *Newsweek*, *New York Magazine*, and *Websight* magazine, points out[2]—and as just about anyone can see simply by surveying our contemporary landscape—images have now become an important part of our reality: our environments are now so visually saturated that images have become naturalized. Images are so often a part of our meaning-making processes that we have come to see them as real in themselves and capable of generating meanings, rather than as being somehow opposed to the real, capable only of representing or delivering the meaning of the real world. Because images now mean more, viewers tend to pay more attention to the structure of the images they encounter—how individual graphical elements are arranged to suggest value or emphasis; how, in photographs, vectors can suggest particular types of action; and so on. Like the way literate readers recognize the rhetorical elements at work in a piece of writing, viewers who approach images with this "new" visual literacy tend to think of images as composed of a number of meaningful, and meaningfully arranged, elements.

Nowhere is this new way of seeing more clearly at work than in the use and reception of digital images on today's World Wide Web. Images in hypermedia environments like the Web demonstrate principles of new visual literacy on at least two levels, involving both image production and image consumption. In one sense, the fact that visual representations are constructed from constituent elements is even more important when images are digital: the ease with which specific elements from digital images can be cut and pasted and modified draws attention both to their own status as individual carriers of meaning and to how the meaning of the composition in which they appear is conditioned by their combined synthesis. Suddenly, the presence and appearance of any graphic element become newly significant, simply because it could have been so easily seamlessly cut out or modified.

This status is bolstered by the fact that literally, technically, digital images really *are* composed of constituent parts—either vector-based elements (as in non-pixel-based applications like Adobe Illustrator and, in a sense, in image formats like PNG), or, on a more abstract level, the digital bits of which they are made—a floating chain of ones and zeroes. The move from atoms to bits as the building blocks of products of all kinds has made and will continue to make obvious to our Western understanding what the so-called "pre-literates" have known all along: that images are made of parts that are consciously arranged to convey a particular message.

This new way of approaching images has been further confirmed and, in fact, made more obvious by the arrival of the hypermedia image-map. An image-map, of course, is more than just a map: image-maps aren't just digital versions of the visual representations of physical, geographic space we normally call maps.

"Image-map" is a technical term used among hypermedia developers to refer to the background programming or coding maneuver of dividing Web page images into invisibly mapped regions that are each hyperlinked to distinct destinations: other Web pages, multimedia files, and the like. The following illustration demonstrates the basic technical characteristics of an image-map: each of the quadrants of an image like this could be linked, independently of the others, to specific referents.

When regions of an image are clickable in this way—that is, when clicking on a specific image element serves up some specific data—that image has forever lost any semblance of being objective, non-coded, neutral or perspective-free. Its structured status is made literal. Its constituent parts clearly mean something, because, when prompted, they offer a statement—the other Web page or the audio file, for example, that the clickable region links to.

Of course, even though a clickable element in an image-map is granted a certain significance by the data to which it is linked (I call this an element's "click-through meaning"), it also has meaning simply as a visual element: it still functions as a visual element within the grammar of the image in which it appears. The meaning of an image-map, then, is a product of the intersection of several different semantic layers: the meaning of the image as image or as visual artifact, which might include notions of how the image is the deposit of social relationships; the significance of visual elements as constituents of the image (the

Visual Perspectives

hallmark of the new visual literacy); the click-through meaning of elements; and the significance of any overlaid or surrounding text.

The Web's image-mapping capabilities also tend to change the way users of the Web view *all* screen images: on the Web, any image could potentially be an image-map, so all screen images tend to be viewed as being composed of significant elements that might be clickable and that are therefore meaningful. Because so many images on the Web are linked, when one encounters an image that is not linked, the very lack may cause one to re-examine that image. In other words, encountering a non-linked element in an environment whose texts so often point away from themselves prompts renewed attention to that non-linked element, to the meaning itself produces. The possibility of the link, in such ways, is now acting as a catalyst in the development of new types of hypermedia-specific visual literacy. ■

Notes

1. Kress, Gunther, and Theo van Leeuwen. *Reading Images: The Grammar of Visual Design.* London and New York: Routledge, 1996: 15–42.
2. Johnson, Steven. *Interface Culture: How New Technology Transforms the Way We Create and Communicate.* San Francisco: Harper, 1997: 30.

CHAPTER 3

An Ethical Approach

by Paul Martin Lester

Ethical concerns are everywhere. Gruesome images shock viewers, dozens of visual journalists hound a celebrity, picture manipulations present misleading views, visual messages perpetuate negative stereotypes of individuals from various multicultural groups, and images blur the distinction between advertising, public relations, and journalism. What is happening? Nothing that hasn't been a part of photographic reporting since its invention in 1839. What is new, however, is the spread of computer technology that allows practically anyone to produce and disseminate visual messages in massive numbers for a worldwide audience.

Study the Six Philosophies

One way to make sense of the ethical issues that arise because of the increased use and access to images is to study six ethical philosophies that have shaped thought and actions for hundreds of centuries. The six ethical philosophies most useful to visual journalists are the categorical imperative, utilitarianism, hedonism, the golden mean, the golden rule, and the veil of ignorance. These form two major groups: the first four philosophies are applied mainly by visual journalists when justifying photographing or using an image, while the latter two are invoked mostly by victims, their families and friends, readers, and viewers who are often offended by such visual messages.

The Categorical Imperative

Immanuel Kant, born in 1724, was an East Prussian philosopher who greatly influenced Western philosophical thought. He is noted for his categorical, or unconditional imperative in thought or action. However, Kant advocated categorical imperatives to reduce harm and thus propel individuals to be caring and thoughtful citizens. Unfortunately, journalists largely oversimplify Kant's philosophy, mistakenly concluding that once established no exceptions can be made to the rule. Visual journalists may evoke the philosophy with the justification, "The picture was unusual. It was news. And since we publish (or broadcast) news, it had to be used." When all the major networks and cable stations aired the terrorist attack upon America, they justified the coverage by arguing that the event satisfied professional definitions for news or that all the other stations were covering it so it had to be photographed. Either justification uses Kant's categorical approach, but in a limited way. By relying on such strict rules, visual journalists absolve themselves of moral responsibility for possible harm caused by the image. But if a categorical imperative is used that takes into account the reduction of harm, visual journalists are on safer ethical ground.

An example of a categorical imperative-based news photo.

AP/Wide World

AP/Wide World

An example of a utilitarianism-based news photo.

Utilitarianism

English philosophers Jeremy Bentham and John Mill introduced "the greater good for the greater number" philosophy known as utilitarianism. With such an approach, various possible outcomes are imagined as a result of an action. The one that aids the largest number of people is the one that should be chosen. Visual journalists usually try to justify an image of a tragic car wreck or drowning victim with this philosophy. Readers and viewers are urged to consider that they should drive more safely without being influenced by alcohol or avoid a treacherous section of a river, lake, or ocean, since there is a chance that great personal harm could result. Obviously, the printing or broadcasting of such images is most likely distressing to family and friends of the victims, but the greater good is served—more people benefit from the warning message implicit in such pictures.

Hedonism

The philosophy of hedonism is easily the most controversial of the six and is often denied as the motive for a visual journalist's actions. Nevertheless, it is also probably the most widely applied philosophy. From the Greek word for pleasure, hedonism is based on the personal whim of the one who evokes it. Any action that is a result of a purely personal motive—to gain fame or monetary reward, for example—comes from the hedonistic philosophy summed up by the phrases "eat, drink, and be merry, for tomorrow we die" and "don't worry, be happy." When controversial images are used in the mass media for no other reason than to cause

An example of a hedonistic news photo.

Christopher R. Harris

sensational, personal satisfaction, or financial gain, hedonism rules the mind of the visual journalist, and the argument that the images are news or educate readers and viewers rings hollow.

The Golden Mean

The Greek philosopher Aristotle was one of the first to articulate the golden mean philosophy, which tries to find a compromise, a middle way, or a mean between two extreme points of view. Visual journalists often use the golden mean when making decisions about taking pictures and editors apply it when deciding on how a picture or video is to be used. A visual journalist can decide to photograph someone with a close-up lens and a microphone in the subject's face, for example, or decide that no image is necessary, two extremes. But a visual journalist applying the golden mean philosophy would try to find a middle ground. Most likely the compromise would be to use a telephoto lens from far away or to get permission from the subject to take pictures.

The golden mean is also used when deciding how the images should be used. One extreme would be to run a large color photograph on the front page of the newspaper or to lead a newscast with the video footage. The opposite extreme would be not to run the pictures at all. The golden mean would dictate that the images be used but would be smaller and possibly in black and white and on an inside page or, as part of a newscast, not as the lead story, but made brief, with the most controversial aspects of the image edited.

The Golden Rule

Based on the Judeo-Christian tradition of not adding grief to another, the golden rule philosophy teaches an individual to avoid any action that may harm someone else—a "do unto others as you would have them do unto you" approach. Victims, their families and friends, and readers and viewers often base their complaints about a controversial image on this philosophy, since the picture adds to the grief of those directly involved or distresses viewers who would simply rather not see such images.

The Veil of Ignorance

The most recent ethical philosophy of the six described here comes from the philosopher John Rawls and his book, *A Theory of Justice* (1999). The veil of ignorance philosophy can be summed up with the phrase, "walking in someone else's shoes." When readers and viewers upset by a particular controversial picture ask a visual journalist to consider what it might feel like to be a relative or friend of the person portrayed in the image, they are using the veil of ignorance philosophy.

An example of a photo applying the veil of ignorance philosophy.

Christopher R. Harris

The clash between the two groups of ethical philosophies—the journalistic approaches of categorical imperative, utilitarianism, hedonism, and golden mean and the subject or viewer approaches of golden rule and veil of ignorance—is seldom resolved. But when you consider your own motivations those of other visual journalists, victims and their families and friends, and readers and viewers through these six ethical philosophies, you become more aware of meanings and motives that may lie beneath the surface of any action or picture.

Five Chief Ethical Concerns

Because images evoke almost immediate emotional responses among viewers, pictures have tremendous impact. With well-chosen words, visual messages combine to educate, entertain, or persuade. But the flip side to such visual power is that images can also offend, shock, mislead, stereotype, and confuse.

Consider some examples: Violent images from a Miami television station, reporters camped out in front of O.J. Simpson's home, Olympic skaters and rivals Tonya Harding and Nancy Kerrigan digitally altered to look like best friends, an African American cast as a Los Angeles rioter, and a victim of AIDS used in an advertisement to sell sweaters. Such stories can be classified into five ethical concerns of most interest to visual journalism professionals: Victims of violence, the right to privacy, picture manipulations, stereotyping and the mixing of advertising, public relations, and journalism so that you cannot tell the difference.

Victims of Violence

After a gruesome image of dead or grieving victims of a tragic event is presented to the public in either the print or screen media, many viewers are often repulsed and offended by the picture. Nevertheless, violence and tragedy are staples of American journalism. "If it bleeds, it leads" is an unspoken sentiment popular in many newsrooms. The reason for this obvious incongruity is that most viewers are attracted and intrigued by such stories. Visual journalists who win Pulitzer Prizes and other international competitions are almost always witnesses to excruciatingly painful human tragedies that nevertheless get published or broadcast. It is as if viewers want to see violent pictures, but through gaps in the fingers in front of their faces.

When television station WSVN, Channel 7, in Miami lost its affiliation with NBC, it joined the Fox network and had to generate high ratings quickly in order to survive. To appeal to a younger audience, the station began specializing in gory crime news. The programming change was described by a television critic as "a continuous barrage of the body bags on the street and the blood coming out of them." The content of the nightly newscast was so disturbing that nine area hotels banned the station from its television sets, lest out-of-town guests get the wrong impression about Miami. Complaints about hotel censorship from station executives were framed within a utilitarian context. As one television spokesperson said, "To mask crime stories would not be fair to the viewers." But to be honest, both sides presented hedonistic arguments based on a fear of a decline in tourism revenue or viewers.

Editors must be sure that images of murder or automobile victims are really needed to tell the story. Perhaps a more real motive is to avoid being scooped by a rival media organization. Despite well-rehearsed explanations, sensational images of victims of violence are shown more for economic reasons than for categorical or utilitarian imperatives. The media concentration on criminal activity creates an exaggerated perception of crime in the minds of viewers. Rather than focusing on bloody body bags, journalists need to explain the underlying social forces that cause such tragic events to occur.

Right to Privacy

Ordinary citizens or celebrities who are suddenly thrust before the unblinking lens of a camera because of their connection to some sensational news story almost always voice privacy concerns. But viewers seldom complain about violating someone else's right to privacy. U.S. courts have consistently maintained that privacy rights differ between private and public persons, saying private citizens deserve much more strictly enforced rights to their own privacy than celebrities who often ask for media attention. Not surprisingly, celebrities bitterly complain when they are the subjects of relentless media attention because of some controversial allegation.

O.J. Simpson ran from defensive football players for teams in California and New York and over airport obstacles in Hertz car rental commercials. But when his mostly hidden violent personality was tragically revealed, he couldn't run from the media. With video cameras set in front of Simpson's house and from helicopters following his bizarre travel along Southern California freeways, news personnel broadcast live his every move to a worldwide audience.

Critics were divided over the media's obsession with the sensational double murder case. But the attention is easily explained. The story involved one of the strangest entities of any society—the celebrity. O.J. was beloved and respected by countless fans around the world. His fall from grace is at once shocking and extremely interesting. Such a story simply has to be covered. And part of that coverage involves the key and secondary characters caught in the media's storytelling web. When a news story is so compelling as to draw worldwide attention, the categorical imperative is invoked. In such cases, a person—whether celebrity or neighbor—has a legal right to privacy that seems defined by the height of the fence outside his or her house.

For private or public citizens, perhaps the most stressful news story is the funeral of a loved one. A guiding principle for journalists in deciding to cover such a story is whether the event is newsworthy. Newsworthiness is not determined by the number of cameras pointed through the gate at the cemetery; it is rooted in the principles of unemotional, objective, and reasoned journalism. In 1946, the Hutchins Commission issued a definition of news that still applies today: a truthful, comprehensive, and intelligent account of the day's events in a context that gives them meaning. Unfortunately, media officials under pressure from circulation or rating figures make decisions to sensationalize rather than explain complex stories of interest to the public. Live pictures for the nightly newscast of a speculating reporter in front of a brightly lit brick mansion invite the charge of sensational coverage. In an ideal world, journalists tell stories in words and pictures that explain rather than cause a viewer to ask more questions.

Picture Manipulation

Picture and subject manipulation has been a part of photography since it was first invented. But because of computer technology, digital manipulation is relatively easy to accomplish, hard to detect, and, perhaps more alarming, alters the original image so that checking the authenticity of the picture is impossible. Some critics have predicted that in a few years, images—whether still or moving—will not be allowed in trials as physical evidence because of the threat to their veracity created by digital alterations.

Tonya and Nancy. Who can (or would love to) forget the Harding versus Kerrigan soap opera that nearly froze the 1994 Winter Olympic games? In the dead of winter, editors at *New York Newsday* published a slick cover picture of the two cold-faced skaters under a large headline, "Fire on Ice," and above a confusing subhead, "Tonya, Nancy to Meet at Practice." But the color photograph showed the two skating next to each other. Didn't they meet when the picture was taken? The obvious answer (at least in this context) was that the picture was a lie—it was a composite of two separate images manipulated by a computer.

Newspaper editors across the country condemned the computer technique. How dare *Newsday* use an altered photo for a news event? But lost in the criticism was the fact that the editors for the publication did everything they were supposed to do when turning a news picture into an illustration. For also on the cover, in bold, black, sans serif type, is the cutline for the image:

> Tonya Harding, left, and Nancy Kerrigan appear to skate together in this *New York Newsday* composite illustration. Tomorrow, they'll take to the ice together.

In addition, a byline beside the picture identified the visual journalists who contributed the separate images.

So what was the problem? Why was there so much criticism from fellow journalists? The answer is that admitting to a lie doesn't make the lie acceptable.

Cameras and the images they produce are naively thought by many to never lie. But because humans operate the machine, technical, composition, and content manipulations are unavoidable. Computer technology did not start the decline in the credibility of pictures, but it has hastened it. Photographic darkrooms are quickly being replaced by computer workstation lightrooms. But as long as visual journalists do not subtract or add parts of a picture's internal elements, almost any other manipulation once accomplished in a photographic darkroom is considered ethical for news and editorial purposes.

Two factors may guard against a further erosion of credibility in visual messages: the reputation of the media organization that publishes or broadcasts images and the words that accompany the manipulated picture.

Credibility is not an inherent quality of a particular picture, but depends on tradition, story choices, design considerations, and the reader's or viewer's perception of the company or individual that produces the image. Reputation is what separates the difference in picture credibility between the *New York Times* and the *National Enquirer*, or "CBS Evening News" and "Hard Copy."

Words are also vital in assuring the credibility of a news organization and a picture. If a visual journalist or art director is tempted to combine parts from two separate pictures to create a third image, the reader needs to know that such an action has taken place. The cutline for the shot should include the details of the manipulation, and the image itself should be labeled an illustration—not a news-editorial picture. Making the reader aware of the illustrative technique would solve at least one aspect of the ethical problem.

A larger question remains, however: In this age of digital manipulation and desktop publishing, why do computer operators need to turn news-editorial photographs into illustrations? Journalism professionals should be more concerned that visual journalism images are being replaced by illustrations and less concerned about the tool that creates that ethical problem.

Stereotyping

The list is long and always injurious. African Americans are criminals. Latinos are gang members. Native Americans are alcoholics. Wheelchair-dependent individuals are helpless. Gays are effeminate. Lesbians wear their hair short. Older adults need constant care. Anglos from the Southern states are rednecks. Homeless people are drug addicts. These prevalent stereotypes are perpetuated by images presented in the media. Stereotypical portrayals of ethnic, gender, physical characteristic, sexual preference, and job-related cultural groups are a consequence of journalism professionals being lazy, ignorant, or racist. As with the printing term from which the word comes, to stereotype is a shorthand way to describe a person with collective, rather than unique, characteristics. It is easier and quicker for a visual journalist to take a picture of an angry African American during a riot than to take the time to explore in words and pictures the underlying social problems that are responsible for the civil disturbance. Critics complain that at best ignorance and at worst culturalism are the reasons stereotypes persist. *Culturalism* is a term used to describe an attitude that someone's cultural group—whether based on ethnic, educational, economic, or other factors—is somehow better than someone else's. Culturalism may explain why mainstream media are slow to cover human catastrophes in remote sections of the world such as in Rwanda, Somalia, and south-central Los Angeles.

On April 29, 1992, an all-white jury acquitted four Los Angeles police officers of unnecessarily beating Rodney King the year before. The surprising verdict sparked an orgy of violence, vandalism, and looting at a level never before seen in American history. More than fifty lives were lost, over a billion dollars in property damage was reported, and hundreds were arrested. On the cover of *Newsweek* magazine, readers were afforded a close-up picture of a young, angry African American man wearing a turned-around baseball cap yelling in front of a burning building. Although dramatic, the color picture illustrates a problem with the media: African Americans are more often than not shown as criminals to be feared. Research studies have shown that magazines and newspapers publish few photographs of African Americans, but when editors do select pictures that include African Americans, they are almost always concerned with crime, sports, or entertainment. In fact, most people from diverse cultures are shown as their collective stereotype and not as ordinary individuals with everyday hopes and concerns.

Many readers form their opinions about individuals from cultural groups based on the pictures they see in the media. Editors should assess the pictorial coverage of underrepresented groups for their own newspaper or television station. If biases are found, visual journalists, reporters, and editors should attend sensitivity training workshops in order to promote more fair and balanced images. To break the stereotypical sports coverage of African Americans, for example, athletes should be portrayed having interests other than sports. And to avoid reporting errors or omissions, news-editorial staffs should be culturally diverse and have expert knowledge of local and foreign issues.

Advertising, Public Relations, and Journalism Blurring

With names like "advertorials" and "infomercials," advertisers mimic the production cues of print and screen journalists to persuade an unsuspecting viewer to purchase a product. With full-page ads in newspapers and magazines that resemble news-editorial pages and thirty-minute commercials that look like talk shows, corporate executives rely on the credibility of the media to fool its audience of trusting viewers. Most media consumers can easily distinguish an advertisement from a news story, but sometimes the distinction is so subtle only highly observant readers can tell the difference.

In 1992, the Benetton clothing company was criticized so severely for using news pictures in their print advertisements that the campaign was ended. One startling image, of AIDS victim David Kirby on his deathbed surrounded by his grieving family, produced a firestorm of media attention and a public relations bonus, since it was estimated that more than a billion people worldwide saw the picture *because* of the controversy surrounding it. In defense, a Benetton spokesperson said the ad was used to increase AIDS awareness. AIDS activists denounced the use of a family's tragedy to sell sweaters. Media critics were alarmed that the photograph spread across two pages in a magazine appeared at first glance to be a news-editorial image. An unsuspecting magazine reader is briefly fooled into noticing the powerful visual message because of the perception that the picture is a part of a news story. Once the green Benetton logo and "800" catalog ordering telephone number is noticed, it is too late. Advertising, public relations, and journalism have been intentionally fused into the advertorial. From that moment on, the reader may be skeptical of all the rest of the pictures and stories in the magazine, whose credibility—a priceless commodity—is reduced.

In the case of the *Newsday* cover of Tonya and Nancy, the decision to manipulate the cover image was not based on a concern for illustration. In a highly competitive, mostly street-sales environment, an eye-catching cover picture acts as an ad for the publication. If journalism professionals concede the cover or top half of a magazine or newspaper as belonging to the realm of advertising rather than to news-editorial content, the publication will lose credibility for any other story, quotation, or image within its pages.

In a rare exhibition of photo editing agreement, *Newsweek* and *Time* magazines presented a police mug shot picture of O.J. Simpson on their covers the same week. But they drew a vastly different reaction from the public and media critics. Although the *Newsweek* cover image was altered to create a three-dimensional, sensational effect (the top of the picture around Simpson's head was removed), editors at *Time* were severely criticized for printing an artistic interpretation of the police picture in which Simpson's features were blurred and darkened by computer manipulation. Typical of the response was NAACP's Benjamin Chavis's complaint that the image made Simpson look more sinister, guilty, and like "some kind of animal." Even labeled on the contents page as a "photo-illustration," the practice of turning objective photographs into interpretive works of art is considered unethical by many in the profession—a blatantly hedonistic approach. The artist did not intentionally darken the photograph for racist reasons, but editors should have been aware that many readers would come to that conclusion.

Ethics and the Future of Visual Reporting

Visual reporting is undergoing an exciting and challenging period in its history. The photographic medium is currently in a hybrid or transitional period between traditional film and computer technologies. It is reasonable to predict that by the end of the first decade, visual journalists will no longer use film in their cameras.

Print and screen media will also dramatically change as households are linked with fiber optic technology. Newspapers and televisions will be transformed into a medium that combines the best attributes of the printed page, telephone, television, and computer. These stand-alone and portable teleputers (as some have called the new machine) will transform passive readers and viewers into active users with instantaneous links to text and images from sources all over the world.

CONCLUSION

No matter how the tools of journalism change, fundamental ethical concerns still apply. Displaying violent, sensational images for economic reasons, violating a person's privacy without a clear news sense for doing so, manipulating news-editorial pictures to alter their content, stereotyping individuals into preconceived categories, and blurring the distinction between advertising, public relations, and editorial messages were journalism concerns in 1902, are important topics in 2002, and will be carefully considered issues, no doubt, in 2102. Professionals, academics, and students owe it to their readers to be aware of unethical practices that demean the profession and reduce the credibility of journalism. In almost all cases, that means avoiding hedonism as a prime motivation for making and using images.

IDEAS FOR FURTHER STUDY

- Find a controversial image on the front page of a newspaper or from a television news show. Try to justify the image using every ethical philosophy discussed in this chapter. Which one philosophy works best for you personally?

- What are the ways readers can judge the credibility of an image even in this era of digital manipulation?

- Imagine yourself as a reader representative for a newspaper. What would you tell a reader who complained to you about a picture of a car wreck that was particularly upsetting?

From Great Tragedy, Humanity is Found

by Deni Elliott and Paul Martin Lester

Where were you when you learned that:

- President Kennedy was assassinated? (One of us was just back from lunch in Laredo, Texas; the other was in class in Hyattsville, Maryland).
- The space shuttle Challenger exploded? (One of us was in the darkroom in the Journalism School at Indiana University; the other was attending a committee meeting at Utah State University).
- The Federal building in Oklahoma was destroyed by a terrorist's bomb? (One of us was teaching a class at California State University, Fullerton; the other can't remember).
- The World Trade Center's Twin Towers were attacked and destroyed? (We were in bed listening to NPR News on the radio in Missoula, Montana).

These were moments of incredible historical significance, and yet deeply personal. These were personal moments because reporters and visual journalists made us feel those stories. These were moments destined to be forever a part of our visual memory. And soon, after hearing of each tragic news event from a teacher, a friend, or Bob Edwards, we quickly found a television set because we wanted to see, we *needed* to see, pictures.

The moments from those events we most remember are the ones that communicated our enduring humanity—the saluting John F. Kennedy Jr. during his father's funeral, chil-

dren in a classroom crying over the death of their teacher, Christa McAuliffe, Chris Fields gently carrying Baylee Almon after the Oklahoma City bombing, and two dust-covered firefighters hugging each other after both realizing they had survived the collapse of one of the Trade Center's towers.

But conversely, there are some news stories we see, read, and hear that don't make us feel.

Critics cry sensationalism, politicians cry favoritism, and readers cry paternalism when we are inundated with a constant barrage of misinformation and trivia pursuit from stories that take up too much time. Take your pick of scandals, botched investigations, and personal tragedies with these men in the news— Richard Jewel, OJ Simpson, and Bill Clinton.

A recent example comes to mind. When Chandra Levy, a Washington DC intern romantically linked to California Representative Gary Condit went missing and was feared dead, over several weeks, ABC's *World News Tonight* aired 14 minutes and NBC's *NBC Nightly News* aired 60 minutes about the case. CNN covered the story exhaustively with hourly updates on most days. But CBS only ran one, two-minute story.

Ironically, anchor Dan Rather and CBS News were criticized for *not* covering the Levy case. Some industry critics complained that the story had to be covered and so couldn't understand CBS's refusal to air reports. In defense, Rather responded, "What we were seeing, what we were hearing, wasn't always solid.

This article originally appeared in *News Photographer* magazine.

Often, it was rumor or gossip. We chose not to report that until we had something that we thought was important to the story. Without passing judgment on anybody else, I've tried to stand for what I believe in—decent, responsible journalism." Sensational gossip masqueraded as news never propels a people to do the right thing.

But sometimes we need totally saturated, 24-7, sensational coverage because of the nature of the story. The attacks upon the World Trade Center and the Pentagon are examples of stories that are no doubt sensational, yet unite us all out of concern and interest. And journalists should know the difference between the two.

From the morning of September 11, 2001, radio, television, and print media sources along with their website counterparts all went to work to try to inform and explain the horrific personal carnage and destruction that was unleashed against thousands of innocent Americans. Reporters gathered as much information as quickly as possible during the confusing and unbelievable first hours of the attack. With the north tower of the World Trade Center already on fire from a previous direct hit from an airplane, viewers on television saw live and unedited video footage of a commercial airplane slam into the south tower and then witnessed the collapse of both 110-story structures. Thousands were killed and many more were injured. The visual messages seemed more appropriate for a Hollywood movie than actual events.

In fact, it was those striking, unforgettable visual messages that make this story so compelling and memorable. President George W. Bush acknowledged the power of visual communication in his speech to the country the first evening of the tragedy, "The *pictures* of airplanes flying into buildings, fires burning, huge structures collapsing, have filled us with disbelief, terrible sadness and a quiet, unyielding anger."

The major television networks all agreed to suspend their competitive nature and share all footage they gathered at the various scenes of destruction and chaos. Professional and amateur video became a shared community resource. National Public Radio (NPR) News and other radio and television stations broadcast continuous news reports. Several newspaper editors quickly printed special or "extra" editions. Internet traffic on the World Wide Web slowed as information was sought online. In an ironic response to the fear that new media might replace the old, the search engine Google suggested that those who wanted more information should simply listen to the radio or watch television. And although the news reports were sometimes repetitious and incomplete, the earnest efforts of all those involved in reporting the stories outweighed any criticism that might be contemplated.

The challenge of media presentation and analysis is to know when coverage is proper and necessary and when it is gratuitous and shameful.

The visual impact of seeing a 757 commercial airliner slam into a building, the telephoto shot from across the river of the Twin Towers bellowing smoke, the incredible destructive power of buildings collapsing in a hail of concrete, steel, dust, and death, and the ash-filled post-apocalyptic scene of smashed cars, steel girders, and dust-covered rescue workers and photojournalists are images that make the front pages of newspapers and websites around the world.

Visual Perspectives

Pictures. Moments. Emotions. But is every possible moment fair game when the news event is so catastrophic? Is it acceptable journalism to show a woman waving a scarf out of one of the windows of a tower? Is it acceptable journalism to print a desperate soul falling from one of the fiery towers to certain death?

One of us says yes because that is our job and that is what we do; the other one says no because even the most public act demands some consideration for the privacy rights of these victims and their family and friends. We will no doubt continue to argue the issue of privacy in future columns, but fortunately, it will forever be the tiny moments, and not the most tragic ones, we will remember from this story—a doctor borrowing a suck of air from a firefighter's air nozzle, a man and his mother hugging after being lost then reunited, and the mental images evoked by the e-mail sent to the NPPA listserv by Steven E. Frischling, a photojournalist for Corbis Sygma out of Amherst, Massachusetts:

This scene is the most horrific thing I have ever seen in my life, just totally inconceivable. The destruction, the loss of life, finding out shooters were injured, and a firefighter and a medic I knew killed (or believed to be dead). The entire drive down I had no idea how bad it could be, and the entire drive back just wondering how it could have been that bad.

Covered in ash and having yet to sleep or bathe I stopped by my daughter's day care to see her, and since it was nap time just to kiss her and look at her. I am so grateful that the destruction was not

"here," but it still happened in my "home," and I am just devastated physically (burns on the back of my neck) and emotionally.

I do not think I will be sleeping for a while, I think the sounds and the smell will linger very much longer for me as I block the images from my mind.

Be grateful for what you have and remember the sun will rise tomorrow.

This is our job. This is what we do. But we also know that the greater the tragedy, the greater is our capacity to find humanity within the tiniest moments we capture with our machines, our eyes, and our hearts. ■

Steven E. Frischling/Corbis Sygma

Using Photography

In this section a chapter discusses preproduction, camera, lens, recording, lighting, and post-production technical considerations for visual journalists. Another chapter explains documentary photography assignments: spot and general news, human interest and pictorial features, sports action and features, and picture stories, and addresses photojournalism ethics. A third chapter details manipulated photography assignments: mug shots, environmental portraits, and editorial illustrations, along with fashion, public relations, and advertising images.

C H A P T E R 4

Technical Considerations

by Christopher R. Harris

Visual journalists are more than just recorders of news information. They are also information gatherers. Quite often they have to call upon a broad palette of background information in order to properly produce the photographic visuals needed in today's sophisticated world.

Advancements in coverage of news events around the world require that modern-day photographers have a better understanding of the world than at anytime in the past. These photojournalists become a combination of anthropologist, sociologist, political scientist, artist, and journalist.

Many of today's finest photojournalists have extensive backgrounds—and advanced degrees—in fields other than visual communication, or journalism. Often the photography they produce is based on this background knowledge of other fields. Photography becomes their outlet for the information they have gathered. Rather than using a traditional approach to research and publication, the modern visual journalist uses, as a means of validation, the sharing (publication) of her photography.

While a better understanding of the human condition can come about from an awareness of other peoples and cultures, none of that background and research potential counts one bit if the photographer can't produce informative images. It is that mix of investigation, research, and, ultimately, visual explanation that becomes the unique quality of the visual journalist. The work of a photographer does not count if the message can't be communicated to an audience.

Therefore, there is a need to produce the technical photographic message. This chapter addresses the technical concerns of photography.

Preproduction

In order to produce quality photographic images the photographers must lay the groundwork for their successful completion. Knowledge of the basic requirements of the assignment is necessary for any job, and the more successful the photographer the better the preproduction.

First and foremost is the assignment itself. The photographer must have a good grasp of what the assignment entails. What media are the photographs to be used in? Are they to be reproduced in a newspaper, magazine, book, on the Internet, or on television? What possible uses will the images have for those publications? Cover possibilities, horizontal or vertical images, commercial or documentary styles along with short "bites" or longer video essays are all concerns that need to be addressed in preproduction.

Another aspect of preproduction that the successful photographer must address is the possibility of developing more than one assignment in any area. If a photographer covers an event in a foreign country, or even in the next county, it makes good business sense to see what other visual possibilities are available. The more stories that a photographer can produce, the better the business potential is likely to be. However, the photographer must be somewhat cautious in the pursuit of additional photo stories. Obviously, no photographer wants to jeopardize an assignment for one that is speculative. Properly done, however, there should be no conflict in doing multiple assignments in any area. Good business dictates having an awareness of multiple assignment possibilities.

As an example, if you were to obtain an assignment to do a photo story on the French Quarter of New Orleans you would want to research and document the many varied aspects of that unique area. Through research you may decide to photographically cover the architecture, businesses, restaurants and other tourist-related aspects. But you would not necessarily include coverage of the lakefront with its specialty restaurants, or the antebellum homes of the city's uptown Garden

District. These are different stories in the same basic location, with multiple sales possibilities.

The additional coverage could become new assignments from other, non-competing, publications, or self-produced coverage for potential sale in the future. Using the Internet and other sources it is possible to alert others who might be interested in coverage of any area to your proposed travel plans and availability.

Conflicts of interest must be avoided, but that does not eliminate the possibility of shooting multiple assignments if they come about.

Equipment

Equipment selection can make or break an assignment. No job can be successfully completed without paying attention to the specific equipment needed to produce the desired results. Just as a surgeon requires certain specific tools, so does the successful photographer. While basic equipment is all that is required for most assignments, awareness of specialized equipment may yield unexpected, often exciting, results.

The Camera

The camera, a basic element of any photographer's arsenal, functions as a device to hold the exposure medium, whether it is film, videotape, or computer-coded information. Most cameras

- hold the lens in relationship to a specific "film plane,"
- determine exposure (if the camera body has a built-in meter),
- allow adjustment of the shutter speed, and
- advance the film or other media.

Edward Steichen, a famous photographer of the early twentieth century, is known for best showing that the function of the camera is universal. It is reported that Steichen, while on assignment for a publication in Greece, was about to photograph the famous dancer Isadora Duncan, at the Parthenon, when an American tourist came upon the scene. Pointing out Steichen's tripod-mounted, large-format view camera, the tourist announced that of course he would get a good picture—he had a fine expensive camera! Steichen was so taken aback that he purchased the tourist's box camera loaded with roll film, and promptly completed the assignment. One of those photographs later became a classic image.

Steichen's awareness of the primary need for content, composition, and style versus technical, mechanical equipment makes a valid point. Equipment should aid creative discovery. But equipment alone does not yield a creative product. That is the purview, and proper goal, of the creative photographer.

In addition to specific cameras for different media, such as film, video, or digital, cameras come in different standard styles and formats.

Film-Based Cameras

The standard styles of film-based cameras include the single-lens reflex (SLR), twin-lens reflex, rangefinder, and view cameras. While all have multiple format capabilities each camera style has its own unique qualities and attributes.

The Single-Lens Reflex   The single-lens reflex (SLR) is the most common still camera style in use by the active professional today. The SLR allows focusing and viewing through the lens, using a pentaprism and mirror scheme. As the shutter button is released, the mirror moves out of the way and allows the film to be exposed through the lens. Once exposed, the mirror drops back down into position for further viewing. All this occurs in the blink of an eye.

Since the SLR depends on through-the-lens viewing the result is generally a what-you-see-is-what-you-get quality that only the SLR and view camera have in common. Some SLR cameras show 100 percent of the image as it appears on the film, while others show less than the actual picture area, sometimes as little as 94 percent.

This ability to view and focus through the lens is particularly well suited to zoom and telephoto lenses. No other camera style allows a full complement of lenses, from super wide-angle to telephoto, to be used so easily. These camera and lens combinations are usually the lowest priced, and are available throughout the world. Most modern SLRs use either 35mm or medium-format roll film.

An example of a medium-format single-lens reflex camera.

Twin-Lens Reflex   The twin-lens reflex has two lenses mounted in specific relationship to each other, which allows viewing, and focusing, through the top lens
while the bottom lens is used for exposure. Most of these cameras have fixed, normal focal length lenses, which do not allow for interchangeability. There are a few
manufacturers who have produced add-on wide-angle and telephoto lenses, and
others have added removable lens pairs.

While viewing through the twin-lens reflex allows for a what-you-see-is-
what-you-get quality, any time close-focusing lenses are used the viewing lens does
not yield exactly what the taking lens sees, because of the distance between the
viewing and taking lenses. This inability to adjust for the difference between the
taking and viewing lens is called parallax. Simple parallax adjusters for use on
tripods are available for making exact corrections for the distance between the two
lenses. Most twin-lens reflex cameras are medium-format and shoot roll film.

The Rangefinder Camera   The rangefinder camera, sometimes called a viewfinder camera, depends on an optical rangefinder for focusing. In most instances
this is accomplished by using a double image spot that comes sharply into focus
when the two images merge.

The scene is then viewed through a viewfinder.
That viewfinder often contains multiple frames for individual focal length lens. Advanced rangefinder cameras
offer interchangeable lenses with automatic viewfinder
adjustment.

*The Leica M-6, 35mm
rangefinder camera.*

While most rangefinder cameras are 35mm format
and use roll film, there is a new trend towards medium-
format, roll film cameras.

The View Camera   The view camera is most often thought of as a studio camera. View cameras have no rangefinder or SLR capability. They are focused by viewing the image directly on the film plane, usually using a ground glass back.

They are normally large-format, and use sheet film. The most common sheet
film sizes for view cameras are 4 × 5 inches and 8 × 10 inches. Many view cameras
do offer medium-format, roll film back capabilities, however.

This style of camera is more stationary than the other camera styles. Due to
their bulk and focusing technique they almost always require a tripod for support.
This style of camera offers the most control of distortion and perspective, and,
because of its large-format capability, finer grain and contrast control.

Equipment—The Camera

The Lens

The lens has as its function the precise focusing of an image onto the film plane. Common attributes of any lens are the ability to be focused and to change the aperture, or opening, of the lens. Some lenses have as unique qualities speed, specialized focusing abilities, magnification, and distortion correction.

Proper selection of lenses to convey the photographer's scene is essential. There are several attributes that are shared by all photographic lenses.

Lenses can be of different focal lengths. Prime lenses are specific to their focal length, for example, 24mm, 50mm, or 85mm. Zoom lenses vary over a specific set of focal lengths, for example, 35–70mm or 70–210mm.

Lens speed is determined by the f-stop of the maximum aperture. Thus an f/2.8 lens is "faster" than an f/4 lens—that is, the f/2.8 lens allows in twice the light of the f/4 lens.

Photographic lenses fall into four general categories: wide-angle, normal, telephoto, and special purpose.

The different categories of lenses are based on one focal length for each film format being referred to as "normal."

The Wide-Angle Lens

The wide-angle lens offers a wider than normal view of a scene. It is usually in the 21mm to 35mm focal length for 35mm cameras.

These lenses afford a view that has a wider angle of coverage than a normal lens and are particularly well suited to "street" photography and photojournalism. The wide angle of coverage can be successfully used for photographing in tight quarters, and for making the viewer feel more closely involved with the scene being recorded.

Wide-angle lenses can be fast, with a wide-open aperture of f/2 or larger for ease in focusing and low-light situations. They have the ability, because of their wide angle of coverage, to distort a scene, however. The competent photographer will pay close attention to this troublesome quality, and learn to recognize any problems before they detract from the final image.

The wide-angle lens offers an increase in depth-of-field, which gives the appearance of more sharp detail over an extended range from close distance to infinity. This is an ideal choice for scenic photography.

The Normal Lens

The normal lens offers the least amount of distortion of any of the lens categories. It is visually fast, f/2.0 or even f/1.4, and focuses over an extended range, down to a normal close-focusing distance of twelve to eighteen inches.

The same scene shot with various lenses.

14mm lens

28mm lens

50mm lens

100mm lens

200mm lens

300mm lens

Photos: Christopher R. Harris

Normal lenses differ in their focal length according to the size of the film used in the camera:

- normal focal length lens for a 35mm camera is 50–55mm;
- for medium-format cameras the normal lens is 75–80mm; and
- for large format cameras the normal lens is in the 135–150mm focal length range.

The normal lens is invaluable in low-light situations. It is usually lightweight and is the least expensive of all lens types. Most photographers have used the normal lens in their basic training. It is by far the most common lens, yet for the advanced photographer it may become one of the least used.

The Telephoto Lens

Telephoto lenses have a longer focal length than the normal lens, generally in the 85mm to 300mm range. Telephoto lenses are usually slower than their normal or wide-angle counterparts and cost more. Specialty telephoto lenses can be fast, for example, the common photojournalists' f/2.8, 300mm lens, and also in "long" focal lengths of 400mm, 600mm, 800mm, and even 1200mm. These lenses act like a pair of binoculars in that they bring the scene closer to the photographer.

Telephoto lenses are widely used in sports and general news coverage as well as for portraiture. This type of lens is generally free of the distortions found in wide-angle lenses, though it has its own common type of distortion known as compression. The greater the focal length of the telephoto lens the more compression shown.

Compression is simply the general enlargement of the background scene as well as the subject scene. The background and foreground appear to be closer together than in real life. We have all seen images exhibiting telephoto compression, as, for example, a shot of a street crowded with pedestrians. We know that people do not really walk crowded like sardines, yet that is what the telephoto lens will show.

Telephoto lenses are favored for special effects, such as in movies when we see an actor dive safely away from an onrushing car. What appears to be hairsbreadth closeness is really several feet of space. The telephoto lens compresses the image, tricking the viewer into believing the distance between objects is smaller.

Special Purpose Lenses

Special purpose lenses cover a broad spectrum of optics. They may be extremely wide-angle, like the 17mm, or a specialty wide-angle, like the fisheye (8mm) that yields a circular image and has an angle of coverage of 300 to 320 degrees, or they may have special uses like the perspective control (PC) lens. Some have corrected optics for extreme close-up capabilities, like the modern macro lens.

Extreme telephoto lenses are often large and bulky, usually requiring a monopod or tripod for support. They are also quite expensive.

Specialized close-up lenses are corrected for flat-field coverage and have an extremely long focusing range of infinity to 1:1 reproduction. When used in conjunction with a bellows and focusing rail, image reproduction can increase to more than life size. Perspective control, or PC, lenses have the ability to shift part of their optics, thus correcting for lens tilt. They are extremely valuable for photographing architecture. Adjustments on the PC lens allow the photographer to correct any of the common leaning effects that occur when a camera is tilted in order to photograph something tall. Proper selection of lenses can make a photographic

Christopher R. Harris

Using a PC (perspective control) lens, the photographer can shoot corrected architectural photographs without having the buildings lean.

Equipment—The Lens

assignment proceed easily and without surprises. However, special attention needs to be paid in selecting the sharpest and most utilitarian of lenses. Carrying too many lenses can be as bad as not having the proper lenses to complete an assignment.

Supplies

Film or recording media are the next step in preproduction planning. Whether using traditional emulsion-based film, videotape, or SmartCards® to record the scene, the proper choice of media means less correction later and a better end result. All media are rated as to their relative speed in light-capturing qualities. Additionally, film is rated according to its properties of grain structure, sensitivity to the color spectrum, and whether it is negative or positive in nature.

Video media properties can be corrected as it is shot. A white balance can automatically correct for color sensitivity. Grain is usually not a concern for video media, with the exception of low-light situations, which cause the most problems. SmartCard® sensitivity is easily controlled prior to shooting in a range of 100–1600 ISO on some professional digital cameras. Today's cameras have the ability to capture 3–5 megapixels of digital code, yielding image results that rival traditional film in its qualities.

Film

Film is by far the most popular medium available to the photographer. Traditional film is the most common and most widely available of all recording media. Literally anywhere in the world a familiar yellow box of Kodak, a black box of Ilford, a green box of Fuji, or orange boxes of Agfa films are available to the discriminating photographer. All films have in common the general qualities of spectral sensitivity, speed, contrast, and grain.

Spectral Sensitivity

Black and white film is generally panchromatic, orthochromatic, or infrared in its spectral sensitivity. Color film is usually daylight or tungsten light-source responsive. Panchromatic film is responsive to most areas of the color spectrum. Orthochromatic film is limited in its response to the color spectrum, and usually records only in the areas of the red end of the spectrum. Infrared film only responds to the infrared end of the color spectrum. Both black and white and color films may be either negative or positive in nature.

Color film has two general light temperature qualities. It may be daylight- or tungsten-balanced. Daylight-balanced film is rated for the color temperature sensitivity of daylight. This is indicated as 5500°K. Tungsten-balanced films are made to be properly exposed in light having the spectral sensitivity of 3200°K. While these color balances may be obtained by filtration, they may also be easily balanced by exposing to light sources equal to the Kelvin temperature requirements. A special color temperature meter can accurately measure the Kelvin degrees of any scene. Filters may then be used to successfully color-correct the scene.

Film Speed

Film speed is rated according to the general standards of the International Standards Organization (ISO). The ISO speed is a relative speed rating with the higher the number being the faster film. A film speed of 100 is often considered a medium-speed film. Several qualities can be related to the individual film's ISO rating. In general, the slower the film speed the more contrast; conversely, the faster the speed, the less contrast. Faster film has more grain and slower film has less. Modern

Supplies—Film

Color is subjective. This scene in a nuclear energy control room (below) *was shot using tungsten film. Another shot of the same facility* (left) *was shot with daylight film.* (See CP-6 and CP-7.)

Photos: Christopher R. Harris

Christopher R. Harris

With high-speed films like this Kodak Delta 3200 film, available light photographs can be made anywhere.

film technology has lessened the impact of film grain. Today's 1600 ISO film has a tighter, smaller grain structure than the 400 ISO–rated film of just a few years ago.

Specialized films that work better when scanned into computer code for use in electronic darkrooms have also been developed. These films usually offer wider contrast and better highlight control.

Contrast

Contrast quality is dependent not only on speed but also on the type of developer used to process the particular emulsion. Where high-intensity developers can increase contrast, compensating developers often lessen the inherent contrast of the film. Developer/film contrast combinations apply only to black and white film. Most photographers do not develop their own film. It is their responsibility to tell the processor if any special developing requirements are needed.

Contrast in color film is generally controlled by film selection. Most color film is developed in special processing kits with standard developers. Excessive contrast is more pronounced in the positive, or transparency, films, and is more evident in the highlight areas.

Film contrast is easily controlled if a film is to be scanned. Modern computer software such as Adobe Photoshop® can be used to easily correct film contrast problems as well as most other problems.

Proper preproduction planning for the type of recording medium is essential for optimum results.

Miscellaneous Equipment

The modern visual journalist also uses other equipment than just the camera and lens in the production of photographic images.

Strobe—or flash—lighting, different styles of meters, filters, and camera bags generally round out the visual journalist's tools-of-the-trade. But by far the most common need in the miscellaneous category of equipment is the battery. With the advent of the modern camera came the utter dependence on the battery for power.

While many batteries are rechargeable, some of the most common batteries used in cameras and auxiliary devices are not. The lithium battery is currently used throughout the camera industry and is generally not rechargeable.

Batteries are expensive and quickly expended by modern equipment, so an adequate supply of fresh batteries is always needed. If using rechargeable batteries, make sure you know the voltage requirements for the recharging equipment and for the location of the assignment. A recharger with a plug oriented to U.S. electrical wiring is useless in a country that uses a different kind of plug receptacle. Typical American plugs use two blades and one round pole, for example; U.K. outlets use three rounded poles. A simple voltage converter and set of international plugs will usually cure any problem.

Light Meters

Different types of light meters and spectral sensitivity meters are available to the photographer. Light meters fall into three general categories: reflected, incident, or spot meters. They all measure light as an 18 percent gray tone between 0 percent (black) and 100 percent (white). Whatever subject matter they cover is translated to a value of 18 percent gray. After the value is computed, a combination of shutter speeds and apertures at a specific film speed is determined.

Reflected light meters, usually aimed toward the subject from the camera position, measure the light *reflected off* the subject. Incident light meters measure the light *as it falls on* the subject. These meters usually have a "golf ball" style light-measuring dome. They are held at the subject and aimed mid-way between the camera and light source.

Spot meters measure a small angle of coverage, usually 5 degrees or less, and measure reflected light only. Care must be taken to choose a proper mid-tone gray as the reflected measurement area.

Lighting

Many assignment locations will lack proper photographic lighting, but the photographer can choose among several types of lighting sources to correct for any deficiencies. Strobe (flash) and tungsten lighting are the two most common forms of photographic lighting.

Strobes

Strobe lighting equipment is available in lightweight portable hand-held models, larger self-contained light-stand–mounted units, or more powerful heavyweight units. Each has its special qualities. Most strobes are light-balanced at 5500°K, or daylight.

Lightweight, hand-held units are the chosen light source of the photojournalist. They offer enough light to handle almost any situation with medium and fast films and many have an automatic light-measuring capability for automatic exposure.

Self-contained lights offer more power and can often be easily controlled. This style of strobe may be electric or battery powered.

Small hand-held strobes can give many different results with the use of reflectors.

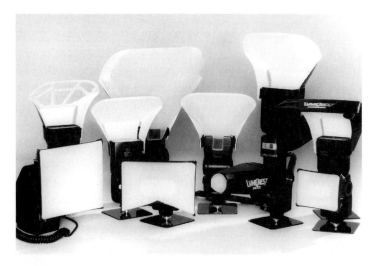

The most powerful strobes are powered with large electric capacitors that store enormous voltage. They are capable of emitting large amounts of light which would allow the photographer a choice of "stopping down" for the maximum depth-of-field. These strobes are often used in studio locations.

Strobes vary in the speed of the light given off. The less powerful strobes may fire off at a speed equivalent to 1/1000 second or less, while the more powerful units may yield a speed of 1/100,000 second or faster.

All strobes synchronize with cameras and lenses at specific sync speeds, which differ from camera to camera but are usually in the range of 1/60 second to 1/250 second. While the camera may be set to any speed on its shutter speed dial, only those speeds at, or slower than, the sync speed will give proper results. A setting higher than the stated sync shutter speed will produce only partially exposed film frames because the shutter will not be fully open during the exposure process.

Filters may be used on any strobe in order to yield a multitude of desired corrections or color effects. Because strobes are "cool" light sources the photographer is not concerned with heat given off by them.

Tungsten Lighting

Tungsten lighting uses electrically powered bulbs corrected to either 3200 °K or 3400°K. Their light intensity is measured with traditional light meters and is continuous, so any shutter speed can be used. These light sources can generate high temperatures and are considered "hot." Attention must be given to position these "hot" lights so that they do not damage the subject matter they are illuminating. Their heat can present risks if any object, including filters, is placed too close to the light bulbs. Gelatin filters placed over a tungsten light source have started many a studio fire.

There are many ways to alter the intensity and contrast of light sources to yield different qualities of light. Soft lighting can be obtained by using photographic umbrellas or soft-boxes, while harder, more contrasting lighting can be achieved by using focusing (fresnel) lenses to concentrate the light source.

Lighting effects are covered more fully in Chapter 6.

Equipment and Camera Bags

Since anything you take with you on an assignment can be damaged during transportation, camera and equipment bags are essential. Equipment bags can be hard or soft sided; some come with heavy duty metallic hardware and locks, some with nothing more than clips to keep a flap covering the equipment secured.

Equipment and Camera Bags

Each style has certain advantages that must be weighed against disadvantages. For instance, hard-sided bags allow for more protection but are heavier and bulkier, whereas soft-sided bags are usually less bulky and easier to work out of. A photographer would not want to carry an aluminum-clad attaché-style case when shooting a football game; the soft-sided, snap-closure canvas bag would be efficient and sufficient. On the other hand, the soft bag might not be appropriate for photographic coverage of a scientific expedition on location in a desert. The hard-sided, gasket-equipped, compartmentalized box could definitely help to prevent sand and dust from damaging the equipment inside. But many photojournalists carry all of their photographic equipment in a soft-sided bag worn on the shoulder for instant access, and they often ship lighting and special-purpose equipment in hard-sided bags for protection and then load it into soft bags for use in the field.

Another risk to equipment is theft. Frequently, it is best to carry what equipment you can without drawing attention to the fact that it is cameras and lenses. Where aluminum hard-sided bags offer physical protection, they are a signal to any thief that they contain valuable equipment. One solution is to ship equipment in the best protection possible and then transfer to less noticeable common, soft-sided bags.

Travel Logistics

The general logistics of the assignment is another concern to the photographer. Some logistics involve the social and economic values of the area and people to be covered. Others strictly relate to the physical and general safety of the traveling photographer. The well-traveled photographer knows that paying attention to the logistics of an assignment during the planning stage can mean the difference between success and disaster.

First in any logistics analysis is the location of the assignment. Once the geographic location of the assignment is known a photographer must ask, how do I get there? What local customs do I face? What equipment can I take with me? How can anyone get in touch with me? Traveling in your own country or local region is relatively simple, but leaving home turf on assignment may present difficulties. If you have interested an editor of a magazine in an assignment to cover the fabled butterflies of Belem, Brazil, in the heart of the Amazon, what is entailed in getting there and back? Researching airline connections, car rentals, and hotels would be in order. But what about more basic questions, such as, what currencies will be needed? What language barriers are there? What customs documents, legal and business forms, or certifications are needed? What about insurance coverage for equipment and personal safety?

Currency

Find out what currencies you may need on your trip and their rate of exchange for U.S. currency. Should foreign currency be purchased before you arrive in the country? You bet. There is nothing worse than struggling from airport to hotel only to find out that you have no way to pay for the cab in the local currency. You will be paying more if you have to use American dollars or exchange large sums for local money at your hotel. Be smart and obtain enough of the destination currency to see you through at least a day of living expenses. Then after settling in you can search out a bank or exchange house to obtain enough of the local currency to last the journey.

A common safety factor to consider when traveling is to carry travelers' checks in addition to hard currency. American Express and Thomas Cook and Sons are the international banking and travel authorities recognized throughout the world. Any of their major offices can assist the traveler in currency exchanges along with another important service; they can function as a message center, where you can leave as well as receive messages. These international offices will also have information about local hospitals, doctors, and lawyers. If the need arises, there is nothing like a well-informed local contact to assist you in solving problems in the field.

Local Customs and Business Needs

Some countries and localities require specific documentation in order to gain admission. In addition to entry visas and passports these may include specialized business, medical, or legal documentation. You may need, for instance, work permits in order for you or anyone you hire in the local area to be allowed to work in a region. Legal documents may also be needed for banking or for importing or exporting your equipment and finished work. Your host country may control even the amount of film and photographic equipment you can bring in with you. Medical documents showing immunizations and inoculations may also be required before entry, and you may need special insurance coverage. In many foreign countries you need an International Drivers License. It would be wise to check with a consulate or embassy of the country where you plan to travel for guidelines.

Customs Registration of Photographic Equipment

Be sure to register your photographic equipment by serial number with your insurance agent and then using your insurance policy apply for U.S. Customs registration of your equipment before you ever leave the United States. If you don't, you may have to pay U.S. Customs duty on items you already own and have paid taxes

A U.S. Customs declaration form.

on. You must make this declaration before you leave the United States. (Contact your nearest U.S. Customs bureau for full information or go to their Web site www.customs.ustreas.gov.)

After the Assignment

Post-production concerns include proper maintenance of your equipment, image cataloging, sales of the resultant imagery, and support and application for reimbursement of expenses.

Once the job is done and you and your equipment have made it home it's time to send your film for processing, assess your equipment for possible damage, and check your supplies.

Travel can damage photographic equipment, especially from vibration during transportation. Check for loosened screws and other effects of the constant abuse. Use dry, canned air to blow dust out of cameras and lenses. Check for battery leaks, and discard any old batteries. (Never leave questionable batteries in your equipment; they can cause extensive damage that can be very costly to repair.) And examine photographic lighting for loose or damaged electrical connections and possible bulb damage.

Once you have checked your images for technical and aesthetic quality, edit and identify the pictures for your client. If photographs are to be submitted to an agent for stock purposes, make sure to have proper credit and caption information placed with your images.

Be sure to check on any embargoes of your work that may be in place. If a client has requested that no photographs from the take you have been hired to produce are reproduced for a specific time period, be sure to honor that commitment.

When you return from an assignment take the time to fill out any expense forms from receipts you have collected. Major sums can be lost when out-of-pocket expenses are not properly reimbursed. It is up to you to report them. Be sure to keep records of any expenses not covered by your client—they may be deductible from your income taxes.

After the Assignment

This photograph of a Cape Cod–style house was "property released" so that more, higher-paid, sales could be made. So far this image has earned over $10,000.

Photos: Christopher R. Harris

A stock image of the marketplace at Chichicastenango, Guatemala. Travel stock is one of the biggest moneymakers for the freelance visual journalist.

CONCLUSION

With proper attention to preproduction any photographer can make every job easier to complete. But remember, having all the technical details worked out in pre- and post-production will still not guarantee satisfactory images that will be useful to others. A firm grasp of the types of assignments you are most likely to encounter will bring a better chance of favorable results. The next two chapters focus on assignment concerns.

IDEAS FOR FURTHER STUDY

- Research images showing photographers covering a news story. What type of equipment are they using?
- Try to identify lighting styles when looking at news or illustration photographs.
- How many stock photographs can you identify in a magazine?

A Life in Photojournalism

by Sherri LaRose, Staff Photographer, Columbus (Georgia) *Ledger-Enquirer*

I knew I wanted to study photojournalism when I was in high school. My classes then emphasized the artistic side of photography, which was a good foundation.

I had not worked at a newspaper in high school but I wanted my work published so I began working at my college newspaper. There I got experience in shooting spot news, features, and sports assignments. I learned photo page layout and how to write a cutline. I became the chief photographer at the school paper and helped the editors organize the photo assignments. That included calling the pool of photographers to find someone to cover an event, and if no one could take the assignment, I would.

I was close to graduation and began to worry about finding a job in the career I had chosen. I decided to look for an internship at a newspaper but I was too late. It was March of 1994 and many of the newspapers I contacted had either chosen an intern or did not have a program. Through a family friend I contacted the Tennessee Valley Authority (TVA), who publishes a monthly news magazine and seemed interested in a having a summer intern. The TVA chief photographer liked my portfolio and said he would be in touch with me if he could get approval from his boss. I would live with my family so I was willing to take an unpaid internship just to get experience and tearsheets. He called a month later to say that cutbacks had eliminated the entire staff except for the chief photographer and that they couldn't have even an unpaid intern.

After sending out resumes for months I took a vacation, moved home, and called a weekly newspaper in my hometown in early June. Within a week the publisher contacted me, saw my portfolio, and offered me a non-paying internship. There I first learned that driving around looking for features is part of the normal workday. I also learned I never wanted to work at a weekly, with its "grip and grins" day after day. An occasional interesting story would keep me going, and so did seeing my hard work published and appreciated. I was touched by a letter to the editor from a woman who just wanted to say that she enjoyed my photographs and looked forward each week to seeing them. I went back to college for my last semester as chief photographer for the college bi-weekly paper.

I was a member of the National Press Photographers Association and checked the job bank listing every couple of weeks to find what jobs I was qualified for and what employers wanted. I sent out resumes and portfolios from August through December until I graduated. My portfolios came back with comments like "very nice portfolio." Apparently other applicants were more qualified. I had graduated and had no job and I was exhausted. Two days later I decided to move to Atlanta to live with my brother.

I assumed Atlanta would have more opportunities for newspaper photographers. It was almost January and a new year. I applied at almost every small newspaper around the Atlanta area and the state of Georgia and no one was hiring, though some said I should apply again in a few months, when they might be hiring. After working six months in a photo lab I saw a classified ad for a part-time photojournalist at a daily in Douglasville, just outside of Atlanta.

I was hired right away. Then I wondered if I could live on the salary. But I enjoyed working at the paper whose circulation was around 11,000 and getting to know people in a small town. I had to look for feature art every day but I could usually find something going on, from saddle maker to tattoo parlor. I worked there five months, when on a rainy Saturday afternoon while covering a high school football game I met a photographer for a larger daily paper in Marietta, Georgia. We were wearing the same Fuji film professional poncho that was given out at an NPPA conference. We talked for a while about the newspapers we worked at and how we liked photography. He told me there was an opening at the *Marietta Daily Journal* (MDJ) and that I should apply. (Always be friendly to other photographers because you never know who you will meet.) I didn't really give the job a second thought—I was poor but happy working twenty-seven hours a week at a small paper with a great staff.

On Monday that friendly photographer phoned to say the chief photographer wanted to see my work. I was excited by the idea of advancing to a larger paper with a 35,000 circulation, but it happened so quickly I was pessimistic. But I got the job and began work two weeks later.

My first exciting assignment was at Dobbins Air Force Base in Marietta a few days into the job. Immigration and Naturalization Service marshals had arrested fifty or more Mexican nationals working illegally in the Atlanta area and were deporting them to Mexico. The only rule I was told to follow was to not photograph the marshals' faces for safety reasons because they should not be identifiable. The reporter and I complied because we had a good working relationship with the Air Force base and were lucky to be there to capture the event. Helicopters from three Atlanta television stations were hovering over us trying to get footage as the Mexicans were being loaded into a jet. My portfolio still includes a photo story of one of the illegal immigrants being led to the plane in handcuffs and chains.

In October of 1995 on the morning after a horrible fire had ripped through an apartment complex, I was told to go cover the residents sifting through items they had lost. When I got there I wasn't sure how the residents would like being photographed just then. But I met a young teenage girl with a Red Cross volunteer and was invited to many of the apartments. After about an hour I saw a woman looking through her bookshelf. Suddenly she picked up a Bible and I shot frame after frame. I was shooting up through a second story window that had been knocked out and the ceiling was gone so the lighting was perfect. I then yelled up to her and asked her if the Bible was undamaged and she answered, "Yes." I walked around and waited until she came outside and I asked her name. She asked if I was with a large paper and when I said I was with the MDJ she told me her name. I asked about the Bible again and she replied, "The only thing that is important are pictures of my mother and the 'good book.'" That day had an effect on me for a long time, making me want to stay with journalism and share my photographs with others.

You beg for the opportunity to cover some stories and then find yourself wondering if you can do it or whether you will be physically sick. I wanted to cover a feature that involved flying in a stunt plane during the air show at the local naval air station and thought the opportunity was worth the risk. I was excited and ready to fly that morning until I saw the two-seater plane sitting on the runway. I talked to the pilot for a few minutes about the plane and was even all right with the whole parachute idea. The pilot was an amateur photographer and had affixed a Nikon N90 to the wing with a 14mm lens and a remote. I grabbed the remote and we were off. As I glanced back at my reporter I noticed a man sitting up against a car tire in the shade. I would later learn that he was a photographer with the largest paper in Atlanta. He became airsick on a flight with the same pilot only minutes before I arrived. My reporter didn't tell me about the photographer's nausea because he feared I would change my mind and there would be no story. I have an image in my mind of my reporter waving happily to me as the plane taxied down the runway. I didn't get sick and I shot some wonderful photographs.

You don't have exciting news events at a medium-sized newspaper every day, so you must keep yourself motivated. The other three photographers and I often find ourselves sitting in the office listening to a scanner. We use this "down time" to discuss photo story ideas, equipment problems, and tips we have discovered on the job. I cover the afternoon and evening shifts, which means a lot of sports. I had thought sports photography was not as interesting as spot news, but I've improved at it and now I love it.

Social events and the bad story ideas reporters sometimes give me are frustrating, but if I just do them I might get a story with more potential later. I try to photograph each story as well as I can, and I look for a new story every day.

I found a new job at a bigger newspaper in a smaller town through the NPPA Job Bank Listing in 1998. A friend once told me, "Just send the portfolio and forget about it," and that is the best advice I could pass on to someone interested in photojournalism. My job as a staff photographer at the *Columbus Ledger-Enquirer* lets me spend more time on assignments, and the quality of my work has improved. The town is very diverse and the newspaper is very in tune with the community.

Why do I work for such a small salary? I honestly love my work. Every day is different from the next. I have grown to love capturing and documenting the daily events of a city. Living on a photojournalist's salary is not easy if you're used to a comfortable lifestyle, but I had already endured the financial hardships of four and a half years as a student, a photo lab job, and part-time employment.

When I photograph wealthy people I wonder what it would be like to live like they do, but I also photograph poor people and then I thank my family for the opportunity to go to college and have a job with so many possibilities. Being out there on the job can teach you so much about real life and about people. I guess what keeps me there is not just working on exciting stories with opportunities for great photographs for your tearsheets, but the stories of little boys who didn't receive Christmas gifts and the policeman who helped get them presents. Those human-interest stories touch me and I know they touch others.

My passion is photography; I've wanted to capture wonderful, meaningful images ever since I was twelve when my father introduced me to it. I take my camera everywhere I go and I even have a hard time enjoying an event if I can't photograph it. ■

The Visual Journalist

Visual reporting combines the roles of writer, photographer, infographics creator, researcher, and graphic designer. The visual journalist must bring together all that words, images, and technology can do to communicate a message.

Both of these illustrations make use of conventional studio photography, shot on film, and then scanned into digital format. The images are manipulated at the computer to create a range of interesting effects.

CP-1 (see page 4)

CP-2 (see page 27)

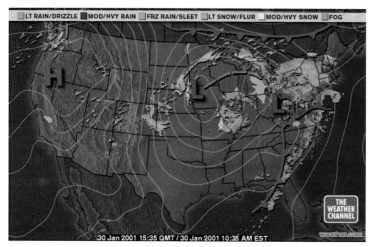

Infographics can convey information that would be tedious to explain in words alone. For example, a weather map, which can quickly and effectively show the progress of complex weather patterns, complements the broadcaster's spoken weather report.

CP-3 (see page 210)

Using Visual Cues

The brain perceives four basic visual cues—color, form, depth, and movement. Graphic artists create designs with these four cues alone and in combination to convey a message effectively.

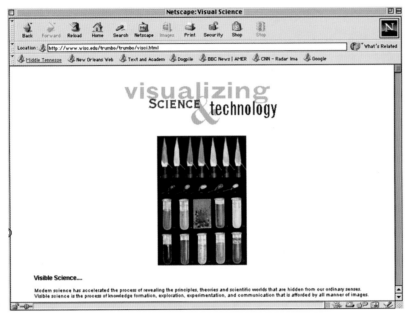

In planning a color-intensive design like this one, graphic artists consider each color's objective, comparative, and subjective qualities. Subjective qualities include emotional and cultural associations linked to particular colors.

CP-4 A web page design based on color (see page 31)

Use of form (dots, lines, and shapes) helps determine how an audience will respond to a given design. Visual journalists need to know how these elements will affect the viewer.

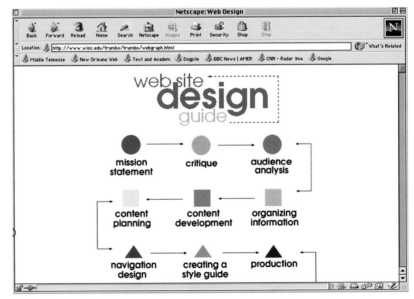

CP-5 A web page design based on form (see page 33)

Spectral Sensitivity

Choice of film can help the photographer achieve subtle tonal effects. Different types of black and white and color film respond to different areas of the color spectrum.

This photo was shot on daylight film, yielding a warm tone.

CP-6 (see page 73)

A similar shot, made on tungsten film, achieves more neutral tones.

CP-7 (see page73)

General News Photography

This form of documentary photography records ordinary events. General news photography is never staged, and these images should not be manipulated—their aim is to capture an authentic slice of life.

CP-8 (see page 99)

CP-9 (see page 99)

General news photography often portrays famous people taking part in everyday life. In these photos, presidential candidate Jimmy Carter attends Easter Sunday services and enjoys a campaign picnic. His daughter Amy sells lemonade on the front lawn. Several general news photographs may be combined as part of a well-rounded feature story.

CP-10 (see page 99)

CHAPTER 5

Documentary Assignments

by Christopher R. Harris

Visual messages affect us all. Most people can't speak of a time when the influence of visual journalism hasn't been felt. Whether informing an absent public of the movements of politicians, armies, citizenry, or reporting a news event for its historical value, photographic documentation has been with us since photography's inception.

It was in the late 1800s that printing technology progressed to the point that the popular press in both magazines and newspapers first had the ability to publish photographs directly, without a woodcut artist's interpretation.

A mere one hundred fifty years old, photography is in its infancy. Because of its relatively young age we can trace its history fairly well.

In 1856 the British journalist Roger Fenton sailed on the ship *Hecla* to cover the ongoing Crimean war visually, becoming the first reporter to use the new medium of photography for the print media. He became, as photo historian Beaumont Newhall has written, the first "faithful witness," a photographic witness for those who could not be present.

Use of photography in news magazines began with "The Illustrated American" in the 1890s. This page shows a typical story, the coal mines of Wilkes-Barre, Pennsylvania.

Since the first photograph appeared in halftone reproduction in the New York *Daily Graphic* on March 4, 1880, viewers have come to trust what they see in publications. That scene of "Shantytown, New York" so changed the ability to tell a story that a new form of journalism was to take shape: photojournalism.

It wasn't long before those faithful qualities of the documentary photograph could be reproduced in most magazines and newspapers. Until then the documentary evidence of photography was not printable directly, and it suffered through the translation of woodcut artists. As time progressed the advances of flexible roll film and halftone screen reproduction allowed the photographer to record life as witnessed, for all to see—with no outside artistic interpretation.

As the twentieth century progressed so did the value of publications that used photography to enhance coverage of events worldwide. In the United States *Life*, *Look*, *National Geographic*, and other photojournalism-intensive publications changed this country, and perhaps the world, with their examples of quality photojournalism. As they displayed the different aspects of cultures and peoples around the world on their pages, they presented for generations of viewers a universe that had not previously been known to them. These images visually documented scenes that forced viewer response.

These reader-viewers learned about what was happening in the world through the information contained in news photographs. They learned to trust these visual messages for their news content and they discovered that photographs often told more than the accompanying written stories.

Images of poverty and racism, and power and abuse became embedded forever in the mind's eye, as did the images of violence, sorrow and grief. Margaret Bourke-White and Arthur Rothstein visually recorded with photographs the Great Depression of the 1930s for all to see on the pages of *Life* and other publications. Robert Capa, W. Eugene Smith, Carl Mydans, Joe Rosenthal, and others documented World War II. David Douglas Duncan eloquently documented the war in Korea, while Alfred Eisenstadt and Peter Stackpole covered the growth of the boom era of the 1950s. Henri Cartier-Bresson and Robert Frank documented the general worldview. The peak of modern photojournalistic coverage came about during the tumultuous 1960s and 1970s.

Many still recall Jack Thornell's photograph of James Meredith being gunned down, with the would-be assassin still crouching in the distance, Charles Moore's coverage of police dogs attacking and biting peaceful protesters in Birmingham, and Bernie Boston's image of a peaceful protester putting a flower into the gun barrel held defensively by a National Guardsman.

These images are so believable that they speak of a unique truth that sometimes forces us to confront our personal faults and beliefs. The constant flood of news images during the 1960s and 1970s forced the people in the United States to view and examine anew themselves and their morality. These were the news images that helped a nation pass the Civil Rights Act and force the end of an unpopular war in Vietnam. These same images changed personal beliefs that were the tradition or norm for decades. News photos made it possible for everyone to see new aspects of everyday life.

A new awareness arose from the public's reaction to these images that changed the way Americans thought about themselves and others. The veracity of

The famous photograph by Dorothea Lange entitled "Migrant Mother with Children" was shot at the height of the economic depression of the 1930s.

the photojournalism images countered the articulated statements of those who would say that the event was different. What words attempted to describe, photographs stated for all to see.

It was known that dogs tore at innocent protesters' flesh in Birmingham. It was known from the documentary photographs that a different form of confrontation between protesters and authority took place in Chicago during the Democratic national convention. It was discovered from news images published in news magazines and on television that what was really occurring in Vietnam was wrong. The face of Mary Vecchio at Kent State recorded the horror of the consequences of confrontation between peaceful student protesters and authority. These vitally important images were believable because they offered visual proof, veracity, of what those involved in the individual conflicts told us about, not what some powerful group would want people to believe from press releases and false information. Veracity means conformity with truth or fact, that is, accuracy. And photojournalism's documentary basis in journalistic practice depends on accuracy.

Photographic Credibility

Everyone has experienced the truth of a photograph. The snapshots on fireplace mantels and on office desks are truthful representations of those we hold dear. These images are so believable that copies are sent to others to show what individuals look like at different times in their lives.

Most viewers believe what they see. Eddie Adams's horrible scene of Colonel Loan executing a suspected Vietcong terrorist won him the Pulitzer Prize for news photography and helped show the world the horrors of that war. The truth of what was happening on campuses was shown in the face of that horror-stricken, unbelieving fourteen-year-old runaway, Mary Vecchio, kneeling over the body of Jeff Miller in the Kent State parking lot. And, as John-John Kennedy gave his public good-bye salute to his father, the people of the world mourned. The images of the family's grief served to symbolize the nation's grief. These images were more than representations of actual events; they were visualizations of deeper truths.

Because they were measured, perhaps subconsciously, against an individual's personal reality, these images reinforced each person's instinctive "knowledge" that news pictures don't lie, that pictures are worth a thousand words, and that seeing is indeed believing. Once again, the images were accurate in what they depicted; they exhibited veracity. It is the responsibility of the visual journalist, when doing documentary coverage, to maintain veracity.

The very turbulence and catharsis created by those examples of photojournalism for society as a whole may foreshadow the turbulence and tension within the ranks of photojournalists as they struggle with new technologies and old ethical problems.

Photojournalism Ethics

When photojournalists falsify photo situations, whether by setting up a picture or manipulating an image in any substantive manner, their actions damage the reputation of the individual, the publication, and the craft of photojournalism in general.

And now there are new technological advances that have an impact on documentary photography. These new computer-driven technologies make it possible to more rapidly "capture" and transmit photographs of momentous events, but they also allow for image distortion and manipulation at a level unthinkable a few years ago. In the process, the "new age" photojournalist may be destroying the credibility of news images for the future.

Not that the history of photojournalism is spotless. One of the earliest cases of manipulation and distortion of the documentary image came from the photographic coverage of the American Civil War.

The author of one of the most famous images from that war, "Home of a Rebel Sharpshooter," was Alexander Gardner. The image of the dead Vermont sniper, Andrew Hoge, was photographed by Gardner on the battlefield in the uniform of a Confederate soldier. The dead soldier was also posed at different locations in the uniform of the Union army. The implication from this discovery is that the accuracy and truth of most photographs of the war are suspect. They no longer are photojournalistic, but fall into another genre of photography often associated with journalism, illustration. This distortion of photographic accuracy, or veracity, is one troublesome consequence associated with modern computer technology.

An ethical "slippery slope" develops from casual manipulation of any image. It is easy to approve the manipulation of a new image if another image has previously had "minor" corrections made to it with no ethical concerns being raised, for example. Once on the ethical slippery slope an editor may disregard a deletion of a bothersome antenna from a photograph as being of no consequence. The basic substance of the photograph isn't changed, some would argue. Except that this minor manipulation then opens the door to others. This is when we start sliding down the ethical slippery slope. If it is acceptable to delete portions of a photograph, then maybe it is permissible also to add something to a photograph.

This slippery slope syndrome has allowed bodies to be combined with different heads and pyramids to be moved, despite the images' basic photojournalistic untruthfulness or inaccuracy. Besides ethical dilemmas there are legal concerns. The photojournalistic craftsman now runs the risk of losing inherent legal rights associated with authorship, such as rights to control derivation, right of paternity, ownership, and intellectual rights. Possible loss of authorship identity is another concern, as defined under the Lanham Act, a federal trademark statute.

Computer Manipulation of Pictures

It is now possible to have news images that are unverifiable. Because of advances in computer technology, it is possible to manipulate minute elements of a photograph so that the manipulation is undetectable, untraceable, and seamless. This capacity for manipulation and/or distortion exists at two different levels. The more serious may be at the transmission and editing level, the less serious may be the "image capturing" equipment itself.

In the new computer-driven transmission and editing systems, the visual message, whether produced through traditional film-based photography or new digital imaging cameras, is scanned into a transmitting computer and broken up into a digital binary code of 0s and 1s. This code can then be transmitted by radio signal to a satellite or over traditional telephone cables. The signal, containing the code that makes up the image, is then sent to an electronic picture desk: a computer base. Here the coded image can be enhanced, color corrected, or manipulated in any other way the computer operator or "picture editor" commands. Specific elements of the binary code, picture elements, or pixels, may be individually manipulated before the reconstructed photograph is sent, either electronically or as traditional hard copy to the press for printing.

These forms of computer manipulation leave no "fingerprint" to prove that the news image as originally seen and photographed has been manipulated at any stage of the operation. Without an original image for comparison, it is impossible to prove whether the manipulated image is a faithful representation of a news event or a falsified and deceptive manipulation of fact.

All the major news organizations worldwide have installed and are using these new technologies. The photo departments of *San Francisco Examiner* and other newspapers have become totally digital, with no traditional "wet darkroom." This new technological revolution in news photography is being hailed by some as a time for photojournalism's coming of age; others predict the demise of accurate, believable visual journalism.

Some publications have installed security systems to protect against unauthorized computer manipulation of news images, but that security usually applies only to access, and not to the amount or type of manipulation that can take place in the newsroom. There have already been harmful transgressions of the gatekeeping security commitment of non-manipulation of imagery and its resultant deception of the public by the media. Photo documents of historic Soviet-American events have been manipulated, for example, and two or more images spliced seamlessly together have been passed off as one.

Gratuitous manipulation of digital images have consistently altered skies, not only changing the photodocumentary nature of the finished product, but violating the integrity of the photographer's intent. This kind of unauthorized manipulation both creates ethical dilemmas and jeopardizes the legal rights afforded to the photographer under the Revised Copyright Act of 1976. The rights of freelance, non-staff, photographers are particularly threatened. Staff photographers usually sign away their rights in a "work for hire" clause in their hiring agreement and so they have no copyright protection for the photographs produced on the job. Freelance photographers should avoid signing "work for hire" agreements.

Computers are not to blame, however. On the contrary, the new computer technology is exciting and vital to the field of photojournalism. It is the operators of the computers and those in authority, usually editors, who oversee the manipulation of images who are at the heart of the matter. The over application of computer manipulation is a most troubling cause of concern to the field of photojournalism and the visual journalist.

The general public should be aware of the potential for both good and bad new processing technologies. Just as people should be aware of bad reporting, they should be aware that manipulated photography is being passed off as photojournalism.

Computer Manipulation of Pictures

The truth is that individuals would not generally be aware of any problem in a photograph's content, due to the subjective qualities of photography. Because photographs are assumed to be accurate, verifiable representations of events, it is uncommon for anyone to question veracity. If it looks believable, and no one says differently, it will most likely be believed by the general public.

Whether with new technologies or the old traditional methods, the general public is the party deceived when unacknowledged substantive manipulation of news photographs occurs. In every one of the manipulations commonly referred to (for example, the *National Geographic* cover that brought two pyramids closer together than they are in reality, and the *TV Guide* cover image, in which Oprah Winfrey's head was spliced onto the body of Ann-Margret), the manipulations were unannounced and unacknowledged. They were manipulated untruths, kept secret from the public served by the publication.

The photojournalism community faces a two-fold dilemma. First, the problems inherent in the technologies must be recognized, and not just dismissed as a fear of technology. Second, concrete solutions must be formulated to handle foreseeable situations involving photo manipulation. The mere existence of new technologies does not mean that they must be misused to the point of abuse.

Perhaps Mark Twain said it best when he declared, "To a man with a new hammer, everything looks like nails." The problem with these new technologies is that, whereas anyone with a hammer damages only wood, someone with a computer may damage forever the veracity of photojournalism.

Documentary Styles

In the realm of documentary photography there are several different types of photojournalistic styles, which can be divided into four general groupings: spot and general news, human interest and pictorial features, sports action and features, and picture stories. Each group of styles, while having their own values and structures, is rooted in a common style: documentary photography. All documentary photography is based on accurate rendering of a scene, without manipulation of its content. Documentary photography should visually document an event and give as much verifiable information as possible.

Spot and General News

Visual news photography can be basically defined as faithfully recording for those not present anything that has an impact on society. Spot and general have individual requirements.

Spot News

Spot news is documentary photography of an event that is usually unplanned, and cannot be reshot. It occurs once and only fleetingly. For example, a spot news image might be a photograph of a race car flipping into the air after a collision at the Indianapolis 500, or an image of an execution taking place after the overthrow of a government.

Spot news is best covered by attending to the technical expertise needed to get a good visual message in "the can" as soon as possible, and then spending time trying to make a more creative image. Suppose you come upon the scene of a blazing fire with flames streaming from a window. It is a hard news situation. What pictures will you take?

Solve the initial problem of news value by immediately documenting the scene, as you walk into it, as you see the scene play out in front of you. Don't search for new vantage points without first documenting the exclusive vantage point you already occupy. Don't look for greener pastures. A newly hired security guard may

Photos: Christopher R. Harris

An aerial view of destruction along the Texas Gulf coast after a hurricane. When access to the scene is blocked along the ground, aerials become a good way of documenting the news event.

Aftermath of the siege of the Howard Johnson sniper in New Orleans, Louisiana. This shot was taken from an adjacent building as police searched for accomplices to the slain sniper, shown in the lower right-hand corner of the photo.

be just around the corner waiting to prevent you from taking any more photographs. Do as the old newsreel photographers of the 1930s and 1940s did. They quickly learned to shoot film as soon as they arrived on the scene and then removed the roll to the safety of the film can—thus the phrase "getting it in the can"—for shipment to be processed. Later, the photographer could round out the initial coverage by searching for the unique angles and compositions that might better document and inform about the specific news event.

A photographer should also begin accumulating the textual information needed to accompany the visual coverage. Photographs without appropriate subject identification have a far smaller chance of being published than do properly identified visuals. As a photojournalist you are involved in presenting as factual an account as possible. A good photographer searches out facts, including the subjects' names and ages that can make his visual message more informational. The photograph of a spot news event will likely have a cutline. Most graphic designers name the headline text above a photograph the "caption" and call the lines of text under a picture the "cutline." It is up to the photographer to make sure correct information is associated with her work—in fact, photographers are legally responsible for the accuracy of their pictures and words.

General News

General news is also a form of documentary photography but it is evidentiary, that is, the recording of ordinary, general, often unspectacular events in the world community. Students on their first day of school would be general news. While having some feature coverage aspect (discussed with manipulated assignment concerns in Chapter Six) general news, like spot news, is never staged. News is news and is not to be manipulated.

The general news quality of storm coverage is graphically illustrated by an aerial that shows flooding in a cemetery.

Christopher R. Harris

A unique kind of general news photo is the "enterprise" picture, a found photo often depicting such general events as the weather, humorous scenes, and cute babies. If you drive around your area on a rainy day searching for images that show the effects and impact of the weather, for example, you are searching for a general news image that will show the news of the day: It rained, and look what happened.

While returning from coverage in another area, aerial photos of results from a sudden downpour lead to another successful solution to the "enterprise" picture.

Young children enjoying life. A typical enterprise photo.

Another found scene. Shooting on the street in New Orleans.

Photos: Christopher R. Harris

The "grip and grin," or shaking hands, picture is another general news example. The photo may depict someone handing a check to a community service volunteer but it is really more than that. The image is public verification that a donation, in the form of a check, was made on a certain date, by specific participants. It may not be earth-shattering news, but it is news nonetheless.

Of all of the documentary styles, spot and general news photography requires the most commitment by the photojournalist. It takes dedication, guts, and patience to cover the gruesome and horrifying subject matter often encountered in this line of work.

The best photographers will wait for a photograph to happen. They know from experience that to force a story along, usually to save time, yields ordinary images. Strong images come to those who wait for them to happen.

It takes keen awareness of the world to be able to decipher what news is today, and what news will be tomorrow. That is why the best photographers of news events, spot or general, are those with interests in sociology, anthropology, political science and the arts. They are inquisitive and always searching for insight into the human condition.

It's not always a close-up photo that shows the impact of a natural disaster. The monumental qualities of such a storm can often be best shown with an overall view.

Christopher R. Harris

A more casual view of Democratic Party candidate Jimmy Carter, during a picnic lunch for the press at his mother's home in Plains, Georgia. (See CP-9.)

Photos: Christopher R. Harris

Jimmy Carter and his family at the Plains, Georgia, church they attended on the Easter Sunday before his election. (See CP-8.)

A news feature image that was reproduced in more than fifty publications throughout the world. Photographic coverage of a presidential candidate, without the candidate appearing in the photograph! (See CP-10.)

Though covering the news can make one cynical and bitter toward power and society in general, the best visual journalists are never satisfied until they know they have done their best to clarify the visual information about an event. Their images answer more questions than they raise.

Human Interest and Pictorial Features

Perhaps the most common photographic images we see are represented by human interest and pictorial feature styles.

Magazines, newspapers, television, and other media use a huge number of these images. They are visually oriented to the end user: a specific periodical or medium. Each publication knows what its images and stories should represent. The visual needs of *Ladies Home Journal* and *National Geographic* are different, yet they both publish human interest subjects and pictorial features.

Human Interest

The human interest photograph is a documentary image of a subject that holds interest for the target market or consumer. A human interest photograph for a fishing publication may involve a visual story on a fly rod maker. The human interest aspect of the story would be the human qualities of the person making the fly rod. Similarly, a human interest story for a business publication might be a study of how a stockbroker works. The human interest aspect of the story may not necessarily

The scene at dawn of a "human interest" story on fly-fishing in the salt marshes of southern Louisiana. Coverage might include a close-up of the type of fly tackle used to fish in the salty marsh waters of Louisiana. These pictures add to the other images in forming a more complete picture story.

Photos: Christopher R. Harris

concern how much she makes as a stockbroker, or her position in the company, but be simply about the day-in, day-out drudgery and long hours. Human interest stories are driven by two basic tenets: First, they are documentary, and second, they are interesting to the viewer.

In newspaper work the human interest story is often concerned with the uniqueness of the region or its people. Publications in south Louisiana might report on local fishermen or cooks, whereas publications in the Midwest might report on farmers and manufacturing companies.

Pictorial Features

Pictorial features are often positive in approach, not necessarily news-oriented, and always documentary in nature. They usually appear with a brief supporting text. Most pictorial features fall into several subcategories including but not limited to

The use of color, as well as light and shadow, in these photos of historic Jackson Square and details of the aboveground cemeteries and decorative iron work enhance a pictorial feature on New Orleans.

Photos: Christopher R. Harris

travel, sports, leisure, and hobbies. The travel pictorial feature is a group of images related to one common theme, a specific geographic location or people. Most stories in the *National Geographic* are pictorial features, since they depict people and places. Airline magazines, newspaper travel sections, Sunday supplements to newspapers and many other outlets, including cable television and the Internet, are prolific users of pictorial features.

One other important aspect of the pictorial feature sets it apart from the picture story. The pictorial feature requires no beginning, middle, or end, but is more freeform. It can be a hodgepodge of photographs that cumulatively deliver insight and information, without necessarily telling a story. The pictorial has no requirement to be a storytelling group of visuals; that requirement is specific to the picture story, described later.

Sports Action and Features

Sports action and features, while also rooted in the documentary, are specific to sports and sports-related subjects but may be news, feature, or pictorial coverage.

A moment of action captured in stop action with a high shutter speed as the bareback bronco rider leaves the "chute" at the famous Cheyenne (Wyoming) Rodeo.

Christopher R. Harris

Sports Action

Sports action photographs usually are single images, specific to the human subject covered or to a particular group or event. They usually capture moments of high action. Typical sports action coverage of a weekly National Football League game might include shots of a "hot" player throwing or catching a pass, a winning or record-setting run by either team, and general documentary coverage of the event as it progressed (including the now-frequent dumping of the drink cooler on the winning coach). The images would typically be used as single images in the newspaper or short action clips on television.

Sports Feature

The sports feature has all of the qualities of the sports action shot with the addition of bulk, or multiple visuals, which allow the photographer to more completely illustrate, or flesh out, the subject. Sports features are sports-oriented images that, when viewed as a whole, give more well-rounded information to the viewer than do singular images.

Christopher R. Harris

Opening kickoff of the first game in the Louisiana Super Dome. The Houston Oilers run back the kickoff from the New Orleans Saints. A sports feature that is an overall view.

Sports action photographs often dominate the sports feature, however. A good example of a sports feature would be coverage of the Super Bowl game, which would typically include individual sports action pictures along with more explanatory images. General scenes of the game might include scene-setting overall pictures, sideline coverage, and other non-action images. When viewed in conjunction with sports action images these non-action images give the viewer a more complete view of the event.

Picture Stories

Picture stories are documentary in nature and contain multiple images. They can be news or non-news, human interest, or pictorial subjects. But a picture story is more general than a pictorial feature. A picture story can be on any subject, showing a positive or negative viewpoint. Whether it is sports, news, or human interest, the picture story is the most common genre of multiple image photography we see.

A picture story can be three or more images. It can be a single page layout or twenty. It can be from multiple photographers or one visual journalist. It is a more extensive visual report of any situation. *Life, The Smithsonian, Sports Illustrated,* and *People* magazines, while dissimilar in audience and content, all use picture stories to enlighten their readers.

The picture story has specific components, including a beginning, middle, and end to the visual story being told. Most picture stories are cinematic in style, using wide, medium, and close-up views. They also use progressive storytelling, which allows a story to develop and have closure.

By following the two basic techniques of progressive storytelling and cinematic style, the photographer can structure a picture story to make it easily understood. Shooting from various distances and with different lenses can produce images that orient the viewer to the progress of the story. For example, a picture story about the late shift in a hospital emergency room might include an overall exterior shot of the hospital to begin the essay, scenes of emergency room chaos that identify the middle of the story, and images of departing and arriving staff at shift's end to signal the story's end or resolution. Cinematic style would include wide-angle views of the emergency room, medium shots of patients and staff, and close-ups of doctors and staff attending to patients.

CONCLUSION

There are many different styles of documentary assignments, but all have in common the desire to photographically record the scene, as accurately as possible, for those not present. No documentary assignment should ever be manipulated, either in content or in its photographic structure. Documentary photography should indeed be the "faithful witness" of society.

IDEAS FOR FURTHER STUDY

- Identify in a local paper the four general groups of documentary photographic styles: spot and general news, human interest and pictorial features, sports action and features, and picture stories. Now do the same for a national newspaper. Any difference in usage?

- Compare newspapers and news magazine coverage of a spot news event. How often is one picture used as the universal illustration? (An example would be the photograph of firefighters raising an American flag amid the wreckage of the World Trade Center after the terrorist attacks.)

- Identify images that follow a systematic solution, for example, the standard photo during basketball season that shows an armpit view during a jump shot. Search for sports images that do not follow the normal solution pattern. Which holds your interest the most?

An Olympic Moment

by James K. Colton, Former Director of Photography, *Newsweek* Magazine

It is summer in Atlanta. Journalists from around the world converge to cover the Olympic Games. Armed with the tools of their craft, hundreds, if not thousands, of reporters, editors and photographers are here to witness the spectacle of premier athletic competition. Disenchanted with the lack of organization for transportation, pool passes and facilities in the Media Center, the downtrodden plod on, documenting the heavily U.S.-biased coverage. In many ways, it is much the same as Olympiads of the past. That is, until one fateful early Saturday morning when another blast is heard around the world.

Newsweek's photographic representation at the summer games consisted of two freelance photographers, Dave Black and Lori Adamski Peek; one contract photographer, Wally McNamee; the services of a sports photo agency (Duomo); one photo editor (me); and one technical support person, David Berkwitz. The weekend before the bomb blast at Centennial Park, *Newsweek* had planned a fairly substantial section on the games, which would include high-resolution transmissions of the opening ceremonies and a few of the premier Saturday track and field events. But for those who may not remember, this was also the week that TWA Flight 800 went down off the coast of Long Island. And as a news magazine, the cover and much of the inside were devoted to that story. The Olympic section lost much of its space to it, and rightly so.

The venues at the games were horribly lit. There was just enough light for television. Screw the still guys. Sound familiar? It was so bad, that almost all of our coverage was done on high-speed color negative film. Kodak was touting their "multi-speed" film that they claimed was rated at 1000 ISO. After much testing it proved to be closer to 640 ISO. The Fuji 1600 negative and 800 negative-pushed one-stop were also popular choices at the venues where most of the scheduling was geared towards prime-time television (nights from 8:00 to 11:00 p.m.). The only chromes (*Newsweek*'s preferred choice for separation) were shot only during daytime events, again usually scheduled on weekends.

The week after the TWA story, much of the magazine's space was again devoted to the Olympics. By Friday night of that week, the day before our deadline, the section was laid out. A page was being reserved again for substituting the premier Saturday track and field events. Earlier that week, Kerri Strugg had vaulted into history, bringing the women's gymnastic team a gold medal. A gatefold was already printed showing a sequence of Kerri's "Leap of Faith." And after transmitting Friday's events to the magazine, it was time for a beer and a sandwich before hitting the hay. This was around midnight.

As I was watching some awful movie on HBO, with the sound turned up and the air conditioning on high to drown out the noise of the band playing in the beer garden nine floors below at the luxurious Comfort Inn, a blast shook the windows of my room facing Centennial Park. The crowd in the beer garden let out a thunderous roar and round of applause, thinking it was part of the band's act. Or perhaps the speaker system blew. And, as they say, the band played on.

As I looked out my window I could see people running in and out of the park. This was no speaker system that blew. Something was wrong, terribly wrong. I threw on my clothes, woke up our photographers, and dispatched them to the park. I grabbed my autofocus and we scurried out as the sounds of ambulances and fire trucks grew in numbers. When we hit the street, people were streaming against us, coming out of the park as we tried to get in.

All of this was within five minutes. A couple of us made it into the park but were ushered out quickly by members of the Atlanta police force. The park was "locked down" within minutes. Only the people who were in the park, or journalists who were able to gain access immediately from the main press center across the street, were the ones to get the pictures and first-hand accounts of the triage being performed.

After shooting what we could, and recouping film from people who were in the park, we returned to the hotel. There were several messages from New York, wondering (one), Was everyone all right? And (two), Did anyone get pictures? I told them that, at that time, our best hopes were with the film we recouped. Most of our photographers were only able to get photos of the rescue efforts around the park. I knew then that the next twenty-four hours until our actual deadline would be my busiest.

It was now 3:00 a.m. The area around the park and our hotel was cordoned off. No one could leave or enter. There was no access to the press center and no place to process the film I had in hand.

Finally, at 6:00 a.m. the National Guard began allowing escorted groups of journalists to the press center. I headed to AP where I knew I could process the color negatives and also see what had moved on the wires from the bombing. I also stopped by every conceivable newspaper, agency, and foreign media outlets that were open in an effort to see their production.

It was at the offices of *Asahi Shinbum* that I struck pay dirt. With the time difference between Japan and Atlanta, many of their photographers were in the press center when the bomb went off and were able to get into the park immediately. It was there that I bought the magazine rights to the bombing pictures that *Newsweek* eventually ran as its gatefold. (They scrapped the Kerri vault sequence.) But now the trick was to get the image back to the New York offices. *Asahi Shinbum* was shipping their negatives to Tokyo in one hour. I persuaded the photo editor to lend me the negative for fifteen minutes. We had a Nikon 3510 scanner in our workspace that could scan the image as high as 28 megabytes. (Minimum for a gatefold, the equivalent of three full pages.)

The rest of the day was spent tracking down and chasing pictures that eventually made it back to the press center, and coordinating our selections between Atlanta and

New York, and transmitting all day. By the end of the day, it was decided that a digital image taken by Tannen Maury, a stringer for AP, taken with a Nikon with a digital back, was the cover of choice. It was an 8 MB digital file, transmitted over the Leaf system, just barely enough to hold up as a cover. (The usual file size for a *Newsweek* cover is 40 MBs.) Close inspection of the cover will show slight pixellation and degradation of grain. But, overall, not too bad. The image showed two members of the U.S. rowing team (one wearing a U.S. flag as a bandanna) bowing their heads in a moment of silence. Tannen was the only photographer to make that image. The rowing venue was outside Atlanta and Tannen had shown up early to get pictures of the team practicing.

The last time *Newsweek* ran a filmless cover was October of 1992. It was a photo from the presidential debates showing George Bush, Bill Clinton, and Ross Perot. Close inspection of that cover shows dramatic pixellation and degradation of grain. We have come a long way with digital photography. But hold on there folks—don't start trading in your Nikons, Canons, and Leicas for digital cameras. And don't start selling your stock in Kodak and Fuji. As long as there are conventional magazines (no they're not dead) and photography books and high-quality newspaper supplements, there will always be a need for "real" film. What the smart photojournalist is doing is learning the new tools of the trade. That includes when and how to use them, digital transmission and delivery, and absorbing everything there is to learn about the "new" technology.

Yes, grasshopper . . . be a sponge! ■

C H A P T E R 6

Manipulated Assignments

by Christopher R. Harris

Photographers often have to photograph situations that require manipulation of some sort. As we have learned from the previous chapter, with documentary photography there are ethical taboos on manipulating subjects. However, the vast majority of uses of photography do not have as a basic requirement the tenet of documentary non-manipulation. In fact, the most common uses of photography often involve photographic manipulation.

Most of this manipulation occurs when the photograph is taken. It can be referred to as on-site manipulation. These on-site manipulations can be generally classified two ways—manipulation of the subject and manipulation of the scene.

Subject Manipulation

When the photographer controls what the subject does in the photographic scene there is simple subject manipulation. Any manipulation or control of the subject in a photograph makes that photograph a unique style of image: an illustration. Once the photographer has given up the faithful photographic documentation of a subject for the control that manipulating a subject's movements offer, then that photographer becomes an illustrator.

Subject manipulation can be as lightweight as the photographer asking the subject to "walk through a scene as you normally would." Or it can be as manipulated as directing the subject to do exactly as someone else has preconceived the scene to be.

Examples of subject manipulation are seen constantly in advertisements and commercials. An ad showing a child playing with a computer game is more than likely a subject manipulation. An ad agency has thought of a concept and asked a photographer to translate its (the agency's) thoughts into a visual message. A location was found, it was appropriately lit, and a model was paid to play a part. Every part of the resultant ad was preconceived, with even the model being controlled to yield the desired result.

Two manipulated scenes used as illustrations for a non–news-oriented business magazine. The manipulation in the top photo occurred when the subject was directed, under controlled lighting. In the bottom photo, the photographer asked the subject to do a "walk through."

Christopher R. Harris

A photographic rendition of a preconceived advertising illustration.

Scene Manipulation

Scene manipulation involves the control of the entire subject matter including the subject and its placement in a specific arena, or scene. The lighting of the scene is another aspect that can be controlled and manipulated by the photographer.

Just as sets are constructed and a script is followed in a movie, the successful still photographer uses the unlimited parameters of scene manipulation when illustrating a subject.

In scene manipulation, the entire location may be controlled in all of its varying aspects including location, specific elements to be used in the photograph, such as chairs, desks, and other scenery used to portray the scene that is envisioned.

It is because of all of this control over the visual message that manipulated image making is so important in the world of editorial and advertising photographic illustration. Manipulated photographs are used as illustrations in every conceivable type of media. Magazines, newspapers, books, video, advertisements, annual reports, public relations, and Web sites all use manipulated photographs for illustration purposes. These types of manipulation of visual messages are usually confined to control of the subject matter and the set used for photographing the subject matter.

As an example, take a look at any business publication and you will see illustrated feature stories about bankers and corporate officers. Quite often the visuals used as illustration for the story will show the banker sitting on the edge of a desk, arms folded, staring into the camera lens. This is strict subject manipulation. Have

A well-lit banking illustration.

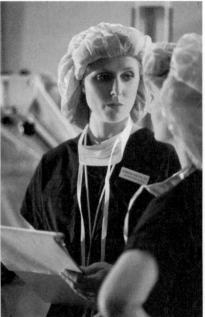

A setup preconceived health services ad.

you ever visited your bank and observed anyone mimicking this vision? Probably not, truth be told; bank officers do not usually sit on the edges of their desks with folded arms. Nor do we usually see situations as well lit as we see in publications or on screen.

But manipulation of images is more than that. Manipulation can yield illustration of the first order, thus expanding the role of the visual journalist.

Illustration, which often demands subject manipulation, can be seen in mug shots, environmental portraits, editorial illustration, fashion, advertising and public relations, and annual reports.

Illustration

Illustration is the term used to denote nondocumentary photography with a preconceived visual solution. Illustration in all of its different forms is the photographer's opportunity to take a general idea and transform that information into a representative visual—with manipulated guidance.

Photos: Christopher R. Harris

Illustration

A public relations shot of Olivia Newton John that was shot as part of an editorial "package."

An editorial illustration for a "back of the book" human interest piece in a leading business publication. (See CP-12.)

It is the photographer's challenge to produce, often in one image, a visual that will grab the reader/viewer's attention and visually explain the accompanying text or story. This type of photographic illustration is used in many magazine articles as the lead, attention-grabbing picture, or as the background on-screen visuals during a television newscast, and as the content "teasers" for television shows such as "60 Minutes."

Other forms of illustration are visually specific and have little or no text other than explanatory information. Fashion illustration is an example of visually specific use of photographic illustration.

Still other forms of illustration involve the visual representation of what the client wants the viewer to believe, with or without text. These types of illustrations are commonly seen in public relations and advertising images. The old advertising phrase, "Sell the sizzle and not the steak" is very descriptive of good photographic illustration. Many photo illustrations used in advertisements try to show what will happen if you use the product, as opposed to a picture of the product itself. Beer ads and automobile ads are good examples of photographic illustration. Drink beer

This is an example of high-quality fashion illustration using documentary techniques. (See CP-11.)

Louis Sahuc

and you will always have fun and get the girls. Buy our car and you will have special lanes to drive in, just because you are the type of person who would purchase that brand of automobile. It is the "sizzle" they sell, not the actual item.

There are many types of manipulation styles. Basic styles of manipulated assignments would include mug shots, environmental portraits, editorial illustration, advertising, annual reports and public relations.

Mug Shots

"Mug" or head shots are used for basic identification of a person. These pictures are not to be confused with police mug shots, however, with their identification numbers under the subject's chin. Those images are specifically representative of the subject. They are used for identification and generally have no real artistic composition. Lighting is usually controlled to evenly light the face of the subject, with no apparent shadows.

In photojournalistic circles the mug shot, or head shot, is often used for rapid identification of the subject. Magazines and newspapers often use head shots as "jump" illustrations to stories on the inner pages of the publication. Additionally, this style of visual journalism is often used when multiple subjects are mentioned in the text of a story.

A good example of the value of the mug shot is its constant use in *Sports Illustrated* in the back of the book section called "milestones." These head shots are used to clearly identify the subject of the milestone in sports. They usually do not show the subject in action, just the visual representation of what that particular person looks like. *USA Today* is another publication that features mug shots, almost exclusively, on its front page sections.

Perhaps the ultimate use of the typical mug shot or head shot is in the obituary section of the newspaper.

Environmental Portraits

Environmental portraits have as a base the same quality as the mug shot, in that they are representative of who the subject is, with the additional artistic aspect of being more creative and informational, not only of the subject, but of what the subject does or represents. They are illustrations that contain documentary information.

An environmental portrait of author Walker Percy. This was originally shot on assignment for Esquire *magazine.*

An environmental portrait of Tennessee Williams in New Orleans. Originally shot for People *magazine.*

Photos: Christopher R. Harris

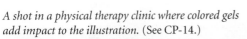

Illustration—Editorial Illustrations

The photographer manipulates these portraits in many ways. They are totally controlled as to lighting, posing, and the elements included in the image. The environmental portrait has multiple uses, and is a standard in the arsenal of the competent photographer.

Editorial Illustrations

Editorial illustrations are broader in scope than all other types of illustrations. Unlike the mug shot and the environmental portrait, the editorial illustration may be concerned with any subject. It may refer to textual content, or not. It may stand alone, as a cover illustration does, or it may be used to illustrate some aspect of the written story information.

With editorial illustration further manipulations may take place than with other styles of visual journalism.

Montage, multiple imagery, and other methods of illustration are included on the palette of the editorial illustration photographer. Post-photography editing

Two images were manually put together and copied onto a new slide. No digital image manipulation was involved. (See CP-16.)

A shot in a physical therapy clinic where colored gels add impact to the illustration. (See CP-14.)

Photos: Christopher R. Harris

Will Crocker

Results obtained by expert digital manipulation can yield images of exceptional illustrative quality. (See CP-13.)

methods use computer imaging software, whose unique capabilities are a perfect match for a photographer when producing editorial illustrations.

Editorial illustration and advertising illustration are very similar in that both are driven by the end-user. That is, the client may give specific direction as to what is to be photographed and, indeed, how the final result will look. This differs from the way photographs are done by a documentary photojournalist.

Editorial illustration is an umbrella term that covers many different types of noncommercial illustrations. In normal terms fashion photography, food photography, and some aspects of travel photography all would fall under the umbrella of editorial illustration. What would not fall under this editorial umbrella would be any type of advertising illustration, including advertising, public relations, and annual report work.

Advertising Photography

In photographic terms no other style of photography is as totally manipulated as the advertising image. Anything is fair game in advertising—within the limits of ethics and law.

This photojournalistic-appearing photograph was a carefully crafted illustration for a company offering protection from terrorist attack.

Christopher R. Harris

Advertising images, as earlier mentioned, are controlled by the end-user: the client. Advertising concepts are developed and refined usually before the photographer becomes involved in the creative process. Rarely will the photographer be involved with the philosophical concepts of the advertising image. He or she will only be the craftsperson who produces the desired end result.

On the other hand, many types of advertising images depend entirely on the eye of the photographer to provide the best usable interpretation of the subject matter. Quite often the difference between working with the advertising illustration creative concept and not being involved is based on the openness and desires of the advertising agency in charge of the project. The best agencies usually work with the photographer during the final stages of the concept development. Good art directors realize that the photographer is a valued member of the visual communication team.

Visual messages are often manipulated in advertising photography with the intent to prod the viewer into believing something that may not be real. Food is lit and doctored to make it appear more appealing. Cars are shown to be roomier, and people smoking cigarettes have clear skin and more fun.

Advertising photography is quite dependent on using manipulated visual messages. When the style of photography used in advertising appears not to be manipulated documentary photography, new ethical, and possibly legal, problems arise. The photographer must safeguard against having manipulated advertising images accepted as documentary photojournalistic coverage.

Subject Manipulation

Positioning or setting up of the subject in any way makes a photograph a particular type of image: an illustration.

Photographer Louis Sahuc often lends a documentary feeling to set-up photographs by waiting for natural light to achieve the effect he wants.

CP-11 (see page 114)

Simply showing the "tools of the trade" that a subject uses can yield an interesting illustration. This CEO's company uses geological charts in their work.

CP-12 (see page 113)

Manipulated Editorial Illustration

Editorial illustrations may involve a whole range of techniques, such as combining multiple images and enhancing color. These illustrations may complement text or stand alone.

Through digital techniques, images can be combined in a collage.

CP-13 (see page 117)

Color filters can produce dynamic illustrations.

CP-14 (see page 116)

Compelling use of shape and form is essential to all successful photography. Tight cropping lends fresh perspective to a subject that might seem uninspiring.

CP-15 (see page 119)

This composite image was made by sandwiching two transparencies together.

CP-16 (see page 116)

Will Crocker first designs an illustration, then shoots original photographs, and finally assembles the illustration digitally.

CP-17 (see page 131)

Lighting

Visual journalists are often confronted by poor lighting conditions. To produce the best possible visual messages, they must often bring lighting to the subject.

CP-19 (see page 124)

CP-18 (see page 124)

Umbrella strobe lighting was used in photographing this environmental portrait.

Simple on-location use of a bounced, hand-held strobe can produce sharpness and contrast.

A two-light setup can capture more detail and add a nice "roundness" of light.

CP-21 One light setup (see page 127)

CP-20 Two light setup (see page 128)

The purpose of advertising is to sell a product by making the consumer want that product. Anything that can be done to enhance the subject can, and often is, used. Advertising photography is based on the ultimate control of visual information about a product.

Annual Reports

Annual reports allow the photographer to employ all aspects of visual message making to produce photographs for publication that have one, and only one, objective: the positive selling of the company to its shareholders. These graphically oriented publications are often creative in the use of photography, and they yield some of the best tear sheets or reference pieces. And the photographer usually earns more for annual reports than almost any other style of photography.

A setup illustration for use in an annual report.

A found illustration used in an energy company's annual report. (See CP-15.)

Photos: Christopher R. Harris

A documentary shot of on-site normal activities for an energy company's annual report.

Annual report photography can involve any of the aspects of illustrative photography mentioned as well as some styles of documentary coverage. Mug shots, environmental portraiture, setup illustration, and other manipulated styles of photography are often combined with documentary coverage of what the company does or manufactures in order to provide a portrait of the company and its activities to its stockholder owners.

Art directors of annual reports often augment their assigned photography by purchasing stock photography of the highest caliber. It is not uncommon to pay usage rates into the multiple thousands of dollars for the proper stock photograph selected for use in an annual report.

Public Relations

Public relations photography is visually controlled propaganda. The images are always positive and freely distributed for publication. The public relations counselor directs all aspects of the photography produced. In almost all instances the public

A public relations photograph of an IBM exhibit.

Photos: Christopher R. Harris

relations agent will acquire all rights to any images produced, as well as control of any and all use of the resultant images. Public relations photographs are controlled from their taking to their use, and are meant to show the subject in only a positive light.

Documentary-*style* photography is often combined with tightly controlled manipulated illustrative photography in the genre of public relations photography, which can include anything from tabletop illustration of a product, behind-the-scenes looks at manufacturing processes, head shots for press releases, to "grip and grin" photographs documenting the passing of a check from the client to a beneficiary.

Whereas the documentary photographer is bound by specific tenets of explanation and veracity, the photographer dealing in manipulated photography must deal more with the desires of the client and technical perfection.

Lighting

Visual journalists are often confronted by poor lighting conditions. As professionals they know that in order to produce the best possible visual messages they must often bring light to the subject—light that can be directed and controlled.

Obviously, photographers are constrained in the amount and style of light that they can use in any given situation. Generally, they cannot use setup lights in photojournalistic hard news coverage, but when they step into the realm of feature photography, or any of the manipulated photographic areas, photographers should use the lighting they feel will give the best possible technical results.

A photographer can choose from among several common lighting styles. They are not complicated and can solve most inadequate lighting situations. Before these lighting styles can be implemented, however, the photographer needs to analyze what type of lighting is required. Basic lighting technique problem solving begins with an analysis of the type of lighting, quality of the light output needed, and number of light sources required.

Types of Lighting

There are two basic types of photographic lighting: strobe, also called flash, which is daylight balanced and functions as a rapidly discharged flash of light; and incandescent bulb, continuous light. Each type of lighting has positive and negative attributes. The competent photographer should feel at home using either type of light source.

Lighting—Types of Lighting

A hand-held strobe.

Strobe

Strobe is balanced for use with daylight film, and its light output is usually rated at 5000–5500°K. Strobes emit a fast burst of light, and therefore are very useful in stopping action, as well as freezing any movement from camera shake.

Strobes must be synchronized with the cameras and are connected by a "sync" cord or by a radio remote sync. Most cameras have a specific shutter-speed setting for synchronizing the burst of the strobe light with the instant that the camera shutter is fully open. On modern focal plane–shuttered cameras this sync speed is 1/125 second or 1/250 second.

Strobe equipment, in general, does not produce a lot of heat. The smaller hand-held strobes produce very little heat, while some of the larger units, which use modeling lights to indicate the spill of the light before firing the strobe, can produce more heat. So beware of using any flammable item near a high-powered strobe head with powerful, hot modeling lights.

As mentioned in Chapter Four, there are many different styles of strobe units. Usually, when using two or more stand-mounted lights, a photographer will be dealing with larger output models. The more power and output, the more light produced for use on the scene. With a low-powered, hand-held unit, the f-stop for a typical scene on a medium speed (100 ISO) film at a distance of ten feet may be f/2.8. A higher powered, AC or battery-driven, stand-mounted unit might produce a working f-stop of f/22, a large difference in output.

While the small hand-held strobe units are lightweight, the more powerful stand-mounted units can weigh a lot and are usually bulky.

Tungsten or Incandescent Lighting

Lighting in the range of 3200–3400°K is referred to as tungsten light. There are many hot-bulb style lights used in photographic lighting. All styles of bulb lighting have three things in common: They operate off a light bulb of some sort, they give constant light output, as opposed to the rapid burst of the strobe light, and they produce heat.

Because this lighting has constant output no sync cord connecting the camera to the light source is needed. Readings of the light output can be taken with a light meter, and any shutter speed and f-stop combination may be used on the camera.

Quality of Light

With both types of light sources it is possible to alter the quality of the light produced. A photographer can control light so that it becomes hard or soft, rounded or sharp, diffused or crisp.

As the photographer makes decisions concerning all other aspects of producing the best visual message, so must he or she control the "feel" of the light on the subject. Does the photograph require harsh, direct lighting for effect, or does it require a softer, more rounded light to convey a particular feeling? These are questions that a photographer must consider when first analyzing the scene to be shot.

Most of the changes to the quality of light are accomplished through add-ons to the light source. Whether strobe or incandescent light, changes can be made to the light source through the use of light modifiers.

Light Modifiers

There are as many different ways of changing the quality of light as there are inventive minds. Photographers have sifted through all of the possibilities and recognized a common group of techniques to assist light modification. Reflectors, umbrellas, soft-boxes, snoots, and scrims are common solutions available to the visual journalist.

Reflectors

Reflectors can be rigid panels, or fabric-mounted screens, a white shirt, or a close wall. Anything that allows a photographer to bounce a light source onto a surface that will reflect light onto the subject works. Some of the best reflectors are compact and portable. Fabrics on frameworks and expandable tension-mounted fabric panels are common and afford some control over the light quality.

Reflectors yield a softer light than a direct light source. But since they reflect back less light power than a light source aimed directly at the subject, a larger camera aperture is required when taking the picture.

The individual qualities of the reflector can be changed to assist the photographer, however. For example, a reflector can be made "warmer" in color quality by using a gold-toned, or warmer, reflector or fabric. And by using a shiny surface, such as reflective Mylar®, a reflector can appear to have more contrast.

Reflectors may have any color used on its surface to effect a desired result. A reflector painted blue would reflect a blue quality of light, rather than the normal, neutral light quality of the light source.

Lighting—Light Modifiers

The top photograph shows the umbrella strobe lighting setup used to produce the environmental portrait below. (See CP-18 and CP-19.)

Photos: Christopher R. Harris

Umbrellas

Photographic umbrellas are made with materials that either reflect back light or allow the light to pass through. They are reflective or translucent. The advantages of using umbrellas are their portability, ease of use, and changeable qualities. Like any umbrella, the photographic umbrella fabric and frame collapses into an easily transportable unit. Some photographic umbrellas have collapsible handles that make them even more compact. Covers may be interchanged on the umbrellas for different results, such as color change, reflective qualities, and translucency.

In normal use a lighting unit is mounted on a sturdy stand, an umbrella is mounted to that unit, and the head of the light source is turned to the inside of the open umbrella and bounced into the material. The umbrella-mounted light is then trained on the subject and adjusted for height, direction, and distance. Umbrellas afford the largest range of changeable attributes of any of the portable light sources, and are an inexpensive method for achieving a wide range of lighting results.

Soft Boxes

Another light diffuser often used in photography is the soft box. A portable soft box is a lightweight frame, covered by fabric, with an opening for the light source. In use it looks like a rectangular box with dark material on all sides, except the front, which usually has a translucent fabric for light diffusion. The soft box and light source are stand-mounted and aimed in the direction of the subject.

Soft boxes give a very soft, low-contrast, rounding light that is ideal for fashion, portraiture, and food illustration. They break down to a small, easily transportable size and are fairly inexpensive.

With the addition of attached scrims, light output can be further controlled.

Snoots and Scrims

Snoots are used to modify the light coming from both strobe and constant light sources. Snoots are stovepipe-looking additions that can be attached to the front of the light source to allow a more direct, funneled light effect. Snoots sometimes have optics built into them that allow a focusing of the direct light.

Snoots are often used to highlight a particular part of the photographic scene with additional lighting while yielding enough light to expose the rest of the scene properly. Snoots cannot be used with reflectors, umbrellas or soft boxes, however. They are only used directly on the front of the light source and are aimed directly at the subject.

Scrims are attachments that are used in conjunction with either type of light source and any of the light modifiers. The function of the scrim is to shield off some of the light falling from the light source. Scrims are often used to cast a shadow on the scene. Scrims can also be used to mottle the light behind the subject in multiple light setups. With the use of snoots and scrims any photographer is given more control over the overall quality of the light applied to any photographic scene.

Number of Lights

The next decision the photographer must make is how many lights are needed to properly light the scene. Usually no more than three lights are necessary for most situations. There will be exceptions to this rule, but most assignments can be adequately covered with just a few light sources.

A natural light setup, properly metered, can be quite pleasant.

Christopher R. Harris

Remember, most of the work of photographers usually relies on only one light source: the sun. So, when confronted by lighting setup decisions, keep in mind the old adage: less is best.

The visual journalist should strive to use similar light sources. If using strobe, all the light sources should be strobe. For most situations light sources should not be mixed. There is one big exception to this rule, however: When using strobe lighting, or sunlight, within any scene where table lamps or other normal incandescent light sources are shown, you may wish to leave those lights on to create natural warmth in a scene. When properly exposed, strobe light/daylight and ambient light sources can be very effective tools for the visual journalist.

Lighting Setups

Lighting setups are as simple as one, two, three. In fact, basic lighting setups consist of one, two, or three or more lights. Photographers must make decisions on lighting keeping in mind that the best photographic lighting doesn't look as though the scene has been specially lit at all! Multiple shadows and subject matter that is poorly lit or lacking desired shadow detail are signs of poor photographic lighting technique. Basic lighting remedies can make a photographer's life easier. Learn to develop lighting styles that you feel competent and comfortable with.

The One-Light Setup

There is one light in the sky and there is one light on the camera. Now, the important part is to learn how to get the most out of the one light you control. Whether with a strobe mounted to the camera, or a constant light source mounted on a light stand, the visual journalist has many ways to "shape" the light for use. Using the light modifiers already mentioned, a light can be bounced off a reflector, attached to an umbrella or shot through a soft box. Many different types of light outputs can be achieved with one light.

One-light setups are the basic tool of the documentary photographer and a starting point for photographers involved in feature and illustration work. Professional photographers know when to use the one light source and, more importantly, know when to advance to multiple light setups.

Lighting—Lighting Setups

Photos: Christopher R. Harris

This portrait of writer Alice Walker at work was lit with a hand-held bounced strobe. It was shot on assignment for the New York Times.

A banjo player at Preservation Hall in New Orleans was lit with a bounced, hand-held strobe and a slight telephoto lens. Shot on assignment for Travel & Leisure *magazine. (See CP-21.)*

Two-Light Setups

Two-light setups allow the photographer to add depth and detail to the photographic scene. Rather than just having more light because of multiple light sources, the two-light setup can be best used to enhance the scene. Keeping one light as the main light source, a second light may be added as a fill light to that main source, a hair-light in portraiture, or as a background light.

With strobe lighting, a remote sync must be used to set off both light units at the same time the shutter is tripped. The light sync is attached to the second strobe and is tripped by a photoelectric cell in the second unit as it responds to the light output from the first flash. With a constant light source, synchronization is not needed.

Three or More Lights

With the addition of three or more lights most photographic scenes can be lit to more exacting needs. While the normal two-light setup is adequate for most jobs, a multiple light setup allows the photographer to give better shadow information or address specific subject needs, such as lighting a large area.

Multiple lights can be modified and used to illuminate any aspect of the photographic scene. From minute lights used to open up shadow areas, to rim and hair lights, to background-enhancing lights, the photographer can ultimately control any aspect of the scene desired. It is the craftsmanship of the photographer that

A typical two-light setup. It gives shadow detail and roundness to shapes and forms. Shot for Fortune *magazine.* (See CP-20.)

Christopher R. Harris

Christopher R. Harris

A three-light setup used to cover the expanse of the entire classroom. Shot on assignment for Newsweek *magazine.*

will show in lighting techniques. The successful photographer should experiment with lighting and multiple light sources and use those techniques to yield the best results.

Additional lights should only be used if they help the photographer to portray a scene. Using additional lights does not necessarily mean that the photographic image will be better. Lighting only assists the technical quality of the image.

CONCLUSION

When you think of the profession of visual journalism, the first type of assignment that will most likely come to mind is news. Documentary assignments are vital to the continued growth and respect for the visual journalism profession. But more and more visual journalists also need to know how to produce a wide variety of manipulated assignments. It is important to remember that even though an assignment is manipulated, you should always strive to produce images that have legal and ethical integrity.

IDEAS FOR FURTHER STUDY

- Compare several mainstream business and news magazines, and identify documentary images and manipulated images as described in this chapter.

- Some questions to consider when looking at publications: In what sections of the magazine are photographs more documentary? And in what sections are they manipulated illustrations? Are the covers of the publications illustration or documentary in nature? Can you find any "blur" in the use of documentary images used in illustrations?

How Has Digital Photography Affected Me as a Photo Illustrator?

by Will Crocker, Freelance Photo Illustrator

The digital revolution has brought wonders and woes to the modern photographer. Special effects and image combination have always enthralled me as a professional photographer, and using a computer has given me the ability to create anything that I can imagine. That sounds a little lofty, but I used to dream up things where I could not hide the strings or drop in the background. Now, if I can sketch it, I can realize the photograph.

I worked in special effects long before computers were affordable to photographers. I would spend more time thinking about how to solve a problem than I did on the actual implementation. Now, with the assistance of computers, I can create images with far more precision, in less time, and accept fewer compromises along the way.

The impact of digital imaging on commercial photography has turned the market upside down. The improvements to cameras, films, and the post-production computer-generated processes make it far easier to create an image that is reproducible than at any time

A sample of Will Crocker's commercial/industrial still digital imaging. (See CP-17.)

in the past. So much so, that many clients and art directors now self-produce images that would have been assigned traditionally to a photo illustrator. Where once photographers were revered as artists and wizards, they are now regarded in a more subordinate manner. They are logistics organizers.

Before digital retouching and other effects, photographers had the responsibility to create flawless images (although there has always been film retouching, as well as other corrective techniques). The fact that it is easier to create images today means that people with less experience can do the assignments that would have gone to more established photographers, and do it within a lower budget. Today, I sometimes hear photographers referred to as "content providers."

With more client advertising dollars going into Web site production today, there are fewer dollars left for traditional print ads. Print exposure or the effectiveness of an advertisement could always be estimated by the number of copies published. That was a concrete measurement of worth to the advertising client. As yet, there is no valid measurement for the Web.

Everything about the Web erodes the worth of the finely crafted photograph. Clients are unsure of the new medium. The idea that a beautiful photograph in a magazine is a powerful attention-grabbing sales tool has not yet translated to the Web. Even tiny photographs slow down the speed that a Web site "loads." Except for pornographic Web sites and the like, most images used are so small that finesse is lost and the photographer's individual approach is often homogenized. Even the number of colors that a photograph renders is usually severely limited.

High-definition monitors gave us a new medium to view photographs with amazing clarity. The digital process has given us new ways to store images perpetually without loss.

Programs like Adobe Photoshop® have made photographers more analytical about the science of creating an image. The new technologies have expanded our picture-making vocabulary. Digital cameras capture images with incredible ease and superior accuracy. They are fast and put no chemistry down the drain.

My computer enables me to work for clients who I have never met face to face by e-mailing previews of a photograph in progress or a snapshot of a location or model choice. Digital technology in printing has brought amazing benefits to reproduction of photographs. Web news providers deliver constantly updated news photographs in color, and with more precision than newspapers ever could. There are innumerable ways that photography as a medium of expression has been enriched by digital technology.

It is only through the synergy of the new technology and the mind of the image maker that new and exciting images will continue to illustrate our world. As conscious human beings we should always be aware that the world of images that we create recreates us. ∎

Using Words

The two chapters in this section concern the words you use to tell stories. In this era of media convergence, visual journalists must be able to use words as easily as using settings on a camera. In this section you will learn how to find good news stories, how to report on them, and how to write stories with the facts you compile. Once you become comfortable with using words, you will find that your power of observation and your visual messages will improve. Learning to write well leads to better quality visual journalism.

CHAPTER 7

Reporting

by Steve Doig
Arizona State University

The right picture may be worth a thousand words. But quite often a few well-chosen words can say things no picture can convey as well.

Comedian Stan Freberg once demonstrated the point in a sketch about the power of imagination and the effectiveness of radio advertising. Using just his voice and the appropriate sound effects, Freberg vividly described a five-hundred-foot mountain of whipped cream being shoved into a hot chocolate–filled Lake Michigan, then a ten-ton maraschino cherry dropped on top by the Canadian Air Force to the cheers of twenty-five thousand onlookers.

"Now, you wanna try that on television?" Freberg concluded.

Gathering information and using words effectively are skills every bit as important to the modern visual journalist as composing a picture or designing an infographic. In fact, the job of a journalist can be boiled down to this simple formula: Find a story to tell, get the information needed to tell it, and then tell it. That's true whether you do it with words, still pictures, graphic images, video or audio, or some combination of all of these.

This chapter will give you some ideas about how to find stories worth telling, as well as some basic techniques for gathering the information you'll need to tell those stories.

Finding Stories

In a classic "Calvin and Hobbes" comic strip, young Calvin is standing waist-deep in a hole he has dug in the back yard, holding out a handful of grubs, rocks, and worms for the admiring inspection of Hobbes, his imaginary tiger.

"There's treasure everywhere!" exclaims Calvin.

Calvin has the right attitude for a good visual journalist: There's treasure—in the form of stories to be found and told—everywhere.

Many stories, of course, don't even have to be found. Instead, they grab you by the throat and demand to be told. These are the so-called hard news stories that fill a significant portion of each day's papers and broadcasts. Crimes, accidents, elections, political decisions, wars, press conferences, jury verdicts, disasters—all are the meat and potatoes of a journalist's daily diet.

In fact, so much hard news occurs in any given day that the problem isn't finding it but deciding what to use. The famous *New York Times* motto "All the News That's Fit to Print" would be more truthful if it read, "All the News That Fits, We Print." When the verdict was reached in O.J. Simpson's wrongful death civil suit at the same time as President Clinton's "State of the Union" speech, many broadcast stations used a new, but controversial, solution—a split screen showing both news events.

Reporters and editors weigh several related factors when making decisions about how much time, energy, money, and space should be spent to cover a hard news event. These factors include:

- *Proximity:* The nearer to home, the more compelling it will be to cover it. A fender-bender involving a local school bus probably will make the news; a fatal bus crash in another country (or maybe even another county) probably won't.

- *Prominence:* All else being equal, things that happen to well-known people are more likely to be worth news coverage than the same things happening to someone less known. If your neighbor's car is stolen, it probably isn't news. If the mayor's is taken, it certainly is. The murder of someone unknown to the public won't get much attention. The murder of entertainer Bill Cosby's son will.

- *Impact:* Something that will have a real effect on the life of many of your readers or viewers is going to be worth attention. A change in the federal income tax rate certainly will mean a big story; a tax deduction for rutabaga growers probably won't.

- *Rarity:* News almost by definition is the unusual. In a big city, most murders will generate perhaps a couple of paragraphs in an inside-page crime briefs column. In a small town, the armed robbery of a local convenience store might be front-page news. As generations of editors have noted, "dog bites man" isn't news, but "man bites dog" is.

- *Competition:* Often, the decision to cover something will be driven by what reporters for other newspapers and stations are doing. If you broke the original story, you'll want to stay ahead of it. If someone else did, you'll want to catch up and perhaps even find a new angle.

- *Interest:* Sometimes, events will be covered simply because the reporter (or her boss) is interested in the subject. As one veteran *Miami Herald* reporter likes to grumble, "Every time some editor gets rained on, I get assigned to do a weather story."

Other Stories

Happily, there is much more to life than accidents, crime, and scandal. A paper or newscast filled with nothing but breaking news would quickly grow tedious. That's why newspaper editors and broadcast news directors seek to spice the daily onslaught of event-driven hard news with other kinds of stories they hope will intrigue and attract readers and viewers. Even sensationalist tabloids and "if it bleeds, it leads" newscasts will include a mix of other stories in their offerings.

Such non-breaking stories include:

- *Investigative projects:* Print and broadcast news outlets alike take justifiable pride in their watchdog role of "comforting the afflicted and afflicting the comfortable." Aggressive and courageous reporting has gotten innocent men off Death Row, helped send scoundrels to prison, uncovered official corruption, forced government and business to change bad policies, and alerted communities to hidden problems. But as with the judgment against ABC in investigating the Food Lion company's handling of perishables with hidden cameras, some investigative reporting methods are despised by the general public.

- *Features:* This catch-all term covers a huge variety of stories—a day at the circus, the opening of a boutique microbrewery, the fuss over a visiting celebrity, the celebration of a religious holiday, the closing of an old school, a behind-the-scenes look at a firehouse, a preview of next fall's fashions, or anything else that lets readers and viewers experience, at least secondhand, some thing or place of interest.

Finding Ideas

- *How-tos and reviews:* In some ways, newspapers and newscasts might be considered survival manuals for coping with the complexities of modern life. Readers and viewers love stories that explain how to accomplish something they might want to do, whether it's to appeal a property tax assessment, choose a new stereo, use an online computer service, select vintage wine, or run a fantasy baseball league. Reviews, whether of movies, records, concerts, books, or restaurants, also help your audience spend their time and money wisely.

- *Profiles:* People are interesting. Stories about well-known celebrities and newsmakers obviously will attract many readers. But good reporters can find fascinating stories in the lives of everyday people, as well, whether it's an engineer who restores antique automobiles for a hobby, a teacher who inspires her students to excel, or a grandmother who raises orphaned squirrels. It's like the old TV show used to say: "There are a million stories in the Naked City." It's true in your city, too.

- *Backgrounders:* Sometimes, you can help your audience understand complex news events by doing analysis stories that explain the background, the why, of such events. Stories like this might include using exit poll data to show how different kinds of voters acted in an election, or comparing the strengths and weaknesses of opposing football teams, or a detailed look at the genesis of a city's budget crisis.

Finding Ideas

As you can see, newspapers, newscasts, and online news services offer journalists a virtually unlimited range of story possibilities. That makes journalism a wonderful career for curious people who like the idea of doing something different every day.

The flip side of that opportunity, though, is the relentless demand for more stories and ideas. In a given year, a general assignment reporter might do two hundred or more stories, enough words alone to fill more than twenty-five pages of newsprint.

Keep a file of story ideas as they pop into your head. Some will be too lame ever to get done, and others will be timeless enough that they can get put off when more pressing news occurs. But thumbing through that file will help during idea-droughts. It's great to have something slow-cooking on a back burner, so to speak, when your editor is looking for someone to go to the scene of the big spill at the municipal sewage plant.

How Do You Keep Those Story Ideas Coming?

Aside from the gotta-cover hard news events, you also will get some significant portion of your stories in the form of assignments from your boss. These may be perennials, such as the first day of school, the annual downtown art fair, the opening of the legislative session, and the deadline for filing income tax returns. Other assignments may have started as ideas from other reporters who didn't have the time or the expertise to do the story themselves.

Moreover, lots of ideas will come from your readers. Many prizewinning investigative stories started as a whispered tip from an anonymous source. Many wonderful feature stories began when someone called to say "Why don't you guys ever do a story about . . . ?" But if you're going to succeed in the news business, you'll have to come up with lots of ideas yourself.

For instance, you are expected to produce most of your own story ideas if you are a beat reporter who covers some particular area. Your beat may be governmental, such as city hall, the legislature, and the courts. It may be functional, such as transportation, or growth management, or welfare. It may be institutional or organizational, such as public schools, higher education, or the local pro basketball team. It may be geographic, such as the inner city, the suburbs, or a bureau in an outlying county. Or it may be a specialty, such as science, technology, medicine, or law.

Whatever your beat, your editor will expect you to know what needs to be covered. You'll do this by immersion in your beat: reading meeting agendas and professional journals, having frequent "What's up?" conversations with officials and office workers, staying in contact with past sources of information, keeping a good tickler file of coming events.

An aggressive beat reporter enjoys a great sense of satisfaction in doing a story that the competing reporters on the beat will wish they had done and will be scrambling to follow. Conversely, there's not much worse than the sinking feeling of seeing a competitor do a story you should have done—and then getting called into the boss's office to explain how you missed it.

Get a Life

Aside from following a beat, another great source of story ideas will come from your life outside the newsroom. The trick is to make sure you have such a life. Some young reporters make the mistake of putting all their time and energy into their job; as a result, they rarely talk with anyone who isn't a news source or another journalist. In fact, a valid criticism of some journalists and news organizations is that they are out of touch with the communities they purport to cover.

Consider the case of the *Miami Herald*. South Florida has been one of the nation's most ethnically diverse, polyglot metropolitan areas since the early 1960s, when Cubans fled to Miami to escape the Castro revolution, followed by waves of refugees and opportunity-seekers from all over the Caribbean and Latin America. But it wasn't until the mid-1980s before the *Herald* newsroom stopped looking mostly like an Ivy League fraternity house. Today, thanks to the deliberate recruiting of reporters who are bilingual or raised and educated in South Florida, the *Herald* is much better able to do its job.

The lesson is that good reporters are members of their community. They talk to—and more important, listen to—the supermarket cashier, the mail carrier, the neighbors, the hair stylist, the homeless guy who asks for small change. They read not only the big metro daily, but also the suburban weekly. They notice signs of change: the clearing of a once-empty lot, the arrival of the first robin of spring, the opening of a new store, the appearance of a new teen fashion. They notice bumper stickers, T-shirt slogans, and billboards and pay attention to new slang, new gadgets, and new faces.

And they take an active part in their community. They might belong to a church, work with the PTA, coach youth soccer, vote, teach a night school course, or join a bridge club. But there are limits. Most news organizations won't want you running for public office, publicly supporting political candidates or controversial causes, or otherwise jeopardizing your ability to cover such things objectively. Obviously, if there is a story to be done about some organization to which you belong, it should be done by another reporter whose objectivity can't be questioned.

From all this, countless stories will suggest themselves. Here's a good rule of thumb to remember: If something interests you, chances are good that it will interest significant numbers of your readers or viewers.

Interviewing

After finding a story, a visual journalist's next step is to gather the information needed to do the story. The most essential facts in most stories are the famous "five Ws and an H"—Who, What, When, Where, Why, and How. Those facts are necessary, but almost never sufficient. A story worth telling deserves a wealth of supporting detail and description and dialogue, all of which you'll have to gather.

Good reporters get their information from many places. Later chapters in this textbook will tell you how to research your subject in the library, online, or in your newspaper's archives. But one of the best methods of information gathering for journalists is the interview.

You may be thinking that an interview is something only writers do. But the best photojournalists and graphic artists know how important it is to talk with their subjects, to ask questions about the subject's work and life. Not only does the conversation put the subject at ease, it also can guide the visual journalist to discovery of better, more revealing images.

Often, story interviews are fun and interesting, a chance for you to meet and talk with fascinating people from every walk of life. You may be asking a rock star about the new CD, or the governor about next year's budget, a scientist about her discovery, or a young boy about how he saved his neighbors from a housefire.

Occasionally, though, some interviews and photo assignments are gut-wrenching and emotional. You might be asking anguished parents to talk about their murdered child, confronting a respected politician with evidence of accepting bribes, or getting reactions from relatives of plane crash victims.

Either way, the words and images of your news sources—whether they're famous, infamous, or unknowns—are the heart of the stories you will tell.

When you conduct an interview, you are looking for two things: information and color. The information you get, of course, will form the structure of your story. But the color, the details you observe, the words you hear, and the images and sounds you record, are what will help you tell that story in a way that will interest your readers or viewers.

Preparing for an Interview

Many of your interviews will be impromptu, conducted on the scene of a news event with little time for preparation. In such cases, it's a good idea to talk to as many persons as you reasonably can; you never know who will have seen something others missed or will say something in a particularly interesting way.

Often, though, you will be able to prepare for an interview. The first step in preparation is studying whatever background information you can find, both about the topic of your story and the person or persons you might interview. This advance work will help you decide who to interview, focus your questions, and suggest aspects of the story you might not have considered before.

Just as important, it will help you avoid wasting time and aggravating your subject by asking questions you easily could have answered on your own with a little research.

The next step is deciding whom to interview. Obviously, many times there is no choice: You must talk to the winner, the loser, the victim, the perpetrator, the eyewitness, the star of the show, the goat who missed the game-winning shot, or anyone else who is central to the story.

However, particularly when you are seeking comment or expertise, there are lots of occasions when you will choose who to interview. A strong temptation for reporters is to keep going back to sources that have been good interviews in the past. Some experts and public figures have a knack for saying the right thing in a succinct and even colorful way. They not only "give good quote" or "soundbite," they don't mind when you call them at home on deadline. But don't get lazy about choosing whom to interview, always going back to the same small circle of "usual suspects." Instead, look for opportunities to widen your pool of sources and fatten your phone file.

Doing the Interview

The next step is to set up the interview. Call your subject, explain who you are and why you want to do an interview, and arrange a time and place.

Often, particularly when you are on deadline or your subject isn't in the local area, you will do the interview over the telephone. Ideally, though, you and your subject will have the time to meet in person. This is preferred, because it gives you the opportunity to gather much more than just information and quotes.

A face-to-face interview gives you the chance to pick up the color that will tell you and your audience more about your subject than just her words. Be observant: Note the family pictures on the desk, the plaques on the wall, the titles on the bookshelf, the pattern on his tie, the way she gestures when making a point, the southern accent, the bead of sweat on the forehead. This kind of detail will help you paint a word picture of your subject when the time comes to write.

A few tips on the mechanics of doing an interview:

- Have your important questions written down. Give the list a quick look before you conclude the interview so you don't forget to ask something you need to know.
- When doing a phone interview, take notes using your writing terminal by typing shorthand. You say you don't know shorthand? Sure u do . . . jst drop som vwls when poss, use lots abbrevs, n dont bothr w/ caps . . . its ez.

- Never assume you know the spelling of your subject's name just from the sound of it—always confirm. "Steven Smith" might be "Stephen Smythe," and you'll be the fool.

- Try not to ask yes-or-no questions. You won't get many usable quotes out of someone who mostly is responding "uh-huh" or "nope." Instead, use open-ended questions such as, "Tell me how you did such and such" or "What was it like to do so and so?"

- Listen to the answers you get and be prepared to wander from your pre-conceived notions about the story. A good interview will reveal things that you didn't know about the subject, suggesting follow-up questions and story angles that won't be on your initial list.

- To get your subject at ease, particularly if the interview might cover some painful ground, ask a couple of easy questions at first.

- Be sure you know how to get in touch with the subject again if you have some last-minute questions or need to confirm a fact.

- On the other hand, do not agree if the person you're interviewing asks to review your story before it is printed or aired. Gently but firmly say you certainly will check back with them if you have to clear up any questions of fact, but that you alone are responsible for the content of the story.

- When the interview is done, review your notes immediately and fill in any abbreviations or incomplete phrases that you might forget if you waited too long.

Taking Notes

What about audio tape or DAT recorders? This may seem like counterintuitive advice, but generally you're better off if you don't tape an interview unless you need proof of the conversation or you are a multimedia reporter who'll use the actual voice in a broadcast or online.

For one thing, a tape recorder makes the session seem more like an adversarial court proceeding and might make your subject speak more cautiously than you would like. Some people, when seeing you pull out a recorder, will want to make their own tape. (However, you should bring a recorder if the subject, particularly a hostile one in a confrontation interview, insists on taping the interview herself.)

Another reason is that too much can go wrong with a tape recorder. Batteries go dead, tapes break, nearby electrical devices drown the recording in static. At the least, you will be distracted during the interview, watching for when to turn the cassette.

And taping tends to make your note-taking perfunctory. Thus, when you get back to your desk, you're going to have to listen to the whole thing all over again to transcribe it.

Instead of relying on audio tape, learn to take good notes in an interview. This does not mean scribbling down every word uttered; you're a journalist, not a court reporter. To help you know what notes to take, figure that everything in an interview falls into these four categories:

- *Verbal pleasantries and other nonessentials:* Don't bother writing these down.
- *Good, colorful quotes:* Something you may use in your story as the subject said it. Develop an ear for good quotes. When you hear one during your interview, write it down accurately, and put quotation marks around the words to remind yourself later that you got what was said well enough to use it as a quote.
- *Information:* Facts, dates, addresses, descriptions, and so on. If pertinent to your story, you need to get these down accurately, but you can paraphrase. In other words, change "Well, as it happens, I was born in Glendale, California, on April 21, 1948" into DOB 4/21/48 Glendale CA. The information is good, but the actual quote is too boring to use as is. Remember, don't put quotes around paraphrases.
- *Your observations and insights:* [Desk impossibly messy.] [Martini shaken, not stirred.] [Nervous twitch when asked about the money.] Put brackets or some other distinguishing mark around these so you don't accidentally attribute them to your interview subject, even as a paraphrase.

Using Quotes Properly

Here's a guideline to follow when writing down and using quotes: Be as accurate as possible, but not necessarily literal.

If you have ever read a court transcript, you'll realize that few people actually speak in perfect, grammatical sentences. They false-start, cough, punctuate their phrases with "uh . . . ," mismatch verb tenses, run on and on, hem and haw. When the mayor says, "Uh, okay, let's see, the budget this year, er, next year that is, is gonna be, uh, two percent—George, it is two percent, isn't it? Ah, good—yes, two percent higher than this year," you can accurately quote him as follows: "The budget next year is going to be two percent higher than this year's."

In short, it's often necessary—and proper—to lightly edit what your interview subject says. In fact, you'll do much of that editing automatically as you take notes. Your standard is to stay as close as possible to the original wording and—most important—to ensure that you do not change the meaning of what was said.

Interview subjects who use obscenities, slang or dialect create other problems. On occasion, you may get an otherwise good quote marred with impolite language; consult with your editor about how to handle it. Generally, you'll either turn the quote into an indirect paraphrase, or use dashes or some such typographical device to blunt the offending word or words.

But don't change the word itself. If a politician says, "My opponent is an asshole," don't turn it into "My opponent is an ass." Very rarely, the quote and its circumstances may be so powerful that you will use it as spoken. A few years ago, when a powerful state senator unleashed an obscenity-laced tirade at a colleague during a near-fistfight on the floor of the Florida Senate, his words made the front page of most of the state's papers.

As for slang or dialect, normally you should not try to recreate those speech patterns in print. Such quotes are hard to write and harder to read. If your subject says "Pahk the cah in Hahvahd Yahd," turn it into this: "'Park the car in Harvard Yard,' he said in a thick Boston accent." A little slang or a snippet of dialect sometimes can be used well in a quote for color or effect, but do it sparingly.

Working in a Newsroom

Journalism is very much a team sport. To succeed as a visual journalist, you need to work well in an organization full of people who have other, sometimes conflicting, responsibilities. Two of the most important of those newsroom responsibilities, theirs and yours, are meeting space limits and deadlines.

When your editor says your story needs to be fifteen column-inches, don't hand in twenty inches. A paper's newshole, or amount of space available for news on a given day, is determined mostly by the amount of advertising space that has been sold. Only in the event of unexpected major news will additional space be given to the newsroom. Thus, your too-long story either will run as written at the expense of someone else's work or—much more likely—will be hastily chopped down to fit. Your editors won't like having to do that, and you won't like the result.

Story length is even more critical for broadcast journalists. With a change in layout or some typographical tricks, a newspaper editor sometimes can squeeze a little extra into the day's paper. But newscast space is measured by time, and you can't squeeze seventy seconds into a minute.

Deadlines also can't be ignored, or even stretched very much, whether you're in a newspaper, broadcast, or online newsroom. A disheartening reality understood by all journalists is that the story or picture or graphic they submit at deadline is never as good as it could have been with just a little more time. There are always better turns of phrase, additional facts, and other picture viewpoints, all of which would have improved your work. But "okay right now" almost always is more important in journalism than "better later."

CONCLUSION

Finally, an important key to success in the newsroom is communication between all reporters and editors. All too often in some newsrooms, photos and graphics are afterthoughts assigned close to deadline. The result is pedestrian images that don't illustrate the story well.

Reporters and editors who work with words should learn more about how visual journalists do their jobs, in order to improve that process. But good visual journalists shouldn't sit back waiting to be asked. Instead, they should be aggressive about seeking early entry into the stories they will illustrate. They should talk with the writer before the assignment to make sure they are clear on the intent of the story. Moreover, while on the assignment they should keep an eye out for story angles or information the writer might have missed, and talk again with the writer after it's over.

The ideal is real teamwork, where writers and visual journalists understand and complement each other's tasks and skills. The writer, for instance, might work something otherwise unplanned into the story to justify using a particularly striking image. And the visual journalist acts as a second pair of eyes and ears for the writer, perhaps taking not-for-publication scene-setting shots that help the writer recall details or helping interview additional witnesses at an accident.

Remember again that simplest description of what reporters do: Find a story to tell, get the information needed to tell, and then tell it. When writers and visual journalists are working as a team, the result is a coherent story told with words and images. And that's the best kind of journalism.

IDEAS FOR FURTHER STUDY

■ Volunteer at a nursing home or hospice to interview residents and patients about their lives. Use a tape recorder and make a transcript of your conversations. Print out a copy for them and their family members.

■ Practice being observant. Go to a city park or some other outdoor area on a warm, sunny day. Sit yourself down on a blanket. Write in a notebook all that you see and hear within a five-minute period.

■ Ask to spend a day at your local newspaper or television station watching city editors working with reporters, photographers, and other news personnel. See if you can go along as a reporter works on a story.

The Saga of a Great Headline: The Genesis of "Harvard Beats Yale, 29–29"

by Alan Schwarz, Senior Writer, *Baseball America* Magazine

It was supposed to be easy. Asked by *American Heritage* magazine to select the most over-rated and underrated newspaper headlines in history, I knew the winners immediately. The *Chicago Tribune*'s "DEWEY DEFEATS TRUMAN" 1948 banner took the overrated category be-cause, after all, it gained its immortality simply by being wrong. Meanwhile, the underrated headline would be one that *appeared* wrong, but was deliciously right: "HARVARD BEATS YALE, 29–29." Somebody at the *Crimson*, with only one little word, had brilliantly captured the essence of the Harvard football team's leg-endary comeback (sixteen points in the final forty-two seconds) to tie Yale in November 1986. I would find that somebody.

How hard could that be? "HARVARD BEATS YALE, 29–29" had to be the most famous head-line in *Crimson* history, its author surely spo-ken of reverently through the generations, perhaps even honored with a shrine in the newsroom. This would take two or three phone calls, tops. Instead it became the longest, most frustrating, undulating, teasing, and exhausting search I have undertaken in ten years in journalism—lasting three months and consisting of 117 phone calls, eighty-three Internet searches, and thousands of hairs I'll never see again. I tracked down a Federal Court of Appeals judge, an Internet magnate, Ring Lardner's grandson, and ten other candi-dates before finally finding my white whale.

Phone call number one went to the Har-vard sports information office, whose copy of the famous paper listed Peter Lennon and Scott Jacobs as co-authors of the main story. Well, Lennon's phone number wasn't listed anywhere, but Jacobs's was. Jacobs said that, while he didn't come up with the headline, he knew four candidates who either did or would know: Joel Kramer, *Crimson* president at the time; James Glassman, the managing editor; the newspaper's longtime typesetter, Pat Sor-rento; and Esther Dyson, then a seventeen-year-old freshman who ran around helping out however she could.

Four more people. No problem.

My confidence was swiftly punished. Kra-mer, now a senior fellow at the University of Minnesota's School of Journalism, had no idea who came up with "HARVARD BEATS YALE." Glassman laughed and said, "People over the years have congratulated me on writing the headline, but I'm not sure I did it." He then sent me off on a detour, saying I had to call Bill Bryson, a news staffer who had given Glass-man tickets to The Game (whoops!) and stayed in the Crimson office to handle that Saturday's postgame extra edition. Six phone calls uncovered Bryson's whereabouts—but have you ever tried to phone a U.S. circuit court judge?

"I'm sorry, Judge Bryson isn't available at the moment," the woman said.

Reprinted from the November–December 2000 issue of *Harvard Magazine*.

"Uh, do judges have voice mail?"

They don't, it turns out, but Bryson returned my message within three minutes. "I wish I could plead guilty," he yukked, "but it wasn't my headline. I would have been much more pleased with myself. I think it wasn't until the following Monday's paper that that headline ran."

Could that be true? Before I could determine the ramifications of this—to that point, everyone had assumed the headline had run in the Saturday extra—Dyson returned my e-mail. (Now an e-publishing force dubbed "Queen of the Digerati" by the *New York Times*, e-mail is the only way to contact her.) Whichever edition it was, she had no idea who wrote the headline. Neither did Josh Simon, the current *Crimson* president. But he did clear up one small point: Bryson was right, the Saturday extra ran a different headline, "HARVARD, YALE DRAW, 29–29." It *was* the Monday edition that featured the famous banner. But still, who wrote it? Simon offered two more names from the paper's masthead: sports editor Richard Paisner and night editor Bill Kutik.

No dice with Paisner, now a healthcare technology investor in Washington, D.C. He said try Jim Lardner, the grandson of Ring, and now a writer himself in New York City. "Far be it for a Paisner to take credit for a great line when a Lardner was part of the team," he declared. Like everyone else, though, Lardner charmingly declined his chance to seize any credit. "My role," he said, "was taking pleasure in the whole thing."

Every person offered two or three others to try, the candidates multiplying like bacteria.

I even tracked down Sorrento, the production supervisor who spent thirty-two years helping the *Crimson* hum before retiring to Chelsea last year. He remembered Bryson saying, "Run with it!" but added, "I have no idea who wrote the headline. All I did was set it." Two months into this process, and after sifting through eight more names with no results, I was about to give up. My last call would be made to Kutik, the night editor whom I had forgotten about. I caught him as he was walking out the door and gave my spiel about trying to find the author of history's most underrated headline.

"You got him," Kutik said. "You got the guy."

At last! As night editor, Kutik explained, he edited copy and wrote headlines that Sunday afternoon after The Game. He was hunched over a page of scribble, fiddling with "HARVARD TIES YALE, 29–29," horribly dissatisfied because every reader knew the score. "It didn't reflect the feel of the game," Kutik recalled. Then photography editor Tim Carlson looked over his shoulder.

"How 'bout 'HARVARD *BEATS* YALE, 29–29'?" Carlson asked.

"But—," Kutik reflexively balked. Then he realized how perfect it was. He convinced skeptical higher-ups to accept the headline, and hours later, it was flying off the *Crimson* presses.

The problem, I gingerly explained to Kutik, was that I still hadn't found the person who thought of the headline. Carlson's was the flash of inspiration: Kutik had only implemented it. Where was Tim Carlson? All Kutik remembered was that he had worked for a Los Angeles newspaper at some point. Seventeen attempts to find him there or through phone, Internet, or Harvard alumni searches didn't work, until finally an old friend said he had an old e-mail address that surely was out-of-date. Desperate, I pecked out an e-mail to Carlson detailing my quest and begging his reply.

He called the next day.

"I was taking photographs for the *Crimson* in the end zone," said Carlson, now the editor of *Inside Triathlon* magazine in Boulder, Colorado. "When the game ends, I'm running across the field, people are dancing, and this very drunk undergraduate sees my camera and press pass and says, 'You know, Harvard *Beats* Yale,' as if he'd gotten a vision of it. Like he had just seen God.

"I was like, 'Oh my God, that's right.' I was smart enough to know it was good, but I didn't think of it. The person who had the vision of it was an anonymous undergraduate. It would be nice to say I was smart and take all the credit. I guess you could say I wasn't dumb enough to drop it. I was present at the conception."

With that, Carlson and I said our good-byes and hung up. I just started laughing. Three months into this odyssey, there would be no reward. The hunt was over. Rather than finding a fact, I had confirmed a mystery. Maybe that drunken undergraduate will read this story, recall that magical moment of delirium, and identify himself. Or perhaps the afternoon's alcohol forever erased his memory.

Either way, his headline has become almost as legendary as the remarkable Game that inspired it. And as for my quest, like the tie itself, no answer became the best outcome of all. ■

CHAPTER 8

Writing

by Gerald Grow
Florida A&M University

Writing comes naturally to some visual journalists. Others, through effort, luck, and good instruction, have learned to write well. For other visual journalists, writing seems like an unnatural act—yet no other skill would be more valuable to an accomplished visual journalist than learning to write well. This chapter is designed to help you recognize some of the writing problems many visual journalists encounter and to help you become better at writing.

You can gain important insights into writing by considering some ways that pictures and writing differ from one another. This chapter will focus on a few key distinctions:

- Pictures can exist without words; writing consists of words.
- Pictures often contain important information about their contexts; it is easy to write words without specifying the context that clarifies their meaning.
- The same picture can be "read" from a variety of perspectives; in writing, one word follows another in a specific order and it is the duty of the writer to establish the perspective.

We are at the age of progressing from text in print to digital delivery.

Will Crocker

Finding Words for Things

As a visual journalist, you may not need many words. You are skilled at communicating with pictures. You can point to things without having to name them—"that," "over there," "it," "that thingamajig." It is amazing how much human beings can accomplish with few words. Early humans may have coordinated their hunts largely with hand signals. Today, point-and-click computers enable us to work for hours without writing or uttering—or thinking—a single word.

Writers can't point. They have to spell everything out, using words. Finding the right words, then, is the first task any writer faces. In order to write something, you have to name it. Your high school English teacher gave you this advice: Develop a larger vocabulary! But the old joke about the book reviewer who read the dictionary points out a problem with vocabulary: "Great vocabulary; terrible plot." Vocabulary counts for little without a "plot" that connects the words meaningfully. Finding the right words, then, also means finding the right story that connects those words.

Words do not have meanings in themselves, but only as they refer to patterns in the world and in society. The meanings are in the patterns, not in the words. Even when you write well, readers still have to bring with them knowledge of how the world works. They must also apply this knowledge to your prose in order to understand what you have written.

When you write, you don't "use" words to "convey" meaning; you send out certain words that signal readers to activate the knowledge of certain specific patterns. For example, if you write this cutline: "President Bush hugs his wife, Laura, before leaving on a weeklong trip to Japan for an economic summit," you are not telling readers the meaning of "president," "wife," "hug," or "Japan." You are cueing readers to recall their knowledge of these things and use it to interpret the picture. You are anchoring the visual message in your readers' knowledge of patterns in the world and in the culture. In order to do this effectively, you have to use the same words your readers use to label these patterns. Thus, tapping the shared vocabulary of your readers is the first step in writing—along with the societal patterns that give that vocabulary meaning; unless you use a shared vocabulary and shared meanings, you write for yourself alone. Writers have immersed themselves for decades in the river of words we all swim in, but some visual thinkers have been too occupied with other things to have automatically picked up the skill of thinking in a shared language.

How do you learn the words? Two ways: Develop the habit of listening very carefully to what people call things. Take notes, draw diagrams, and label the parts, so you can learn the names. In any publication you work for, readers will know certain things by certain names. Learn that vocabulary. Use it. Practice it.

But second, and more important, learn what people understand by the words they read. For every field, there is a specialized vocabulary—in tennis, auto racing, fishing, finance, health care, education, farming, retail, computers, international news. Learn the vocabulary of the subject you write about. Learn it so deeply that you can anticipate how your readers will interpret the words you use.

Above all, don't use words in a private or eccentric manner. You'll know you're doing this if you ever find yourself saying to your editor, "Well that's just what I used the word to mean." Writing offers many opportunities to be creative, but words are not decor: You cannot change them around just because you like their sound or color. Words already have meanings to your readers. Respect those meanings.

As a creative person, you may be tempted to use a creative vocabulary. But unless you are working for an unusually creative publication, you should write primarily with the clean, clear, limited vocabulary of journalism. Be creative not with the words you choose, but with the stories you tell. The key to journalism is learning the difference between someone with only a ninth-grade vocabulary and a well-informed, intelligent writer using a ninth-grade vocabulary by choice. Learn to use words as a choice.

Context

Words gain meaning through context. Even though the vocabulary of the English language is vast, nearly all common words have more than one meaning, and readers decide which meaning is meant by the context in which the word appears. "Shoulder" means one thing in the context of a torso, another in typography, and another on a highway. "Run" means one thing applied to football, another applied to stockings, another applied to creeks, another in the stock market. "Blue" can be a color, an inflection in a musical chord, an emotional state, or one team in a soccer game. This situation creates a problem for some visual journalists when they write.

A word may label more than one reality. You have to be exceptionally specific to identify which reality you are talking about. Don't hesitate to use extra words to clarify your meaning. In an article, it is seldom enough to state something, even if you state it clearly. You have to repeat, clarify, and explain. Above all, you have to give the context.

Unpacking Words

Pictures can carry layers of meaning; they often invite interpretation and reflection. Part of the joy of a great painting is that you may experience different responses to it at different times. Visual thinking is, in part, a way of layering multiple meanings into a single image. And that meaning does not always have to be clear. Readers may find themselves unclear about the meaning of a picture, yet they may also find that the picture is compelling and effective.

Visual journalists may try to make words carry more meaning than words can bear—as if the words were labels for unseen pictures: "Then he gave her a funny look and picked the thing up and dropped it into the bag." If readers had in mind the same images the writer did, everyone would interpret that sentence in the same way. As it stands, however, this sentence needs to be "unpacked," clarified, specified—something like this: "The new butcher, confused by her remark, glanced up to see whether she intended it as a criticism. Concluding that she was only making friendly conversation, he softened, hefted the oddly shaped package of dog bones, and dropped it into the string bag she awkwardly held open for him."

Sentences that are compressed, telegraphic, and marked by such unclear words as "this," "that," "it," and the like probably come from depths of the mind that are too private for effective journalism. You need to drag them out into the light, open them up, unpack their compressed meanings, and spell out what you mean. Doing this takes more words, but the results will almost always be better.

This advice goes against the usual instruction to be "clear and concise." As a visual journalist, you may need to learn first to write at greater length, with greater detail, explanation, paraphrase, and redundancy. Afterward, you can shorten and tighten your work. Or an editor can.

Sequence

When you look at a painting, your eyes can move through it in many different ways. A painting does not tell you where to begin looking or where to look next. True, your eye can be drawn to parts of the canvas, but a painting does not control the sequence of glances you give the work. Prose, by contrast, is based on sequence. One thing follows another, and the order in which they appear is crucial. Much of the art of writing comes from finding the right order in which to present material.

Before you can put your thoughts into sequence, you have to decide what is important in the story. This step is difficult for many visual journalists, because visual messages give you the freedom to present more than one point of view, and the artist can leave viewers to find their own way through it.

Not so in writing: Here, you must decide what is important, what comes first, second, third, and lay everything out for your readers. One of the writer's most important tasks is to organize each story around what is most important in it.

Visual journalists are prone to think of all elements in a picture as equally important. This is true in a way—each line, color, and shape makes a contribution to the whole, which is greater than its parts. Indeed, some art teachers think that artists go into a special state of mind—what one called "aprene"—where they consider every detail significant, magical, crucial, and all equal. This almost mystical state may produce superb art, but writers in this state will have a difficult time producing journalistic writing.

How do you decide what is important in a story? When you write for journalism, you nearly always start with a collection of facts, quotes, and information. Often, there is no obvious way to arrange it, so you begin by asking: "What is this story about?"

Imagine a plane crash. Is the story about the technical failure of the equipment that may have caused the crash? The rescue effort? The human drama captured on the traffic controller's tapes? The death of a famous person? The death of a local person? The grief of the family of a local person who died in the crash? The history of crashes by this type of airplane? Freak weather conditions that may have contributed to the crash?

Nearly every story can be told in several ways. One of the first steps toward becoming a better writer is to realize that every time you write, you make a choice among many options. Learn to see what those options are, what choices you are making, what options you are eliminating. When you feel yourself making real choices that affect your readers, you will feel more of the creative excitement that comes with writing. And you will write better.

Photographers learn their art by practicing—taking pictures in different light, from new angles, using different development methods. Writers practice, too—recording dialogue, describing people and scenes, capturing actions in words, finding ways to convey facial expressions, gestures, intonation, irony. And they practice writing stories in different ways—trying it first as a story about a technical problem, then as a story about a person solving a technical problem, then as a story about an organization dealing with a technical problem, then as a story about the danger this technical problem poses for readers, then as a story about specific steps you can take to avoid this technical problem, and so on, until they learn to think through story options without having to write each one out fully. It is a good idea to try several different outlines for a story before committing yourself to one approach.

Not "To Be"

One verb causes more grief in writing than anything else: "to be" and its forms—is, are, am, was, were, be, been, being. Remember: Nothing "is" anything else. Everything relates to other things in some way other than "is." Writers must find that relationship and express it with a strong verb. When you revise your work, circle every instance of "is," "are," "be," and other forms of the verb "to be." If you find one on every line, take this as a warning that you are "is-ing" rather than relating. Challenge each instance of "to be." Revise as many as you can, to draw out the real relations among things, to tell the real story.

Challenge especially every instance of the passive voice, which leads to statements like "the ball was hit by the boy." The active voice says it this way: "The boy hit the ball." Concentrate your prose on telling who did what to whom—and with what effect. When revising your prose, be merciless with the passive voice—change it all. Then add back the few passive sentences you really need.

Work especially hard to identify each action, and to find the person that performed the action. Don't write as if things just happened by themselves ("it was decided"); write about people who did things ("After an acrimonious debate, the five

Republicans on the nine-person committee voted to . . ."). Write about things that made other things happen. Connect. Relate. Show readers how the world works.

Tell a story that starts in one place and moves to another. "Is" just sits there. Write a story that moves, and that moves readers.

Of course, you need forms of "is" now and then to make your prose flow. So, when you have taken out all the "is"s and rewritten as much as you can with strong, clear verbs and definite subjects, add back the "is"s you need to make the prose sound natural.

Writing the Story

Before you begin, anticipate what kind of story you will write. Make a guess about what the story will be about. Make a provisional outline, and use that outline to organize your interviews and other research. Without a preliminary outline, you may not know what to research. Then follow the story wherever it unfolds, revising the outline as you go. After you finish the research, analyze what you have.

Read through it all and divide it into stacks of related material. Consider these carefully, to see what stories you can tell with them.

Decide which story you are going to tell: This is your focus.

Arrange the stacks into an order that will tell that story.

Re-read everything carefully. Do you have enough material in each stack to tell this particular story, or do you need to conduct more research? If you can't tell the story you want to tell, you may have to tell the story your material permits you to tell. Be flexible. Respond to the material you have gathered, and respond to the story you believe that material tells.

Before you begin, decide how each stack will connect to the others. Write out a brief transition to connect each stack with the one that precedes and follows it.

Next, write the ending to your story—the point you want readers to arrive at.

Now go back into your material and review everything one more time. Jot down the main parts of your outline, and, *without looking at your notes,* write the entire story from your outline and what you remember. When you need a quote but cannot remember it, write "Insert quote here" and keep going. Write for the whole, for the flow, for the overall meaning, the overall story. Let it flow, let it breathe and move, let it move you and your readers. Capture the fundamental truth of the matter; capture the feeling of the story; you can fill in the details later.

When you finish this draft, go back and insert the factual material from your notes. Weave in the details. Flesh out the story with your research. Check to make sure everything you wrote is correct and complete.

CONCLUSION

Finally, write the opening, the title, and the subtitle or summary subhead—all the things a reader will need to enter your story. And revise your ending. Writing a story this way is like painting in layers; in order for readers to progress from beginning to end and arrive at what is most important, you have to start with what is most important and build up the story around it.

IDEAS FOR FURTHER STUDY

- Write a story—a personality piece of someone in your town—in various styles. Try writing the profile on a person in the style of a hard news (who, what, when, and where information) and a feature (more descriptive and full of quotes) story. What makes these types of stories different or similar?

- Find a previously written story of about 1000 words. Edit it so that the entire story is 300 words.

- Find a photograph. Write three different cutlines that completely change the meaning of the image for a viewer.

Visual Journalism and the Connection with Word Reporters

by Bryan Grigsby, Photo Editor, *The Philadelphia Inquirer*

For the past twenty-five years I have made my living as a photojournalist, photo editor, and photo teacher. Recently I attended the Wilmington (Delaware) Writers' Workshop. Yes, our colleagues in the newsroom go to workshops seeking inspiration, same as we. I traveled to Wilmington that weekend with a professional agenda quite different from most of the other journalists present. I was in search of evidence to support research I had begun some months before comparing the genealogy of writing and photography. Although I had file folders full of in-house memorandums about my own newspaper's quest for better-written stories, I felt I needed to see and hear for myself what young reporters looked to for professional inspiration. What I heard that weekend confirmed my suspicions.

Writer Richard Ben Cramer told his audience to take their reporting down from the aerial perspective of institutional experts and write instead through the eyes of the people affected by those institutions. Using the words of his former mentor Eugene Roberts, Cramer challenged the audience to find ways to make their readers *see* the thing they were writing about. Indeed, as a photo editor my greatest professional frustration is the daily struggle to stitch together badly conceived photo assignments to stories that are written from a nonvisual perspective. Despite Cramer's well-intentioned remarks on reporting, photographers are often assigned to mate pictures of the experts interviewed about a story rather than the story itself. While this kind of reporting is easier and quicker to complete for busy reporters assigned to fill a few column inches, it also produces a predictable, routine kind of news writing that I believe our readers grow tired of reading.

Several years ago I discovered a small paperback book titled, *On Becoming a Writer* by Dorthea Brande. Originally published more than sixty years ago, Brande's book challenged its readers to find new ways to look at the familiar world around them. Remove their blinders of habit, she suggested. Learn to see the world through the eyes of a child. Brande's book put the hook in me. Her advice to young writers made perfect sense for photographic vision as well. In Wilmington I listened as Richard Ben Cramer told his mostly young audience the same thing. If Dorthea Brande and Richard Ben Cramer were both talking about writing in terms that applied to photographers as well as to reporters, then what if writing and photography shared more of a commonality of vision than most practitioners of those two crafts realized? What if, by a better understanding of this commonality of vision, reporters, photographers, and their editors could somehow learn to act better as a storytelling/news gathering team? The pages of our newspapers are full of the daily failures produced by the lack of understanding between writing and photography.

A growing number of thoughtful photojournalists and photo editors have begun to question the newsroom status quo that prevents the photo department from having more of a say about the content of stories in their newspapers. Unfortunately, for my colleagues and for myself, the editorial power in our newspapers lies with the folks who write the words, not with the folks who take the pictures.

During a lecture in one of those big, industrial-strength conference rooms of the Wilmington Holiday Inn, I couldn't help but notice a khaki-clad young man moving around the room lugging several cameras, lights, and other gear. He was obviously there to photograph the participants at the conference. His appearance and demeanor suggested to me that his perspective on the events that day was probably limited to f-stops, shutter speeds, and depth of field. If he felt any professional kinship to the other people in that room it was probably not a result of any of the journalistic thoughts he was being exposed to. He was probably feeling the usual second-class citizenship that most photographers carry along with their press credentials when surrounded by a room full of reporters. Professionally, he was a colleague of mine, and yet I wondered what kind of a leap of faith would be necessary to convince anyone else in that room that his activities that day had any kinship to what they did for a living. Still, I believe change and evolution will have to come through platforms like the Wilmington Writers' Workshop or the National Press Photogra-

pher's Flying Short Course. Younger minds that are willing to spend money and time to go to workshops or are still in school offer the best vehicle for any change in attitude.

At present most journalism schools give student reporters only a passing glance at photography. A quick course geared to teaching them how to shoot a picture, process a roll of film and make a print in the darkroom is considered sufficient. To me that is as superficial as teaching photo students how to type sixty words per minute and then believing they know how to write. Student reporters and photographers need to experience a teaching environment that is more interactive. Instead of being shunted off to separate-but-equal classrooms, they should learn how the other thinks as they work. Instead of taking a few overlapping professional courses that stress computers and cameras, they need to learn to see deeper into each other's craft. How do photographers and reporters respond to a story idea? How do they plan their coverage? What drives the direction of a word or picture story? Future newspaper managers with this kind of background could be the key to a more thoughtful mix between words and pictures in tomorrow's newspapers. Indeed, it might be a small part of the solution towards newspapers becoming more relevant in today's electronic media–dominated world,

The single greatest difference between photo reporting and word reporting is that photographers are forced to operate totally within the confines of "real time." Photographers have to be present when a story is unfolding; reporters do not. When reporters choose not to write from the perspective of a witness but from the anecdotes of others, then the resulting photographs are usually as predictable as the writing. I believe both crafts use many of the same narrative techniques to tell a story. For example:

- Both begin with the act of looking.
- Both record a story from the perspective of outsider looking in.
- Both require a narrative hook in order to be more than a bland document of something's existence.
- Both can play elements within a scene/ frame against or towards each other in order to generate some level of narrative stress. Juxtaposition is a common tactic. Writers find contrast, contradiction, or incongruity in situations. Photographers look for visual vignettes using the same narrative tactics inherent to juxtaposition.
- Both use the tactic of exclusion of information deemed distracting or redundant. Writers do this through editing. Photographers do this through framing during the picture-making process or by cropping the negative later on.

- Both are often capable of telling a story from a perspective that is more encompassing than the perspective of the subjects of that story.
- Both are capable of great descriptive power.
- Both are the result of a cognitive thought process and at times artistic intuition.

Unfortunately most newspaper photo departments are viewed as "service" departments. Photo assignments are often treated as a necessary tactic for getting better play for stories in the paper rather than as a vehicle for providing additional reader insight into a story. When newspaper management talks about writing they talk about content. When they talk about photography they talk about technology. Photographs are seen as an adjunct of the graphics department, a visual device to draw the reader into a story rather then a formal part of the information process.

A better understanding of what photography and writing have in common rather than the continued status quo of competition between the two crafts could result in improving the quality of both writing and photography in tomorrow's newspapers. ■

Using Design

The three chapters in this section explain the importance of typography, graphic design, and informational graphics for aiding storytelling by visual journalists. It stresses typography because the choices a visual journalist makes concerning how words are presented on a page or screen largely determine if the work looks professional or conveys the appropriate message. Once you are aware of the ways typography is essential to effective communication, you must then learn how to create pleasing and content-filled compositions for print and screen media. The final chapter in this section will provide a background in informational graphics so that you can produce and/or have discussions with designers about how to use words, images, and design to their maximum benefit for readers and viewers.

CHAPTER 9

Typography

by Jean Trumbo
University of Missouri

Many of us read a newspaper, magazine, or computer screen without paying a great deal of attention to typography. In fact, when typography is most effectively used it is unobtrusive; it bows to the importance of the words that it reveals. It is tempting to think of typography as simply functioning to make the text visible. We demand a great deal from it—clarity, aesthetic appeal, legibility, and readability—and with some basic skills it is possible to make type function reasonably well.

But to dismiss typography as a simple, functional element of design is understating its power because typography has great expressive potential. It can clarify, illuminate, and augment content. It can help or hinder the process of reading. Typography can also work with editorial content to establish the personality of the publication. The integration of typography and the other elements of design (color, image, space, and so on) can create powerful and effective messages. Typography is also tied to the technology for which it was created and the culture from which it was designed.

This chapter will introduce some of the basic principles of typographic composition.

Seeing Typography

Learning to look carefully at typography can help the editor and designer understand the subtle characteristics of the type design and how to use type meaningfully. Each typeface is a unique system of letterform built by the type designer to solve a problem or to create a particular visible expression on the printed page. The tradition of typographic design developed from the hand-drawn letterform of the monastic scribe and the chiseled structure of letterform found on Roman monuments.

The adaptations and variations that we see in modern type design are the result of changes in technology and the cultural influences of the time. Computer technology has allowed the type designer to create new typefaces more easily and has also created a new market for typography. Viewing typography on the computer screen is a different process from reading the printed page and many type designers have made adaptations to the letterform to account for the bitmap of the computer monitor. Printing in digital media is also much different from traditional photographic pre-press processes. It is possible to make alterations to the typeface—stretching and skewing the letterform—on the computer, for example. And traditional typesetting, hot metal or phototypesetting for paste-up, has been forever simplified through desktop publishing.

The process of simplifying typesetting and page layout has created new options for communicators, but it has not necessarily made it easier to use type effectively. In fact, with more options and new technologies the role of the communicator is more diverse than ever. Editors are often charged with designing both the verbal and visual content of a publication. Understanding the special vocabulary that accompanies typography as well as some of the functional and creative applications for typography can help make this beautiful system of symbols work to clarify a message.

Typography can be grouped into two big categories that describe structural details of the typeface. These categories are serif and sans serif typefaces. Serifs are the finishing strokes on the letterform. They are distinctive from one typeface to another.

Typefaces can be described in terms of their physical attributes—shape of the letterform, serifs, weight and contrast, and posture. It is helpful to organize the thousands of typefaces that are available into categories or families that share basic characteristics. These type families are: blackletter, roman, script, square serif, sans serif, and miscellaneous.

Blackletter

Johannes Gutenberg in Mainz, Germany, invented the first moveable type printing press in the 1400s. The letters that he developed were based upon the heavy, ornate blackletters of the northern European monastic scribes. These letters had great variation in stroke weight, with strong, heavy verticals and fine, calligraphic connecting strokes. Gutenberg created metal type characters that retained most of the detail of the calligraphic hand. The use of blackletter was limited by its cumbersome weight and complexity. Letterform evolved from blackletter to simpler roman typefaces within a few decades of the introduction of printing.

Blackletter is not legible in text sizes. The most common use of blackletter today is in display sizes for newspaper banners, special invitations, decorative initials or monograms, and diplomas.

Roman

Designers in southern Europe who were inspired by the simple, open forms of the Roman alphabet created roman type in the late 1400s. This letterform was created with a hand-held brush painted on stone and then carved over by stonemasons. Most of the lines within the letterform were created with a single movement of the brush and contrast is created by changing pressure on the brush stroke. This technique produced letterform with varying stroke width and fine finishing strokes on the main body of the letterform. These finishing strokes are called serifs.

Script

Script typefaces resemble handwriting, with slanted strokes and serifs that form connections between letterform. Some script typefaces are ornate, with flowing, curved finishes on the ending strokes.

Examples of blackletter type.

Cloister Black
Blackletter 686

Examples of roman, script, and sans serif type.

Classic Garamond
Cathedral Regular
Futura Heavy

Script typefaces are useful in visual design because they can add a formal, elegant, and sometimes feminine tone to the printed piece. They are often used in wedding invitations or to simulate handwriting in titles or headings. Many script typefaces are more decorative than readable.

Sans Serif

Sans serif, also called Gothic or Grotesque typefaces, have no serifs. They are geometric and uniform in stroke weight. The interior shape of the letterform is often open, which gives the typeface a light, even texture on the printed page. This monotone quality tends to make sans serif typefaces less popular as text faces. Many readability studies suggest that the contrast provided by the serif helps the reader navigate a text block. Nonetheless, sans serif typefaces can be accessible and beautiful on the printed page.

Because of the geometric structure of the letterform, sans serif typefaces have an open, clean efficiency. They are highly visible on the computer screen or in video and film. On the printed page, sans serifs create an even, gray text block that may require the addition of leading—weight or width variation to create contrast.

Square Serif

Square serif, also called Egyptian or slab serif, typefaces have straight, square serifs that are often the same weight as the main letter stroke. These typefaces are sturdy and heavy. They do not work particularly well in text sizes, but are good for display or headlines. Square serifs go in and out of style. Because of their width, weight, and ruggedness, they require adequate space and an appreciation on the part of the designer for the emphasis they will create on the page. On the computer screen, square serifs adapt well to the bitmapped display of the monitor.

Examples of square or slab serif type.

Aachen
Egyptian 505
Ivy League Solid

Miscellaneous

This family of typefaces is often called novelty type and has its origins in the display type created for advertising in the mid-1800s. A common trait among novelty typefaces is that they are seldom subtle; their shape and form are often decorative and attention-grabbing. The readability of most novelty typefaces is limited to its use in display sizes for banners or headlines. The designer must select novelty typefaces carefully. They call attention to themselves through the style or "personality" of their design and thus can be misunderstood if the cultural cues are off-target.

Using Typography

Measurement

Type is measured in points. This small unit of measure is also used to define the thickness of space between lines of type (leading), the width of rule lines, and frames or borders around images or blocks of type. For practical purposes, there are approximately 72 points per inch. Printed text works best when set between 8

Examples of display and text type.

Display Type is Large

Body copy or text type is typically set at between 8 and 12 point size.

Examples of novelty type.

Agincort
Potrzebie
PERSEUS

and 12 points. Display sizes in print are usually considered anything larger than 14 points. Computer display requires a somewhat larger typesize for readable text—12 to 18 points depending upon on the nature of the viewer and the complexity of the typeface.

Leading

The space between lines of set type is called leading from the lead strip that letter-press printers used to divide lines of metal type. Leading is measured in points. In text type, 2 points of lead between lines is considered standard. However, this ideal depends on the design of the typeface, the length of the ascenders and descenders, and the x-height of the letterform.

Line Length

The line length of a text block is measured in picas. There are 12 points per pica or 6 picas in one inch. The line length of the text block has a powerful impact on read-ability. There are several rules of thumb that are useful for the designer.

- The optimum line length should be one and one-half alphabets of the selected typeface (39 characters). This can be applied by measuring in picas the width of a full alphabet (the lowercase letters a through z) set in the selected typeface at the desired size. This width in picas is then added to one-half the total width. For example, if the lowercase alphabet measures 16 picas, a good line length would be 24 picas wide.

Leading is the space between lines of type.

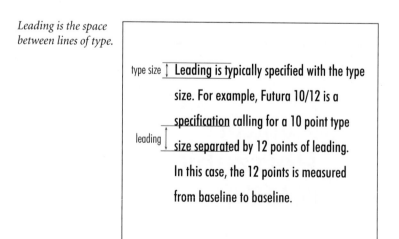

type size ⌐ Leading is typically specified with the type size. For example, Futura 10/12 is a specification calling for a 10 point type leading ⌐ size separated by 12 points of leading. In this case, the 12 points is measured from baseline to baseline.

- The line length should contain at least 5 words per line and no more than 12 words per line.
- The line length in picas should be double the point size of the type. For example, 12 point type should be set in a 24-pica line length.
- As point size of type increases, line length must increase.

Column Setting

In print communication, the options for column setting include flush or justified left and right, flush left/ragged right, ragged left/flush right, and centered. Each of these options has constraints. For example, columns of text set centered down an imaginary midpoint create strong shapes on the printed page. We tend to see the text block as a design element and may be distracted from reading the text. On the other hand, this can be an effective way of adding visual interest to an advertisement. It may also work nicely when the content is an announcement or invitation.

Type set ragged left/justified right works sometimes for short blocks of text in captions or cutlines, but should be avoided for longer sections of text because it disrupts reading.

Type set in columns that are justified right and left creates solid, even text patterns on the printed page. This setting tends to give the page a clean, formal look and it is a good setting to consider when there are multiple vertical columns of text on the printed page. These solid columns require that contrast be added to break the monotony. Contrast can be added through the placement of meaningful subheads, initial capitals that highlight content, paragraph indents, and pull quotes that are used to bring out important comments from the story.

Type set justified left and ragged right is readable when the line length and leading are appropriate. This setting gives the page a less formal structure and provides good contrast for the reader. It works best when there are fewer vertical columns on the page. The raggedness of the right edge of the column can be adjusted through hyphenation. As a general rule, the designer should strive for no more than a 5-character variation at line endings. Lines should not be ended with single character words or numerals.

x-Height

Literally, the height of the lowercase x is the x-height. The x-height is an indicator of the relationship of the letter body to the ascenders and descenders. As the x-height increases, the length of the ascenders and descenders shortens. This changes the visual proportion of the letterform and influences how much white space occurs naturally between lines of type. The x-height also influences the number of characters that will fit per line of set type. Notice these relationships in the examples below. Each example is set 12 points. There is great variation from one typeface to another.

The relationship of ascenders and descenders to the x-height is visible in the examples set below. Each example is set 24 points. The top example, Bauer Bodoni, has a short x-height and ascenders and descenders that are proportionally long. The bottom example, Americana, has a taller x-height and ascenders and descenders that are proportionally shorter.

Americana requires the addition of leading to add contrast to a text block because the shortness of the ascenders and descenders and the relative size of the x-height create a fairly solid setting. Bauer Bodoni, on the other hand, has a great deal of built-in contrast in stroke weight, and the proportion of x-height to ascenders and descenders. Notice the difference in contrast in the text blocks set below. Both examples are set 12/13.

The x-height of various typefaces.

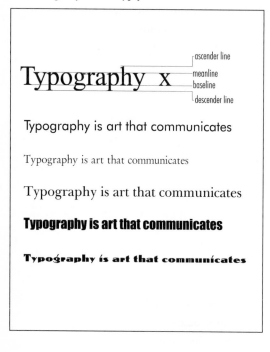

Bauer Bodoni and ITC Americana.

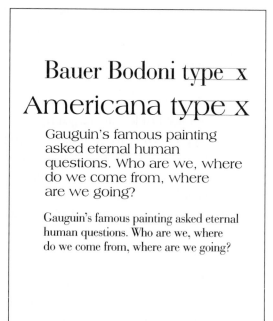

Type Contrast

The creation of a visual hierarchy of information can assist the reader by emphasizing content that is most important or that is capable of offering an overview or introduction to the text. Headline schedules are a common example of using typographic contrast to clarify or introduce story content. The designer uses changes in type size, weight, width, or posture to create contrast and to place emphasis on the printed page.

Some typefaces have dramatic contrast between the thin and thick strokes in the letterform. Others have little contrast in stroke weight. Typically, sans serif typefaces have less contrast than those with serifs. Good contrast adds to readability on the printed page. Ironically, typefaces with relatively little weight contrast work best on-screen.

The effective use of contrast in text can add color and texture to the printed page. Typographic contrast highlights elements of the story that are dominant—the headline and the moral, for example. Each typeface also has a different visual texture. The serifs and variation in the thick and thin strokes give Garamond relatively more texture on the page. Helvetica is fairly uniform in weight and creates a text block that has an even pattern. On the printed page, contrast is important in helping the reader navigate the text. The changing shapes of the letterform provide signals that promote eye movement and consequently help the reader. On the computer screen, sans serifs help overcome the difficulty of reading at low resolution.

Creative Typography

Typography has tremendous expressive potential. The selection of type should reinforce the message through selection that carefully considers the visual personality of the typeface.

- Type can be elegant or casual.
- Type can be delicate or strong.
- It can shout or whisper.
- It can be light or heavy, fat or thin.
- Type can have cultural identity.
- Type can suggest an era or a feeling of formality.
- Type can suggest a particular place and time.
- It can be simple or complex.

Creative Typography

When typography is selected effectively, there is no ambiguity between the intended message and the use of a particular typeface.

On the printed page, typography reveals its content and is a means of creating relationships among elements on the page. The designer uses typography to interact with images, clarify the content of photographs, and establish the mood or emphasis within a story. In a complex communication environment, the designer must view typography as an element among other elements—color, line, and image—and in a multimedia environment type must also work with movement and sound.

Technology makes it possible to manipulate type in many ways. Type can be stretched, elongated, colored, smashed, and overlapped. It can be set in circles or set into irregular shapes. The availability of sizes is nearly limitless. All of these options offer exciting opportunities to the designer. However, they also create the potential to confuse meaning and to create impossible situations for the reader. Creativity should never compromise communication.

Type is a visible voice.

Type is a visible voice and a design element.

Some rules of thumb for using typography creatively:

- If typography is used as a creative element on the printed page, afford it the same consideration as image, color, or other visual elements. Remember that the inherent personality of the typeface is important. Does it match the message?
- Remember that type is read from left to right. If you are making an adjustment to the baseline or setting type on a curved line, at an angle or vertically, you will compromise readability.
- Decorative devices can add interest to the page and many times they are used to augment typographic compositions. Borders, clip art, and ornaments can be used effectively. However, many inexperienced designers rely on these devices when the simple use of space and typography can be more effective. Use the tools of typography—contrast, alignment, and selection of typeface—to build the message.

CONCLUSION

The integration of typography and images can be exciting. Many designers use typography in an illustrative way as an important element within a composition. Make certain that type used in this way is used appropriately. Does it meet the needs of the audience and the message? Does it contribute to our understanding of content?

Typography can be a powerful tool in establishing brand or identity. Advertisers use type effectively in logos, tradenames, or trademarks. Editorial designers can use type similarly to create visual identity for a continuing series, sections within a publication, or publication banners. Remember that type used in this way creates an important relationship with the reader.

The key to using typography effectively and creatively is to design rather than decorate. Design is meaningful, purposeful communication. Decoration is attending only to the "look" of the type. Remember that the underpinning of all communication is attention to the message. Typography is an essential element in that process. It is used most effectively when it is a servant of language and meaning. It is used most effectively when the message and the intended meaning are revealed through the composition. Typography must work in union with color, image, structure, and all of the elements of design. Typography is a subtle and essential element in effective communication.

IDEAS FOR FURTHER STUDY

- Discuss the impact that the Gutenberg Bible has had on the field of typography.

- Describe your favorite use of typography in advertising and editorial work.

- What do you think is the future of typography?

- Find a particular typeface that reflects your personality. What does it say about you?

- Write a paper that discusses any ethical concern about typography.

- Why do you think most typography is hardly noticed by the reader or viewer?

The Current Tendency for Weak Typography in the Web and Interactive Design Arena

by Julia Ptasznik, Editor of *Visual Arts Trend*

Referring to technologists, or technology-based designers in particular, Mark Rattin, one of the judges of Communication Arts' 1999 Interactive Design Competition, says he is surprised by the state of typography on the Web.

You could argue that this is not a new trend, if you consider the history and the present state of both Web and print design. Much of what we see out there lacks—and will always lack—a true understanding of design fundamentals. Some of it is because non-designers are producing a lot of work (the words "secretary" and "PowerPoint" come to mind). And there are plenty of incompetent designers. While none of us would ever recognize ourselves as belonging to this category, it exists in design just as it does in any other profession.

Having said that, typography somehow remains the most overlooked element of the fundamentals. Although we've "come a long way, baby," an ad campaign that uses type in a non-formulaic way is still rare. A solely typographic TV commercial is rarely if ever seen. In print advertising, there are plenty of art directors who subscribe to the old-fashioned headline-photo-body copy formula, and the majority of type is still black or knocked out of a photographic or solid-color background. The primary cause of this is not the perfectly understandable readability issue; it is the fact that black is easy. It happens to be the default color in all software applications.

With the advent of digital royalty-free photography, illustration, and clip art, the use of these elements to "spruce-up" otherwise conceptually weak design work is rampant, in all media, as long as the photo is nice and colorful. Design for the Web and other interactive media gives—let's call them "bad," for the sake of argument—designers yet another opportunity to add eye-candy, in the form of spiffy animation and pretty multicolored buttons.

Think back to when the computer was first becoming a fixture at print design studios. Every help-wanted ad then concentrated mostly on the technical aspects of the job, in much the same way ads for Web designers do today. Today, ads for print designers placed by the better companies focus on design and problem-solving skills, with the phrase "a good understanding of type" being a mandatory requirement. Quark, Illustrator, and Photoshop are simply an afterthought, as every design school graduate is assumed to possess the knowledge of these or other similar software.

If history repeats itself, as indeed it does, we shall soon see the same change of approach in help-wanted advertising for Web jobs. Interestingly, another judge involved in the

First published by Typographer.com, ©2000.

Communication Arts' 1999 Interactive Design Competition, Janis Nakano Spivak, points out that designers are continuing to evolve their technical abilities, "understanding the [applications] as things that [they] use as opposed to being hobbled by them." Just as it happened with print, soon the technical aspects of the job will become academic when it comes to employment considerations in the Web and interactive arena. We'll see a shift back to the fundamentals in the skills employers look for in their new hires. Then we'll see more good design and typography on the Web. Please stand by. ■

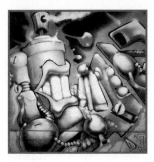

CHAPTER 10

Graphic Design

by Jean Trumbo
University of Missouri

Design, by definition, is concerned with intent. An idea created "by design" is intended to perform in a specific way, typically as a visual form of communication with a clearly articulated message developed for a specific audience. Graphic design is a profession involved in the creation and production of visible products that are meaningful if they are successful. Advertising persuades. Corporate identity attracts and clarifies. Information design informs. Publication design assembles a mix of text and visual content for a well-defined audience. Multimedia design offers an interactive, navigable package of content in multiple media formats. Design communicates through the arrangement of visual elements and the building of form within a variety of formats to reveal content.

Graphic design is a creative process and a strategic process that begins with a message to be communicated to an audience. The designer objectively determines the appropriate medium and through research and refinement develops a concept that meets the client's and an audience's needs. This process requires the integration of a number of disciplines: fine art, mass communication, psychology, business, and marketing. The designer seldom works alone. Art directors, photographers, illustrators, writers, and editors share a common goal—effective communication—and this process requires real partnership among all of the content experts. Graphic designers are visual communicators.

Graphic designers shape the form of the communication effort. They create magazines, newspapers, books, brochures, multimedia, signage, billboards, TV graphics, annual reports, film titles, and hundreds of other expressions all intended for diverse audiences. While the writer and editor work within the realm of the written word, the designer's responsibility is to make the message visible and meaningful through the deliberate, strategic, sensible organization of information. The designer's tools include all of the software and hardware, production processes, and information skills that other communicators depend on. In addition, the designer's tools include the elements and principles of visual design.

The designer must be a solid technician and a diligent researcher. The designer must be well versed in the creation of visual form and must comprehend the needs of diverse audiences. The designer must understand perception, learning processes, and persuasion. The designer must be a type, image, color, paper, printing, and production expert. The designer must have solid business ethics and the discipline to pursue excellence. The designer must be able to evaluate success and failure. The designer must have a foundation in tradition with an appreciation for experimentation within this emerging discipline. Perhaps most importantly, the designer must be a negotiator who can help all of the content developers—writers, editors, artists, photographers—make decisions about the most effective way to tell the story.

The design process begins with a complete understanding of the communication challenge. This includes understanding the intent of the originator or information source, the intricacies of the message, the channel through which the message will be delivered, and the audience. The designer's role is to synthesize this information and to select an appropriate visual response. For example, if the message is a profile of a regional airline company that describes the company's profits for the most recent quarter, the designer's role is to clarify that message. Some possible strategies might include the design of informational graphics that show the numerical demonstration of company profit. But other solutions are also viable. They include photographs of the CEO if her role was important in the company's success, or photographs of employees if this is an employee-owned company. There are often a number of possible visible solutions. The designer's role is to generate visual alternatives and to then suggest the option that communicates most appropriately.

We can distinguish between two aspects of visual design—content and form. Content is the subject matter, the story, the information or message that is to be

Design is the integration of content and form.

This document contains an introduction. It goes on for two sentences followed by four more paragraphs.

1. Paragraph 2 has detailed information. In this case, the type used is Futura Light Condensed.

2. The type is set at 7/10. This means 7 point type size with 10 points of leading.

3. This is a basic example of allowing the content to dictate the form. The page should look like the explanation.

If the content is text with an introductory paragraph followed by three detailed explanations . . .

This document contains an introduction. It goes on for two sentences followed by three more paragraphs.

1 Paragraph 2 has detailed information. In this case, the type used is Futura Light Condensed.

The type is set at 7/10. This means 7 point type size with 10 points of leading. *2*

3 This is a basic example of allowing the content to dictate the form. The page should look like the explanation.

. . . then make it *look like* an introductory paragraph followed by three detailed explanations.

That is the designed integration of form with content.

communicated to an audience. Form is the visual aspect of the result of the format, the organization of visual elements, the production properties, and the application of design principles. Form without content is merely decorative. Content without form is boring. In fact, form that doesn't augment the content may be visually appealing but will rarely be meaningful. Content that has little concern for form will often be overlooked or considered too confusing for the audience. Decisions about the effectiveness of visual form and the development of content depend upon the audience's needs. The designer is an expert in unifying the goals of content with the possibilities of visual form.

The Process of Design

In visual design, the response to a communication problem will take a variety of forms all intended for a particular audience. The struggle for the designer is always balancing the potential for a creative solution with the practical realities of solving a communication problem. Innovation cannot come at the expense of effective communication. This balance of strategy and creativity seems almost contradictory. But the fundamental activities of both processes involve the purposeful exploration of options and their successful application. The designer must be able to plan and produce aesthetically effective form that implements the communication strategy.

A strategic approach to understanding the communication problem begins with research and analysis. Most communication fails because the real problem is not fully understood. The designer needs a thorough understanding of what precisely is to be achieved, who specifically is the audience, and the nature of the production requirements. Deadlines, budgets, and marketing profiles should be factored into the strategic planning.

The designer's arsenal of skills and aesthetic sensibilities are built through an appreciation for the tradition of design and an understanding of the exploration that is a constant part of technology and culture. We are surrounded by visual stimuli whose form and meaning shape our aesthetic tastes and understanding. The designer should examine how and why some design is effective and why other visual solutions fall flat. This is a process of training the eye to be a better resource. As writing improves through practice, so too does our ability to envision and evaluate effective visual design. Sources for observation include traditional media as well as collections of graphic design and visual communication.

Application is an obvious part of the process of design because ultimately if you don't do something with your idea, it will disappear. This is the process of producing the visible result and it involves a series of developmental steps: conceptualization, thumbnail sketches, critique, rough layout, and comprehensive layout.

Conceptualization is the first step in the design process and involves thinking through the communication problem while exploring possible solutions. It is often a process more involved with envisioning and imagining than with generating answers. The conceptualization stage is often messy. Many designers immerse themselves in inspiring visual media, listen to music, take long walks, or simply stare out the window while they are thinking about the problem. Conceptualization is a very important part of the process. It requires openness to new ideas and a willingness to look beyond the obvious answer to arrive at a visual solution. Without it the result will often be borrowed, familiar or uninspired.

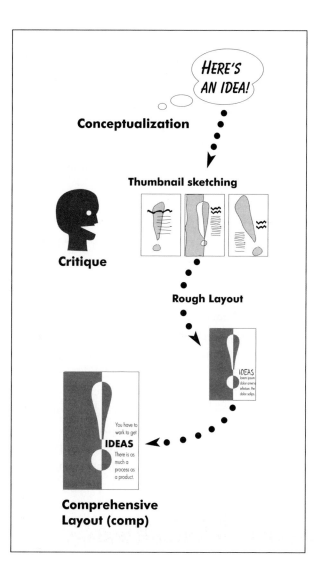

The design development process.

Thumbnail sketches are small, preliminary sketches that show emerging ideas. Thumbnails are often very loose, rough, quick sketches. Many designers generate dozens or hundreds of thumbnails before pushing a concept to the next stage. Thumbnails are idea sketches.

Critique is a necessary part of any communication process. It can be an effective tool for self-evaluation if the process is developed. There are many approaches but some hallmarks of effective critique are to delay value judgments by avoiding assessments of good/bad or right/wrong. Begin with a thorough description of the visual approach—the use of color, image, space, and type. Examine their visible relationships without judging their effectiveness. Then, interpret the potential for meaning that is presented. How will the target audience respond to the solution? What are some possible conflicts or areas of confusion? Are there multiple possible interpretations? Finally, when the visual elements have been described and their potential for communication has been interpreted, evaluate the overall result. Is it possible to produce efficiently? Does it communicate clearly? Can improvements be made? How will success be measured?

The key to effective critique is to continue to assess visual elements and their design without placing value judgments on the skill or effort of the designer. Keep the discussion focused on the communication effort. A healthy response to a good critique is one in which the designer makes changes that are meaningful to help clarify the intended message.

Rough layout is a full-size or proportional rough sketch of the design. It shows the initial size and placement of elements. It is a working document that can be adapted and refined through the critique process. The rough layout is a very useful step in the design process because potential communication and production problems can be identified before the finished piece is produced. It is also a useful document for encouraging discussion among the content developers.

The comprehensive layout is a completed layout that includes all of the details that will appear in print. It serves as a printer's guideline. This is the layout that is typically shown to the client or editor and presented as the fully developed visual solution. If the preliminary stages have included good dialogue and communication among the content developers, the comprehensive will serve simply as a production guide. On the other hand, if the designer has worked independently with little interaction among the content developers, the comprehensive layout is the visual solution that the designer must "sell" to the client.

Reaching the Audience

Any process of visual design requires a clear understanding of the intended audience for the communication effort. There are many business and marketing tools that can help communicators identify the target audience. These include readership surveys, demographic data, or lifestyle research. While these descriptions help put a face on the audience, there are many other concerns for the visual communicator that influence how the message is perceived and understood. Among these are the processes of seeing, reading, comprehension, and action.

Seeing involves the physical properties of vision. There is tremendous varia-tion in vision acuity within any audience. Some people have poor eyesight that re-quires corrective lenses. Color blindness is a factor for many people. The ambient light level and the amount of contrast on the page may affect some viewing situa-tions. In any case, the designer needs to consider how elements such as color com-binations or type size will influence the audience's ability to see the message.

Seeing also involves the audience's overall access to or interest in the material. If the audience is actively involved in the material (subscribers, information seek-ers, or those readily exposed to the message), the design may not need to be overtly attention-getting. The use of color may be subdued and the overall visual appeal may be subtle. On the other hand, if the audience is unfamiliar with the product or message, greater visual emphasis or more contrast may be needed.

Seeing depends on establishing access for the readers or viewers by under-standing reading flow and eye movement patterns. If those patterns are obstructed or changed, comprehension will be affected.

Comprehension is the audience's ability to draw meaning from a communi-cation effort. When the principles and elements of visual design are used effectively the message is very accessible and easily understood.

The Elements of Design

Space in visual design is an area that is defined by visual elements. In visual design it is the area within which the visual elements reside. It is also the area between and among visual elements and media. In the simplest terms, space defines the bound-aries of the design. In a two-dimensional design, space has no depth but the illusion of depth can be suggested through linear perspective, the use of lighting, color, or an effective use of size contrast. Space is not that simple, however. If we think of it only as background we are missing its power as an element of design that is as inte-gral to the success of the effort as color, image, or text. In essence, the space is de-signed, not filled. The use of space is both an aesthetic and a functional concern.

Space can be allocated in publication design through the creation of an un-derlying grid that helps the designer position elements in a proportional, organized way. The grid is an established arrangement of horizontal and vertical guidelines. It is based upon a modular, geometric approach to the page and functions as a frame-work that allows the designer to package elements into rectangular units. In spite of its modular structure, the use of a grid system need not result in boring pages. The designer's role is to allow the grid to function as an organizing tool while adding visual interest through the successful interaction of visual elements. The principles

The Elements of Design

The design space.

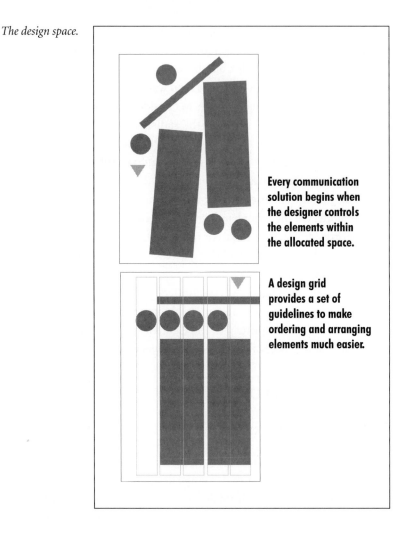

Every communication solution begins when the designer controls the elements within the allocated space.

A design grid provides a set of guidelines to make ordering and arranging elements much easier.

of balance, proportion, contrast, and rhythm offer the designer a palette of tools for creating meaningful and engaging pages within a grid system.

There are many advantages in using a grid system for publication design:

- It is an organizing tool that can help establish visual hierarchy through the ordering and positioning of content.
- It clarifies the position and use of elements. It can define space by making the editorial goals visible through the creation of a visual hierarchy.

- It creates a well-ordered, clean look.

- It establishes a regular structure that adapts well to computer pagination and that offers flexibility for publications that are published on tight deadlines.

- One of its greatest advantages is the routine that can be established for the layout of pages on deadline.

- Story packages and other visual elements can be built to fit the established structure.

- The design approach can be standardized to create a family resemblance among publications.

In spite of its advantages, the grid system can limit exploration and innovation if it is used literally. It can be predictable and boring if the structure overwhelms creativity. Breaking out of the grid can be one way of offering variety in visual expression on the page. For example, all content does not have the same level of editorial importance. Adding variety to the use of space within the grid system offers a way to improve the message by communicating more effectively. Elements that are most important need to be positioned within the space prominently; those that are least important need to recede. This process of establishing visual importance is the creation of a visual hierarchy.

White space is often described as the space surrounding elements within a composition. It is the area that does not contain visual elements—images or text—and it is key to the success of the design. White space is not a leftover ingredient in the design of a page or product. It is not passive or unimportant. In fact, an effective use of white space can highlight important elements and can direct the reader to the area of focus.

Point is the simplest visual element and at the most basic level it defines the location in space of the visible expression. The focal point of a printed publication is the position in space that is most visually important. It is the point that will get and hold the attention of the viewer. The first step in establishing a visual hierarchy is to consider the point at which the viewer should enter the page. This point invites the reader in and the designer's goal is to guide the reader among the visual elements in a meaningful way.

The focal point is not necessarily the biggest, brightest, or busiest element on the page. Often it is the element that is surrounded by space and set off in some way. It is an area of contrast or highlight on the page.

White space in design.

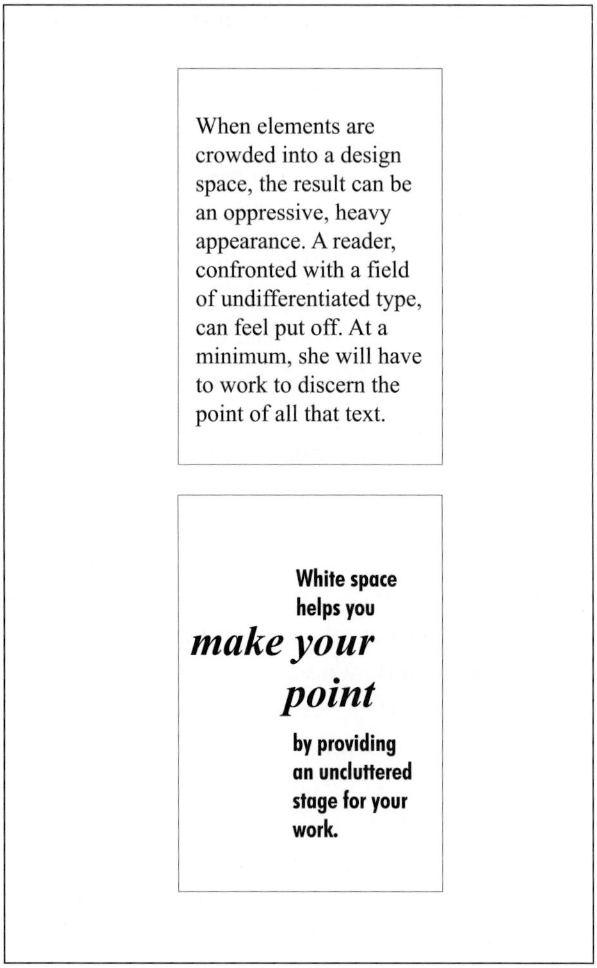

When elements are crowded into a design space, the result can be an oppressive, heavy appearance. A reader, confronted with a field of undifferentiated type, can feel put off. At a minimum, she will have to work to discern the point of all that text.

White space helps you

make your point

by providing an uncluttered stage for your work.

Line is a point in motion. Conceptually it has only one dimension, length. Line in visual design can define the shape of an object or element. It can also be thought of as a manifestation of the direction or movement that is implied by the arrangement of elements. We can think of line as the line of vision that is created by the designer. The use of line can suggest dimension when linear perspective is employed. The use of line can also create emphasis through its relative thinness or thickness. The designer can contain elements within lines that work like frames. Or the designer can point to specific elements by using lines as directional devices.

Shape in visual design can be described in geometric terms as the three basic forms: circle, triangle, and quadrilateral. We can consider the shape to be an expression of an object's exterior or interior form. Shapes have width and height that are defined by their contour and their regularity. For example, a circle is a regular shape with no angles. It is perfectly evenly balanced around a center axis. Its regularity makes the circle appear stable and contained. On the other hand, a polygon may be quite irregular in shape, with tension created through the uneven angles.

A visual composition is a construction of interacting shapes. On the printed page, shapes are the building blocks that establish relationships of content elements to one another. Their relative size, position, and proximity are part of the process of establishing a visual hierarchy.

Form is the definition of depth in an object. Form adds the illusion of depth to shape through the use of tone or texture. Tone helps imply depth by using gradations of light and dark. Texture suggests the surface qualities of an object by revealing how the form might feel when touched. Both tone and texture are visual cues that add tremendous detail to the form.

Point, focal point, and line.

Shape and form.

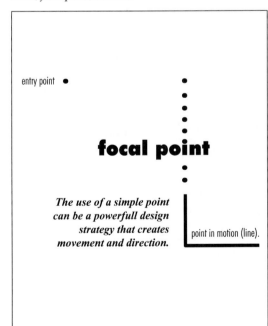

The addition of form makes shapes more interesting and stronger design elements.

Principles of Design

To make meaningful visual form, the designer relies on the principles of balance, contrast, harmony, and rhythm to support the communication effort.

Balance is the arrangement of elements in a composition to achieve equilibrium or a sense of equally distributed weight or proportion. Symmetry is one expression of balance in which opposite sides of a figure or form are equally distributed on either side of a central axis. Symmetric balance is a relatively easy approach to apply since it involves simply centering and stacking elements along a mid-point

Symmetrical and asymmetrical balance.

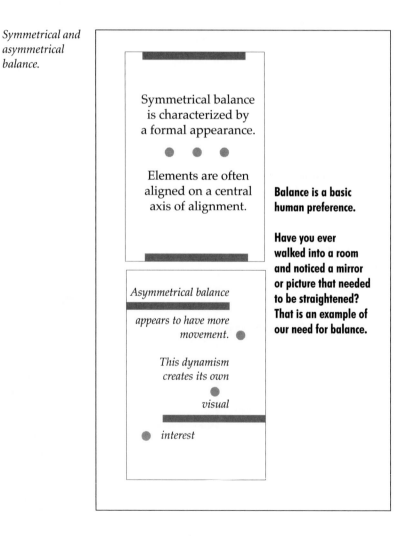

Symmetrical balance
is characterized by
a formal appearance.

Elements are often
aligned on a central
axis of alignment.

**Balance is a basic
human preference.**

**Have you ever
walked into a room
and noticed a mirror
or picture that needed
to be straightened?
That is an example of
our need for balance.**

Asymmetrical balance

*appears to have more
movement.*

*This dynamism
creates its own*

visual

interest

on the page. It results in a formal, stable layout with white space pushed to the outside. It is easy for the reader to access but it lacks real tension or visual excitement. Asymmetric balance relies on an irregular, uneven spatial arrangement that is "balanced" through the effective use of space and an understanding of optical weight. It is a more difficult approach to apply because it requires an appreciation for the interaction of variously shaped, optically weighted elements on the page. The designer must be able to create visual tension and to work within the allotted space to create a dynamic arrangement of elements. A successful asymmetric layout can be very exciting.

Elements that are used in opposition to one another create contrast. In visual design contrast can be an effective tool for establishing emphasis or focus. Contrast can be created with size, shape, texture, color, tone, and direction. Contrast can create a clear point of access to the printed page by grabbing the attention of the reader and by establishing what material is most important. When used effectively, contrast establishes clear connections among elements and adds visual texture to the page. However, a page with too much contrast will be distracting or noisy.

Harmony is the creation of visual order or unity. A harmonious composition is one in which all of the elements relate to one another or work in a complementary way. We can achieve harmony when there is a clear sense of visual style and

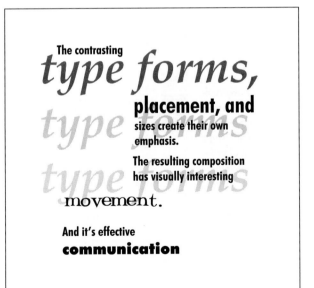

Visual contrast.

when the use of color, typography and image communicates the same message. A composition that is cluttered, chaotic, or visually confusing lacks harmony. Harmony means that there is general agreement between the message and its presentation. All of the visual elements work comfortably together in a harmonious layout.

Rhythm is a regular pattern of visual elements created through the repetition and alignment of form such as line, pattern, texture, color, or shape. Rhythm offers a sense of visual order. Through the repetition of elements, rhythm can create a

Harmony and rhythm.

When all the elements in a composition work together, the result is a harmonious composition

When in the Course of human events, it becomes necessary for one people to dissolve the political bands which have connected them with another, and to assume among the powers of the earth, the separate and equal station to which the Laws of Nature and of Nature's God entitle them, a decent respect to the opinions of mankind requires that they should declare the causes which impel them to the separation.

The rhythmic placement of elements can help bring a sense of order and movement to a static page.

We hold these truths to be self-evident, that all men are created equal, that they are endowed by their Creator with certain unalienable Rights, that among these are Life, Liberty, and the pursuit of Happiness. That to secure these rights, Governments are instituted among Men, deriving their just powers from the consent of the governed.

clear sense of movement or direction. The use of rhythm is a powerful tool for establishing a sequence of information that guides the viewer through a layout. A visual hierarchy that directs the eye to a simple entry point and then moves the reader from left to right, top to bottom, or most to least important has rhythm that maintains movement and helps the reader access content.

The Attributes of Visual Media

All visual media have attributes that distinguish them and that influence our approach to their application. For example, we can describe printed photographs or illustrations as static images that have no movement, sound, or visible change associated with them. Dynamic visuals include video, film, and some interactive media. These visuals have the qualities of movement and time that lead us to consider action and change as part of our experience with them. There are many ways to describe the visual elements used in graphic design. We can describe them in terms of their size, the technology behind their production, their level of realism, or their novelty. Each media form has several unique characteristics.

Text is the words or wording of something that appears in print in traditional circumstances. But we increasingly require that text work within an interactive multimedia environment, with text appearing on a computer screen rather than on a printed page. In either case, the process of reading text is complex. The reader is an active participant in the process with any visual associations made through an interpretation of the text. The reader must learn the system of symbols (alphabet) used to create the text and must then learn how those symbols interact to create more complex symbols (words). It is conceivable that every reader creates a unique sensory relationship with the words that are chosen based upon the reader's prior experience. In addition, many words mean a variety of things.

Typographic design uses the aesthetic and technical skill of the designer to create a visually unique interpretation of the standard symbol set (alphabet, punctuation, numerals) used in text. Each system of letterform is unique and may have been designed to accommodate a particular technology or to convey a particular personality or mood. The skill and vision of the designer are evident in typographic design. Our use of typography is based upon our own unique appreciation for the letterform. We may not have the same understanding or vision as the original designer; thus the intent changes from use to use.

Illustration is a visual interpretation of the message using any of a variety of creative media—painting, digital imaging, drawing, collage, and the like. The illustrator may work in a variety of media, each with unique characteristics. The level of realism or abstraction that the illustrator uses—colors, materials, scale, and composition—influences our understanding of the message. An effective illustration conveys the same message as the text, but with the illustrator's expressive vision readily apparent. Illustration is seldom neutral—each viewer brings his or her own aesthetic sensibility and experience to the interpretation. The illustration style should clarify the message and make a connection with the audience.

Graphic representation seeks to overcome the complexities of the message by using pictographs, icons, symbols, and marks that can be universally understood. It relies on abstraction and simplification of formal elements and may be very complex if the level of abstraction is high. Many symbols fall into this category and their meaning must be learned. Other graphic representation that relies on pictographs or glyphs is easily recognized across cultures. Simple graphic representation is often used in signage and diagrams to convey complex information that must be clearly understood by the audience.

Informational graphics such as charts and diagrams are examples of graphic forms with information organized around a clear structure in an effort to relate a number of complex ideas to one another. Informational graphics call for the data to be clearly organized rather than interpreted through expressive media. Charts and diagrams require an evaluation of the content and its subsequent ordering. Information can be organized alphabetically, categorically, sequentially, geographically, or chronologically. Ideally, the information is clear and the designer's vision is neutral. However, these media can be manipulated to show a false correlation, to distort statistics, or to conceal. The viewer may falsely trust the authority of the information because of its biased organization.

Animation has a wide range of visual possibilities. It can be highly realistic or very expressive. Animation uses many of the tools of print media illustration and applies them to the creation of time-based products. The combination of the animator's visual interpretation with sound, music, and movement can create very evocative results. When realism is used, animation can be an important educational tool. We can see how a satellite orbits around a distant planet or learn how magma is forced through the earth in a volcano. Scenes that would be impossible to capture on film or video can be interpreted through animation.

Pictures, both still and moving, are a form of visual media that are rich with detail and implied realism. The image, photograph, video, or film captures visible light at particular moments in time within the field of view of the camera lens. Making the selected image and framing it within the camera are decisions made by the picture maker that alter the image. Many times we imbue these images with the burden of "realism"—we expect that, since we recognize details within the image, it must be "real." But pictures have great potential to deceive. They also have great potential to reveal and to grab us emotionally. Context is always important to clarify when imagery is used.

Videotape and film are time-based media with an ability to capture a multitude of sensory elements—sound, movement, image, and color. These motion pictures can be highly realistic and can express details in real time. However, as with static images such as still photography, there is great potential for deception—camera angle, composition, and editing all influence the viewer's perception of the recorded event. Nonetheless, complex processes can be explained well in film or video.

Interactive multimedia combines multiple media formats into a dynamic assembly of image, sound, motion, and text. The role of the audience changes from reader or viewer to active participant in an experience that uses many interrelated sensory elements with the benefits of user interaction. The user can make choices about how to view elements and where to move within the presentation. In many cases, interactivity involves the potential for real dialogue with other participants or with the product developers. The design potential of interactive multimedia is tremendous. The palette of visual choice is enormous for the designer and with an active, participating audience involved in the product the result is more mutable and responsive than most traditional formats will allow.

One of the key considerations for the designer of interactive multimedia is defining the level of interactivity in the product. The greater the audience involvement, the more complex the multimedia product will be. Passive multimedia products present information in a linear way and audience choices are limited to adjusting sound, speed, or light while viewing the product. Slide shows are examples of passive multimedia. Interactive multimedia allow users to control their own progress through the content. Hypermedia presentations that combine text, images, sound, and movement and that offer multiple links to other materials within the presentation or games that respond to user choices are interactive. Adaptive multimedia have the highest level of interactivity. In this case, the user can enter his or her own content and can control how it is used. The user may add voice, images, or video, or develop text. Any of these materials may become part of the product.

Ironically, with increased audience involvement in the multimedia product, the designer's role becomes less clear. Initially the designer establishes the visual identity, organization, and composition of the product but then relinquishes control to the active audience. Interactive multimedia require that the designer be responsive to the audience in new ways. The audience is no longer a passive recipient of a communication product, but can become a vital part of an interactive experience. The designer's role as facilitator is most important.

Graphic Design in Practice

The current visual communication landscape offers many choices of media forms and formats: Traditional printed media, electronic media, and stand-alone and World Wide Web interactive media are distinct options for bringing messages to audiences. Magazines, newspapers, and corporate publications are options with established design traditions. Interactive multimedia and the Internet have taken the computer from a desktop publishing tool to a content delivery system and are redefining many established design traditions as these new tools are explored. These changes in orientation have created tremendous opportunities for the communication designer.

Whatever the format, the principles of design are important guidelines for creating accessible, articulate visual communication. All of the characteristics of effective design stress the importance of viewing design as a part of a communication process. For example:

- Design is a strategic approach to visual expression. It is purposeful and should be clearly directed toward the creation of visual form that communicates.
- The use of design elements must complement the editorial philosophy.
- Design is a tool and a process for organizing and clarifying content.
- Communicate. Don't decorate. The aesthetic or style of the visual design must be part of the pattern of visual presentation and content organization; it is never separate from it.
- The decision about how to communicate—whether visually, verbally, interactively, or statistically—should be dictated by the information.
- Technology is a servant of design and communication, not the ruler. In the design of interactive multimedia, design must define how the user will locate and interact with content.
- The visual design must be accessible to the audience and must represent the needs or culture of the audience.

The partnership of effective visual design and compelling content that communicates is possible when the designer, writer, and editor are literally on the same team. Each of these professionals is concerned with specific areas in the process of communication but all share the same ultimate goals—to reach an audience and communicate a message. In some of the most effective organizations design is part of the content development process. The decision about whether the message is best delivered visually or verbally is dictated by the story and becomes part of the planning process. The writer, photographer, artist or illustrator, graphic designer, and editor are collaborators in the process of developing an arrangement of words and images that communicate.

This means that the arrangement of elements and the construction of the form and format depend upon decisions that are made about the most effective way to deliver the message. The selection of images, the use of color, the choice of typography, and the creation of a visual hierarchy are purposeful decisions. The editorial focus and the needs of the audience guide visual communication decision making.

Regardless of the format, one of the first considerations for the designer involves the audience's involvement with the product. Publications are multidimensional, meaning that the reader interacts with the product in several ways and on several levels. One way is by physical interaction. As the reader of a printed publication turns the page, for example, the publication becomes more than a flat, two-dimensional product. The reader introduces movement into the process of reading, aside from holding, turning, and viewing the bound pages. The reader's interaction with the binding, the paper, the organization, and the design is a key ingredient in a successful communication effort.

The designer makes decisions that account for reader interaction with the product. For example, in a perfect bound magazine the pages don't open flat, so the designer must allow for wider margins along the binding edge. In addition, images that span a two-page spread must be used in a way that keeps important content from being trapped in the center gutter. In a broadsheet format typical of most newspapers, the page size is awkward so the designer may need to consider how the reader folds or unfolds the paper to access content.

In a digital product, the involvement of the user is also critical. The designer attempts to create a product that has dimension beyond the "window to content," or what is visible through the computer screen. The designer plans the organization of the product and the visual design to encourage and clarify user involvement.

In both physical and digital formats, successful visual design has several key components. First, the product must get attention by offering a meaningful introduction through the cover or the opening screen to the content inside. Second, the product must involve the reader by allowing easy navigation and access to the content. The designer needs to understand that a reader is sometimes a "skimmer" so the content should be available at a number of levels. Headlines, subheads, and images offer relatively quick and easy access to content while text, charts, and diagrams rely on longer reader involvement. Finally, the product must offer a memorable sense of organization and personality to encourage repeat readership from the audience. There should be a sense of visual identity that clearly relates to content and that is sustained from issue to issue.

Composition is the arrangement of elements within the publication. It is partly an art that requires aesthetic skill and vision from the designer but it is also a strategic means to direct the viewer to the most important content. The process of laying out a physical page or designing a digital product must be an ordered, thoughtful response to the requirements of the message and to the needs of an audience. A newspaper, newsletter, magazine, or Web site that is simply beautiful will be meaningless without clear access to content. The designer's role is to ease comprehension by creating an aesthetically appealing product that clearly reveals content.

Ray Gun Magazine

David Carson, former art director of *Ray Gun* magazine, challenged many of the conventions of composition through this rock and roll–oriented publication targeted for so-called Generation X consumers. *Ray Gun* is visually chaotic with densely layered images and text that challenge most established rules of readability and legibility. Columns are wide, irregular, and sometimes overlapping. Text winds and dances across the page in fonts that appear hand-rendered, digitally manipulated, or altered. Fonts are rough-edged and combined with little reverence for harmony in style. Images are often murky, abstract compositions that are combined, cropped, manipulated, and positioned idiosyncratically. *Ray Gun* is a visual playground with a sophisticated approach to the audience underlying the apparent disorganization.

Ray Gun is designed for readers who are first and foremost viewers of MTV, videogames, multimedia, movies, and television. The organization of elements in *Ray Gun* requires a level of attention and interactivity from the reader that is familiar to viewers raised on MTV. The chaotic visual landscape that is *Ray Gun*'s hallmark requires that the reader spend time with the publication to find an approach to viewing, reading, and comprehension that works.

Designer Neville Brody described *Ray Gun* as "the end of print," which Carson accepted as a compliment and positioned as a slogan on the cover of the magazine. The publication has been in circulation since 1992, and Carson sees *Ray Gun* as a visually expressive response to content and a challenge to the tradition of grid-dependent magazine design.

Time Magazine

Time magazine undertook a redesign in 1992 in response to the changing nature of its readership, news coverage, and technology. One of the editorial goals guiding the redesign effort was to create a publication with a more flexible visual architecture that allowed for greater variety on the pages. The effort was collaborative as the needs of text-oriented journalists and visually inclined page designers were considered. The new magazine design had to work visually with an easy interface to computer pagination. It also had to allow for a different approach to content organization while retaining the integrity of the traditional publication.

One of the most important renovations is visible in the typographic sophistication throughout the magazine. Roger Black and David Berlow designed a new text font, Time Text. It is slightly condensed with a taller x-height and lighter stroke weight than the Times Roman used in the old design. Time Text gives the page a more open look while preserving readability by retaining clean, crisp stroke contrast. The text has a lighter gray tone that calls for greater typographic expression in the use of headline and display type. For example, the magazine uses pull quotes, initial caps and lead-ins to guide the reader through the content. Marginalia and captions interact with the main text and images to clarify content and to add visual variety.

National Geographic Magazine

National Geographic magazine is a publication with a clearly defined visual style and editorial philosophy. The magazine is one of the benefits for members of the National Geographic Society, chartered in 1890 with a goal of increasing geographic knowledge by educating readers about distant cultures and places. Content development and the editorial of the magazine always support this organizational goal.

The cover creates an invitation to the inside of the publication. It is the first impression for the reader and the most important opportunity for establishing the identity of the publication. The *National Geographic* cover uses a familiar yellow frame that surrounds a powerful photographic image, restricted to the vertical dimensions of the page. The frame is a well-established element that adds formality and structure to the cover. Frames tend to suggest importance and are used to highlight something "special." Frames also act as visual borders that keep the eye focused on the subject. The tight composition of the photographic image always highlights the lead story and introduces the reader to the content inside the publication.

The use of typography on the cover is largely restricted to the banner that employs a strong, vertical sans serif typeface set in all caps. The familiar *National Geographic* logo—the globe—rests on the formally balanced type. There is a minimal use of cover lines. This is a banner that suggests tradition while the cover as a whole suggests reverence for the power of the photographic image.

Inside the magazine, the involvement and clear communication among the writers, information designers, artists, photographers, and editors are apparent. It is a publication with a clear sense of the story and a tightly focused visual style. There is no confusion about how to access information. This is a publication designed for the reader. In fact, it is designed for many styles of reading. For example, captions are written and designed to be readable and to work as elements separate from the text. Their narrative style is more revealing than the byline and fact-dominated captions of many publications. This allows the casual reader or "skimmer" to view the images and read the captions separately from the full text. The caption also creates an element of contrast on the printed page that underscores the importance of the photographic image that it accompanies.

The National Geographic Online

The National Geographic online product (www.nationalgeographic.com) is a Web site that retains many of the qualities of *National Geographic* magazine. The site has beautiful photographic images and engaging descriptive text with the added benefit of interactive multimedia. The built-in family resemblance between the two products is important. There is stylistic unity between the traditional printed product and the online version, but there are also some important differences.

The story emphasis in the online version corresponds to that established in the printed product, but the nature of user movement through a Web site is different from the traditional magazine. The traditional ordering of headline/subhead, image/caption, lead-in, and text is given new dimension through the layers and links that are possible in hypermedia. Access to the content of a Web site is different from the sequential chapters in a printed product. Content is less linear in a hypermedia environment.

There are important production concerns in designing online media that relate to the processing speed and low-bandwidth delivery systems that are currently in place. To the designer, this means that the design must account for compact, low-resolution images that take several seconds to become visible to the user. The typographic options are limited in setting and the display varies significantly from one browser to another. Color palettes cannot easily be controlled. In other words, each viewer's screen may be significantly different. And most importantly, how the user enters and departs from the online product is not always predictable. There are multiple paths through content so part of the designer's concern must be user interaction.

In the design of multimedia, the user interface is critical. National Geographic Online has changed this connection to the audience over the years. An early incarnation of the Web site used a travel scrapbook metaphor as the interface. Visitors were greeted by an image of a passport that they clicked on to enter the site. Each page on the passport was a clickable image-map that moved the user to a different section of the site. Navigational icons that complemented the passport metaphor also provided content options for the user. The Web site has evolved into a much more utilitarian interface that resembles an extensive table of contents on the first page. Many of the illustrative characteristics of the early site interface are less dominant. In fact, the visitor today is impressed by the volume and variety of possible choices within the site.

But to ease user movement through the site National Geographic Online still uses icons borrowed from travel experiences (passports) and maps (compass symbols) that make sense to the new visitor and communicate intent unequivocally. These icons also relate directly to the product and the content. One of the more interesting sections of the site is the "map machine," where users can preview the library of National Geographic maps and their descriptions. The user can then download the maps. The image sizes are clearly labeled.

Christian Science Monitor

This tabloid newspaper has a simple, elegant approach to story organization and visual design. The color palette is subdued with pastel spot color used sparingly. A style guide produced for the *Christian Science Monitor* staff describes the approach to color use and suggests it should be applied with thoughtful consideration for its emotional and optical impact. Overall, the publication employs carefully considered design restraint to create an environment for the reader that is accessible. It is also a beautiful example of simplicity in action. The style guide describes this approach to design as being responsive to content by providing a thoughtful environment for words and the straightforward display of fine photojournalism.

There is an elegant geometry to the pages. Typographic contrast relies on subtle size changes and the use of white space to add emphasis. The underlying grid accounts for the dimensions of the tabloid-size page by packaging stories in simple modules with minimal jumps. The simplicity in the design of the *Christian Science Monitor* complements the conservative reputation and editorial philosophy of the publication.

USA Today

This newspaper has had tremendous impact on publishing and newspaper design, particularly with its use of color. Critics argue that sometimes the use of illustration decorates more than it communicates and that the use of color overpowers content. Nonetheless, the color reproduction of *USA Today* is outstanding and has prompted other newspapers to use more spot color, color photographs, and informational graphics.

One of the most impressive design elements in *USA Today* is the full-page weather map designed with the business traveler in mind. Color is used symbolically to suggest temperature throughout the country—cool blues and warm reds correspond to the real weather patterns depicted on the map. Forecasts are described in a typographic table that breaks out regions of the country and uses simple warm/cool colors (which correspond to those used in the map) to reinforce the content. The use of color in the weather map is a meaningful element that augments content.

USA Today also uses bold color to signify the content of sections within the newspaper—for example, the Money section's bold green banner. Each section is unified typographically through the use of similar sizes and a consistent sans serif typeface that relates to the *USA Today* logo.

This is a publication with a clear sense of its own identity and a strong visual personality that is attention-getting. *USA Today* is visible from a distance on any newsstand and its visual style is not likely to be confused with other regional or local papers. It is perfectly suited to its purpose—a quick read for business travelers or commuters who want an overview of national and international events and a very brief suggestion of what might be happening in their home state.

CONCLUSION

Design in any format, delivered through any medium, is a purposeful process of meeting a communication challenge. The designer is a coordinator, strategist, and producer who must work toward developing an integrated product that communicates without hesitation or confusion. Content and form are developed in visual communication design to work as interdependent, inseparable parts of a whole. The result of the designer's efforts is visual form that clarifies content.

IDEAS FOR FURTHER STUDY

- Describe your favorite use of graphic design in print or moving media.
- Lead a discussion about the future of graphic design.
- Make a logo that reflects your personality.
- Write a paper that discusses the ethical concerns with graphic design.

Design Goals

by Brian Callahan, Web Graphic Designer for Clocktower Books,
www.clocktowerbooks.com

My design goals are the same, whether designing a paper brochure or a Web site: I work with the resources I have, keep designs economical, and stay creative. My designs are completely original and I take pride in creating from scratch. I do my own photography instead of relying on stock photos or clip art, and I strive to create original and fresh looks that overstep the limits of the medium.

To obtain dimension and texture difficult to capture on film, I have scanned borrowed tools and paintbrushes directly on the scanner. Some designs incorporate local buildings, people, and the beautiful San Diego skyline, plus more abstract images culled from my travels: carnival masks from Venice (featured on this site), Parisian tombs, New England church towers.

Easy Navigation

Designing a Web site's information space is one of the most important elements; "content is king," but poorly organized content is useless. I arrange information in easy-to-digest chunks, across an intuitive hierarchy that aids comprehension by allowing users to find the information they need. Too many links or too much information on one page lends confusion and causes users to exit a site rather than explore the content. Sites must be easy to navigate, let users know where they are, and help them find the information they need quickly.

Speed and Compatibility

Using Web browser–safe colors ensures that colors don't shift on different platforms. All of my designs take advantage of "safe" colors, and I create graphics that dither minimally when viewed on computers with lesser color depths. Because speed and efficiency of delivery are critical on the Web, I insist on creating "low-fat" graphics that, by design, can be implemented with tiny palettes or high compression.

Attractiveness and Sophistication

Many Web pages are cluttered and segmented with icons and horizontal rules, when all they need is a little white space. Print designers have known all along that white space is a powerful design tool. I strive to make pages clean and easy to read and navigate, with graphics that are powerful, well placed, and focused. As in a magazine ad, they should lend meaning to a Web page, not just decoration.

My background in desktop publishing and digital typography, and my understanding of the Web's intricate technology, helps me create sites that are powerful and sophisticated, using traditional elements of good design in today's most exciting medium. ■

CHAPTER 11

Informational Graphics

by Paul Martin Lester

Whether or not you will actually be employed by a print, television, or computer news service to produce informational graphics, you should be aware of the various kinds of news graphics so that you can collaborate with a designer to produce them. Combining still and moving images with text and infographics not only can explain complex stories in unique ways, but can also satisfy journalism's major mission—to educate readers and viewers.

Informational graphics, often called infographics or news graphics, is one of the fastest-growing fields in mass communications because of the way designers can put together newsroom personnel and powerful computing programs to explain stories that words and photographs have trouble telling. It estimated that more than a trillion single pieces of infographics are published annually throughout the world in newspapers and magazines, for television, and on computer systems. The reason for this tremendous interest is simple—infographics often can explain a story that would be much too tedious for words and much too incomplete with photographs alone. At their finest, informational graphics combine word and visual messages that further the educational mission of journalism and mass communication. And when combined with text and photographs, infographics offer some of the most sophisticated ways to explain complex stories.

Historical Roots

Because chips in the stone used as a background for many animal cave paintings created by prehistoric people were found clustered around vital areas of the animals (usually the neck region), some anthropologists have surmised that these beautifully detailed drawings are actually the earliest examples of informational graphics. Cave paintings acted as diagrams that others in a tribe could use to practice their

A map of the world, circa 1851, showing the influence of Herodotus, Ptolemy, "the ancients," and wind charts of Aristotle and Vitruvius.

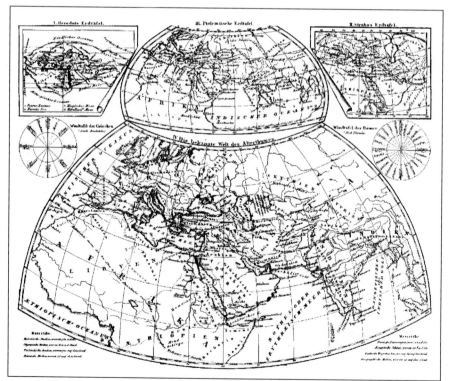

spear-throwing perhaps during inclement weather, when there were no animals in the area, or at night. Intriguing as this hypothesis may be, the more relevant roots of informational graphics come in the form of maps.

Clay tablets from the ancient Sumerian city of Mesopotamia created around 3800 B.C.E. show maps of the city indicating boundaries between properties. Several centuries later, the Greeks and Chinese developed highly detailed maps of local and foreign lands in order to better navigate the oceans for exploration and trade.

Three Infographic Pioneers: Playfair, Snow, and Minard

The field of informational graphics gained respect with the creations by three pioneers—William Playfair, Robert Snow, and Charles Minard. Without their early contributions, the spread of infographics would have been greatly delayed.

The English political economist William Playfair in 1786 invented one of the most common types of informational graphics, the bar chart. In a publication titled *The Commercial and Political Atlas,* he included forty-four charts that helped explain Great Britain's economic well-being during his era. Today the chart is an indispensable component of almost all business-related stories.

Dr. Robert Snow, a London physician, was perplexed and anguished over the many deaths during numerous cholera epidemics. In 1854 there was another devastating outbreak that killed more than five hundred people. Unaware of the cause of the disease, Snow nevertheless had a brainstorm that dramatically ended the cholera epidemic and greatly advanced the field of infographics. Snow obtained a list of names and addresses of all the victims of the latest outbreak. Not being able to make sense of such raw data (imagine several pages of telephone book listings) he superimposed the addresses of the victims on a street map of London. Snow suspected that the water supply might be the cause of the epidemic. He drew little black dots on the map to represent the victims and *x*'s for the water pumps spaced throughout the city (common before indoor plumbing). His data map immediately revealed a huge cluster of victims around a single pump. When city officials replaced the pump at his request, the cholera epidemic ceased.

The third infographic pioneer, French engineer Charles Minard, produced in 1869 what has been described as "the best statistical graphic ever drawn," which detailed Napoleon's disastrous 1812 campaign advance and retreat from Moscow. By combining six separate series of information in one chart, Minard showed the world how powerful an infographic message can be when elegance and simplicity are foremost.

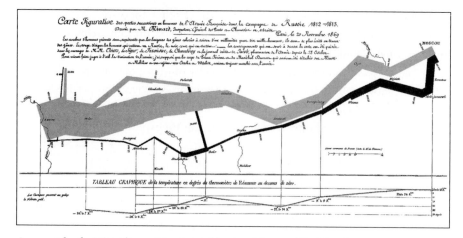

An example of a Minard map, Napoleon's March to Moscow: The War of 1812.

Infographics and Wars

Because most readers are unfamiliar with the location of foreign battle sites, maps have always been used to help tell stories during wars. In fact, whenever a late-breaking news story occurs, a simple locator map is often used to show where the event has taken place before other images from the site have been obtained.

Before photographs could be reproduced in newspapers using the halftone process, introduced in 1888, editors often used maps to illustrate a story because these were more quickly produced than an artist's recreation of a witness's account

President Lincoln examining a map at General Grant's headquarters.

or a still photograph taken at the scene. During World Wars I and II and the Korean and Vietnam conflicts, numerous maps were printed in newspapers and magazines to show battle lines and outcomes. Before the use of computers, artists used traditional methods to draw pictures and letters for these sometimes elegant displays. When the desktop computer and laser printer became common in newsrooms at the end of the 1980s, informational graphics could be produced more quickly and usually with greater complexity and precision.

During the 1991 Gulf War, with Allied forces fighting Iraqi troops in Saudi Arabia, the field of informational graphics gained tremendous prestige simply because traditional journalism methods—battle interviews and photographs—were extremely difficult to obtain due to the remote desert locations, night fighting, and government censorship of the press. One of the only ways many newspaper and television entities were able to tell the story of the war was through diagrams and maps produced by news graphics personnel. The Gulf War is now considered a landmark for infographic production because its coverage demonstrated that stories could be meaningfully enhanced by their presentations.

Historical Roots

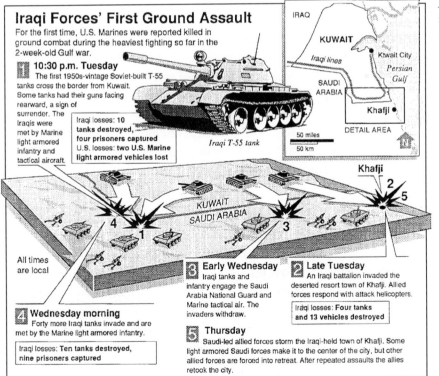

Iraqi Forces' First Ground Assault

For the first time, U.S. Marines were reported killed in ground combat during the heaviest fighting so far in the 2-week-old Gulf war.

1 10:30 p.m. Tuesday
The first 1950s-vintage Soviet-built T-55 tanks cross the border from Kuwait. Some tanks had their guns facing rearward, a sign of surrender. The Iraqis were met by Marine light armored infantry and tactical aircraft.

Iraqi losses: 10 tanks destroyed, four prisoners captured
U.S. losses: two U.S. Marine light armored vehicles lost

Iraqi T-55 tank

IRAQ
KUWAIT
Iraqi lines
Kwait City
Persian Gulf
SAUDI ARABIA
Khafji

50 miles
50 km

DETAIL AREA

Khafji
2
5

KUWAIT
SAUDI ARABIA

4
1
3

All times are local

3 Early Wednesday
Iraqi tanks and infantry engage the Saudi Arabia National Guard and Marine tactical air. The invaders withdraw.

2 Late Tuesday
An Iraqi battalion invaded the deserted resort town of Khafji. Allied forces respond with attack helicopters.

Iraqi losses: Four tanks and 13 vehicles destroyed

4 Wednesday morning
Forty more Iraqi tanks invade and are met by the Marine light armored infantry.

Iraqi losses: Ten tanks destroyed, nine prisoners captured

5 Thursday
Saudi-led allied forces storm the Iraqi-held town of Khafji. Some light armored Saudi forces make it to the center of the city, but other allied forces are forced into retreat. After repeated assaults the allies retook the city.

An example of an infographic from the Gulf War.

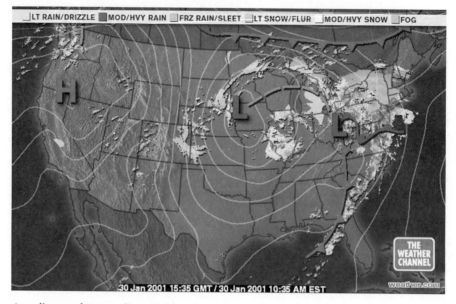

An online weather map. (See CP-3.)

Another landmark in infographic production that has influenced current designers is the large and colorful weather map introduced by *USA Today* in 1982. The Weather Channel coincidentally was begun on cable the same year. The newspaper's critical success with the map and the popularity of a cable outlet devoted to the weather convinced other publishers and local television news producers to enhance their own weather sections or segments. Now most weather pages, in print or online, and weather segments on television are a lively collection of colorful and animated words and images.

Types of Informational Graphics

There are two major types of informational graphics—statistical and nonstatistical. Statistical infographics convert numbers into a visual message. The most common types of statistical infographics are weather maps and charts. Nonstatistical infographics typically either arrange words and numbers into more pleasing and easily read displays or are complicated renderings that illustrate a product or process. Examples of nonstatistical infographics include fact boxes, tables, diagrams, and even icons and television schedules.

Statistical Infographics

Statistical infographics combine numerical data and pictures. The two main types of statistical infographics are charts (also called graphs) and data maps.

Charts

Imagine a business story in which all of the stock averages by the hour on a certain day are reported in numerical figures. Such a long list of numbers would be incomprehensible to most readers and viewers. So charts are used to represent all that information visually. Although detail is sacrificed (someone may need to know the exact average at 2:00 P.M.) a line that represents the ups and downs of a particular market over time is satisfactory for most purposes.

Types of charts include line, area, bar, pie, and pictograph. Charts use lines and bars to visually explain a set of complex data. Sometimes line charts are referred to as fever charts because the data rise and fall as if on a thermometer. When the area behind a line chart is shaded, the chart or graph is called an area chart. Bar charts can be oriented either as rows or columns. When information is displayed as a percentage, a pie chart is sometimes used. Individual wedges of the "pie" stand for various percentages having to do with the story. A type of chart that uses pictures to represent numbers in a chart is called a pictograph. Pictographs were made popular by the work of designer Nigel Holmes for *Time* magazine and the front-page, bottom-left sections in *USA Today*. A designer's choice of chart depends on the relative seriousness of the story and the audience the infographic intends to reach.

A bar chart.

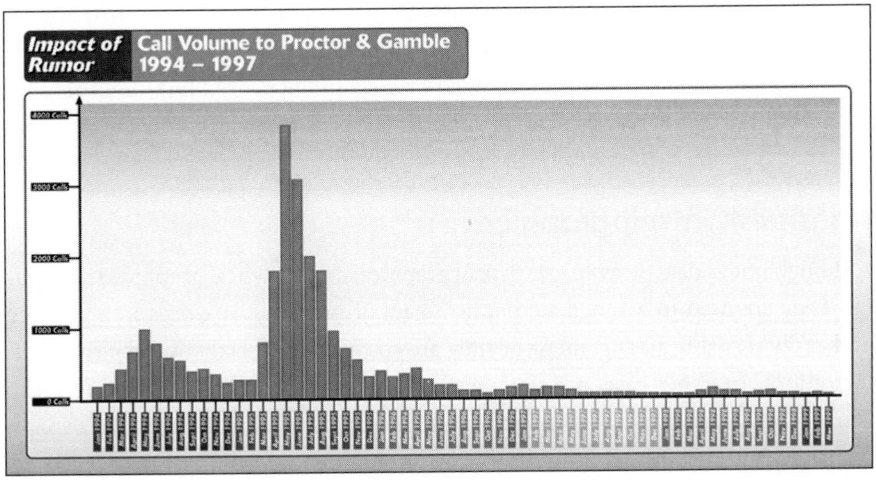

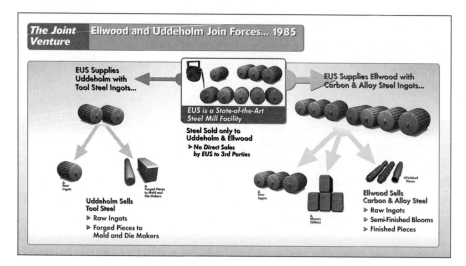

An example of a pictograph.

Datamaps

The maps produced by Dr. Snow and Charles Minard are examples of overlaying numerical data on a simple locator map. Weather maps are another popular example. These may be elaborate, with multicolored bands representing temperatures (as seen in *USA Today* and several other national newspapers) or simple black and white maps with actual temperatures displayed numerically around the map. Television news reports often combine elaborately colored temperature bands with animated graphics for a more dynamic appearance. And online weather sites may include recent satellite images, animated pictures, and hypertext links to other sites where additional information can be found.

Nonstatistical Infographics

Although not as data-heavy as statistical graphics, nonstatistical graphics are popular. They are used to arrange a complex series of numbers or words in a pleasing and easily readable arrangement or they are complex and aesthetically pleasing illustrations. In either case, nonstatistical news graphics can be a vital addition to storytelling. Nonstatistical infographics include fact boxes, tables, non-data maps, diagrams, and miscellaneous items from icons to illustrations.

An example of a fact box. This is for the Silkworm missile used during the Gulf War.

Fact Boxes

Fact boxes merely arrange a set of statements that summarize key points in a longer piece in a graphically pleasing manner that is also easy to read. Fact boxes got their start during World War II when paper shortages forced newspapers to cut back on the number of pages allowed while news of the war increased. To alleviate this problem of more news but with less space to tell it, publishers and editors devised the fact box—an infographic that listed the high points of a story without having to include the details in a long piece. Fact boxes have become a staple of journalism, almost always as a part of a longer story. Readers can look at a fact box, as they do a headline or a photograph, to determine if they want to read the entire story. The information in a fact box frequently isn't included in the main story, however, so readers with little free time can more easily find information that interests them.

Tables, Non-Data Maps, and Diagrams

Tables simply arrange numbers, words, or a combination of both so that the information presented can be easily read. Two of the most common uses of a table are stock market reports and box scores for sports teams. Imagine how much space

Pittsburgh at Los Angeles
Scoring Summary

Team	1	2	3	4	5	6	7	8	9	R	H	E
Pittsburgh	1	0	0	1	0	1	0	0	0	3	7	1
Los Angeles	0	0	0	0	0	0	1	6	X	7	8	0

A box score table.

would be needed if a long story simply explained all of the prices for all of the stocks for each day or if all the sports statistics displayed in a typical box score were written out in paragraph form. Tables, with their emphasis on alignment and white space, can show an enormous amount of data within a relatively small amount of space that is both easily read and elegant in its presentation.

When a plane crashes in a remote part of the world, a picture is often not available for the first news deadline. But a news graphics designer can produce a simple map to show readers and viewers the location of the trouble. Often a detailed map is combined with a larger map that shows where in the world the event took place. The technical name for a non-data map (or street map) is a "locator" map.

1927. Map of Nicaragua with locations of actions involving U.S. Marines during the revolution of 1926–29.

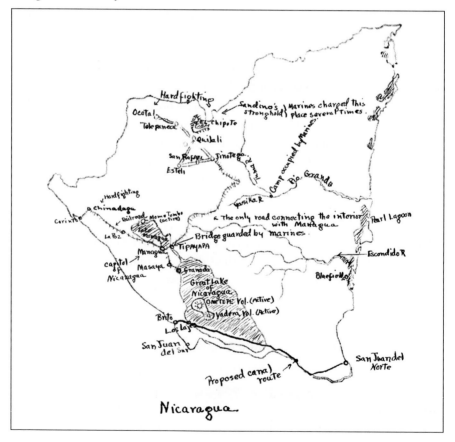

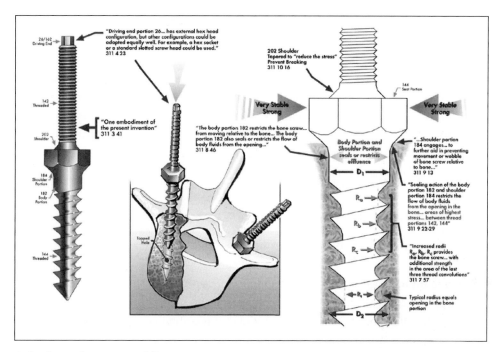

A clearly stated, easy-to-read diagram.

Many of the most elaborate and beautifully rendered artistic drawings in publications are diagrams. Diagrams often are employed to explain the details of a complex operation that simply could not be told using photographs and would be too confusing with words alone.

Miscellaneous Infographics

There are many kinds of informational graphics that don't fit in the categories just described. The most common miscellaneous formats are icons, television schedules, flowcharts, time lines, calendars, courtroom drawings, and illustrations. Icons give a visual cue to a particular section of a publication. The classified ad section of a newspaper is often filled with icons representing various headings. Television schedules are really a form of table that relies on colors to separate movies, sports events, and other types of programming. Flowcharts, time lines, and calendars are often used in business stories to illustrate the hierarchy of a corporation, the history of a product's development, or the schedule of an event. When judges do not wish their trials to be televised, courtroom drawings are the only visual journalism that is allowed. In a controversial spin on the courtroom drawing, the E! cable channel broadcast reenactments of the O.J. Simpson civil case. Actors played participants in the trial reading from actual transcripts—an example of a living courtroom drawing. When an editor decides that a documentary photograph may be too difficult to obtain (as in a story about child abuse), an editorial illustration may be created to portray a mood for the piece. An illustration is often drawn by an artist using traditional techniques, but it can also be a composite of photographic images by a photographer using a computer.

Informational Graphics in Practice

Typically, an infographic designer will work with a reporter, photographer, editor, and researcher and use a variety of software tools to produce infographics. These add meaning to a complicated set of numbers, organize long lists of facts and figures for easier readability, or bring emotional attributes to a story through a high-quality diagram or illustration. Because of this combination of purposes for infographics, a designer must have communication skills, a strong background in journalism, the skills of an artist, and confidence with computer software in order to produce infographics often on short notice.

Greater acceptance by publishers, editors, readers, and viewers of infographics as legitimate facets of complicated stories, along with easier to use computer programs, has pushed their use to record numbers. Consequently, news graphics designers work with quick deadlines or over several days to complete complex full-page displays.

Creating an Infographic

There has been a tragic automobile accident in your community. A van containing two families, with ten people ranging from a six-month-old baby to a seventy-year-old grandparent, collided with a car, careened off a bridge pillar, and landed upside down in a river next to the road. Your editor decides that it is significant and unusual enough to warrant a story, a photograph, and two infographics—a locator map and a diagram that shows the sequence of events that led to the accident. Reporters have been dispatched to the scene and the local hospital. Photojournalists are sent to the accident and in a helicopter to obtain aerial views. You are sent to the scene to draw quick sketches of the accident and learn any details that you can.

When you return to the newsroom, your first task is to meet with the page layout person to find out how much space you have for the infographics. Fortunately, the accident occurred in the morning so there is plenty of time to complete the assignment.

From a map creation software program on your computer or a map-making Web site, you type in the nearest address to the wreck to get a detailed map of the area. Download the map to your computer and use an illustration program (Illustrator®, FreeHand®, or PhotoShop®) to simplify the map. Only use the main streets—do not clutter your map with unnecessary information. If there is space, you may want to create an inset map of the entire county or parish so that readers have a clearer idea of the location of the accident.

Now you must recreate the accident showing the turn of events that led to the tragedy. From your notes and from police, eyewitness, and reporter accounts, you are supplied with details of the accident—the exact location of the wreck, the make, model, color, and location of the vehicles, and any other significant details that help tell the story and explain why the accident happened. Using Illustrator®, you quickly draw a road, a bridge, and a river. From a graphics database of automobiles, you find illustrations that closely resemble the van and automobile involved in the collision. With PhotoShop® you resize and angle the images so they will fit into your infographic. You add text explanations, a background, a headline and sub-head, a credit line, and a border. You then combine the locator map and inset with the diagram, print it out, and run it by your editor to make sure it is clear and accurate. She asks you to make some minor changes that are completed in another fifteen minutes. Then the infographic is combined on a front-page layout with a headline, story, and a photograph.

Ethical Considerations with Informational Graphics

Because of the complicated nature of turning dry, numerical facts into emotionally laden visual messages with impact, an infographic designer runs the potential risk of misleading and distracting a reader or viewer. Information can easily be distorted to emphasize, for example, a particular political view and embellished with unnecessary graphic elements that take away from the content of the piece. When distortion and embellishment are intentional, the news graphics designer may be called unethical. Usually, however, when misleading charts are published it is because a designer simply lacks the time or experience to portray information accurately.

As a rule, infographic designers should always have charts with lines or bars that are "zero based." To do otherwise leads to a presentation that misrepresents the information. The infographic may look more dramatic and exhibit greater emotional impact when a scale for a chart is set above zero, but actually the information is dangerously distorted. The credibility of the information portrayed in print, broadcast, and computer media is vital to the mission of journalism.

Designers should also not give in to the urge to embellish their pieces with unnecessary drawings, which can overpower the content of an infographic. Gratuitous embellishment is often evidenced by a busy array of cartoon images, colors, balloons, or inappropriate symbols. Too often, a cute cartoon or animated graphic with contrasting colors as a part of a presentation—known as "chart junk"—attempts to mask a lack of content. Credit your readers' and viewers' ability to understand infographic presentations that go beyond simple pictographic presentations—they will be better informed and you will have served them better.

CONCLUSION

Infographic design is a highly specialized career that requires knowledge and experience in the art and craft of such varied occupations as reporting, writing, photography, editorial illustration, graphic design, Internet and World Wide Web researching, mathematical quantification of data, and computers. You may not have the inclination or the time to take all of the courses necessary to become an infographics designer. Nevertheless, it is highly likely that you will work on complex stories that require you to converse intelligently with news designers. Being aware of the various kinds of informational graphics displays and their relation with words and images will help you communicate intelligently and accurately with others. A visual journalist strives to use the best tools to explain stories. If those tools require an illustration in addition to a photograph or video clip, you must be able to persuade others of the correctness of that procedure.

IDEAS FOR FURTHER STUDY

- Try to write a story containing all the information within a typical sports box score without using an infographic. Comment on the tediousness of this procedure.

- Make a pictograph for a baseball salary story. Imagine that one footlong hot dog is the salary of a typical hot dog salesman at a ballpark ($100 a day). Compare that salary visually with the salary of a highly paid baseball player.

- Find a chart within a newspaper, magazine, or Web site and, using a spreadsheet program such as Excel, duplicate it and check to see if it is zero-based. If it is not, note and comment on the difference in visual perception of the information between the two charts.

- Use a spreadsheet program such as Excel to create an infographic that is too busy and filled with "chart junk."

VISUAL PERSPECTIVES

Designing the Infograph

by Dennis Cripe, Associate Professor, School of Journalism,
Franklin College, Franklin, Indiana

An informational graphic represents the perfect marriage of information and presentation. The presentation can be in the form of a chart, map, illustration or diagram, in color or black and white, but without total commitment to content (PLUS) presentation, informational graphics are decorations—they underline key information.

—George Rorick, Knight-Ridder Tribune Graphics Network

Pegie Stark, at the Poynter Institute for Media Studies, writes, "To make good, informative informational graphics, a team effort is involved. The writer, artist, and designer must understand the content of the story and discuss in advance what the best possible visual solution will be. The question everyone needs to ask is 'How does it help the reader?'"

Stark offers these tips for good graphics:

- Suggest visual questions the reporters can ask while interviewing.
- Encourage reporters to gather visual information and to sketch on the scene.
- Go with the reporter to the scene to do visual reporting yourself.
- Read your own newspaper and know the stories that will be hot. Be active in the process. Don't wait for information. Ask for it, look for it.
- Initiate graphic ideas. Don't wait for someone to hand you a graphic order.
- Use your imagination. Don't accept the most literal approach.

The best approach to informational graphics is direct, simple, and undecorated. The "1-2-3 strategy" is a segmented approach dictating that artists feature only three activities in the graphic.

George Rorick, the designer of the original *USA Today* weather map, reminds designers that "a major fault of graphics has been the mega graphic, or the graphics for graphics' sake. These are usually graphics that are as intimidating to the reader as the lengthy story with column after column of text."

Daryl Moen, Professor of Journalism at Columbia University, writes, "Properly done, information graphics, like stories, convert data into information, information into understanding."

Research tells that:

- Numerical data are comprehended better in graphics than in text.
- Readers are more likely to read and remember data in graphics than in stories.
- Information graphics attract slightly higher levels of readership than do stories.
- Readers have a low threshold for "chart junk," the artwork some artists build into the data lines. This art sometimes distorts or confuses the data being presented.
- Charts allow readers to grasp trends among numbers more quickly, but comprehension of the numbers in tables is higher than that of charts.
- People read charts on two levels. One is the visual level—a quick scan that picks up trends or relationships. The second level comes from close examination of the graphic.

Two of the most important aids to reader-friendly graphics are the headline and the copy block. The headline tells the reader—in full subject-verb fashion—what's most important. Do not use a label headline here. The text should fulfill all or some of the following:

- Add details to support the headline.
- Tell readers what can't be or isn't contained in the graphic.
- In charts reporting poll results, support headline and give readers critical info like how many were polled, how the survey was conducted, and the margin of error.
- Call attention to something that might be overlooked in the graphic.

Before worrying about what "form" the graphic should take, ask the "design team" these questions:

- What is the point of the story? Some graphics are stand-alone elements. The graphic should make sense on its own, apart from any story it may support.
- Do the story and graphic agree? Sometimes graphics and a reporter's data don't line up. All the more reason to work as a team.
- Ask, "So what?" Just because a story has numbers doesn't mean it's a graphic. If it can be explained in a line or two of text, don't use a graphic.
- Ask, "Compared to what?" Often, a graphic is started on one set of numbers in a story even when the story is not yet completed.

The resulting graphic too often is one dimensional. Asking, "Compared to what?" often leads to a fuller context for the numbers presented.

And be sure to check your charts:

- Are the right numbers used? For instance, if you were reporting on the performance of the newspaper, would you compare circulation or penetration?
- Are the tick marks on the line chart spaced equally and do they represent equal amounts or time periods?
- Do the lengths of the bars and portions of the pie chart reflect the numbers?
- If any of the lines or shapes are canted (made three dimensional), are the data distorted?
- Is the choice of chart appropriate for the content?
- Is the headline specific?
- Is there a copy block that explains the chart?
- Is there a source line?
- Does the graphic use space efficiently? Charts do not have more impact when they get bigger. They ought to maintain the legibility of type.
- If art is included, does it obscure or distort the data?
- Has the story been edited with the graphic in mind? Do the numbers agree? Is there unnecessary redundancy? ■

Using Motion

The three chapters in this section explain video, audio, and interactive multimedia production. The use, meaning, and production of moving images to tell stories are featured first. Then, details of how audio can be used to enhance a production follow. Finally, the last chapter in this section explains what a visual journalist needs to know to produce moving images with audio for interactive multimedia, whether stand-alone or networked.

CHAPTER 12

Visual Motion

by Douglas Mitchell
Middle Tennessee State University

Motion is one of the most important visual cues because of its eyecatching and sustained interest property. Visual journalists need to know how to work with motion—animation and video—as the profession demands journalistic works that tell stories in complex ways. It is no wonder, then, that motion has been of interest to story tellers since the beginning of human history.

Early cave drawings suggest that humans have always been interested in capturing motion. Many of these early drawings suggest motion and a time line of events—ceremonies, hunts, seasons, and so on. But the ability to capture motion in a tangible medium would not appear until late in the industrial revolution.

It was in 1646 that Athanasius Kircher made drawings of a "magic lantern." They were built in the late part of the 1700s. A magic lantern typically used at least two transparent slides in a lantern enclosure. Moving the slides rapidly in front of the light caused an apparent movement of the images on a screen or wall. Improved versions of the magic lantern, called zoetropes, arranged images in a circle around a multifaced mirror. When viewed through a slot, the images would create an illusion of movement.

In order to perceive motion, the eye and brain must be able to complete a mental dot-to-dot process known as persistence of vision. Both film and video technology rely upon a process of fooling the eye into believing that there is motion when, instead, there are a series of individual still shots—like stop motion photography.

History of Visual Motion

The earliest documentation of stop motion photography occurred in 1877 when Eadweard Muybridge was able to photograph the movement of a horse with twenty-four separate cameras. The cameras were set up so that the horse's hooves would trip each shutter as it galloped past. Muybridge had been hired by California Governor Leland Stanford to settle a bet over whether or not all four of the horse's hooves left the ground in full gallop.

By 1882, Frenchman Etienne-Jules Marey designed a camera to record twelve separate images on a single strip of film. By 1888, he had designed the first paper-based flexible film that was followed, in 1889, by George Eastman's development of celluloid flexible film base.

Not to be outdone in this burst of photographic invention, Thomas Alva Edison commissioned William Kennedy Laurie Dickson to build a film camera in the late 1880s. Dickson developed the Kinetograph in 1890. One of the earliest surviving Kinetograph films displays another Edison employee, Fred Ott, sneezing. By 1892, Kinetographs were being used in "peep show" penny arcades.

The inventor Thomas Edison in his lab.

The Lumière brothers.

The French were instrumental in the development of film technology. Louis and Auguste Lumière's Cinématographe developed in 1895 was the first film projector—bringing an audience together to observe moving pictures—rather than private "peep show" viewings. The first public Lumière films included shots of workers leaving their factory, their children, and a train entering a station. The projection of the train coming right at audience members so shocked attendees, it was reported, that many screamed and ran for cover!

French magician and photographer Georges Méliès operated the first public movie theatre, the Theatre Robert Houdin, in Paris, using a modified British projector developed by Robert William Paul. Méliès became known for developing the world's first "trick" photography with cut edits and dissolves. In 1902 he produced Jules Verne's *A Trip to the Moon;* at fourteen minutes long it was three times the length of any previous film. Its thirty separate scenes demonstrated Méliès' genius for editing.

A still from A Trip to the Moon.

Other developments in film included standardization of film stock to gauges we are familiar with today and the movement from silent film to "talkies." (The addition of sound to film is covered in more detail in Chapter 13 on Audio and Motion.) Another development in film that would bear a significant role in the development of future visual technology had to do with the rate at which each individual frame was displayed on the screen. The earliest standard projection rate was 16 frames per second (fps). With the addition of sound, the rate became 24fps. Even at this increased frame rate, however, there was still a tendency for images displayed in a darkened hall to have a flicker caused by the period of black between each frame of light. This was remedied by the use of a shutter that effectively increased the rate to 48fps because the action of the shutter displays each frame twice. As we'll see, this idea would be used again when video was developed.

The Development of Video and Television

It is interesting that Thomas Edison had a hand in the development of television. Although Edison never thought of the transmission of moving images, he did work long and hard on the device that would later make television possible: the light bulb. It was during the development of the light bulb that several of Edison's employees noticed a darkening on the walls inside the vacuum bulb. This effect, termed the Edison effect, was later researched by other physicists, among them Joseph John Thomson, who concluded that the effect was due to the movement of small particles in the vacuum. These small particles, or electrons, could be controlled in their movement with a positively charged plate inside the bulb. These discoveries led to the development of the Audion in 1906 by Lee De Forest and, later, the cathode ray tube (CRT).

A diagram of a cathode ray tube.

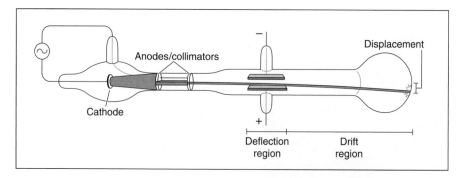

The development of a television system can also be traced to the 1817 discovery of the light-sensitive material selenium. By 1885, Paul Nipkow was able to combine the voltaic reaction of selenium with a special perforated disk he developed to scan an image. This idea for a mechanically based television system was improved upon with electronic amplification and better materials and culminated with the British inventor John Logie Baird's Phonovision in 1927. The Phonovision system was also the first method for storing moving images on a phonographic disk.

The images produced by the Phonovision were quite crude, however, and an all-electronic system of television would be necessary to produce better images. The two most notable inventors working on an all-electronic television system were Russian immigrant Vladimir Zworykin and Idaho farm boy Phil T. Farnsworth (although his birth certificate names him as "Philo," Farnsworth preferred "Phil").

Still a teenager, Farnsworth described an all-electronic form of television in 1922. Zworykin patented the first camera tube, the Iconoscope, in 1923 while working for Westinghouse. Farnsworth filed a patent for his "Image Dissector" tube enabling an electronic scanning television system in 1927. By 1929, Zworykin, then working for RCA, demonstrated his Kinescope tube that was a substantial improvement over existing cathode ray tubes and would make electronic television receivers a possibility. The competition between these two inventors culminated at the 1939 World's Fair where RCA head David Sarnoff demonstrated television for the American public.

The Federal Radio Commission appointed a committee to study this new development and prepare a way for it to be incorporated by American broadcasters. The new National Television Systems Committee (NTSC) was also charged with designing the technical standards for television broadcast. Unfortunately, further development would have to wait while the world became immersed in World War II.

After the war, the NTSC issued its technical standards for monochrome (black and white) broadcast television. These standards were based upon a system of synchronization ensuring that picture could be transmitted and received in synchronism. The synchronization system was based upon the sixty-cycle electrical alternating current rate. Using this system, television frames would occur thirty times per second, with odd and even fields composing each frame and a total of 525 horizontal scanning lines. The screen would be scanned sixty times per second. The first electron beam scan would draw 262½ odd lines from the top left to the bottom right of the screen in the period of 1/60 of a second, followed by a retrace to the top left of the screen when the second scan would draw the 262½ even lines. Like film, two fields composed each frame of television transmission. Unlike film, the frame rate was 30fps instead of 24fps. This caused problems for broadcast of film on television until the development of "telecine" units, which could take film input at 24fps and output a television broadcast signal at 30fps. For some time the telecine was used at virtually all television stations in a "film chain" to broadcast film material.

Magnetic recording techniques were used for film sound tracks shortly following World War II. However, moving images were still recorded on film. Although there had been some investigation of alternate storage media for images (Edison had proposed storing film images on wax cylinders) nothing would come of this until the 1950s. The main problem was that the visual frequency range, while encompassing only one octave (compared with ten in audio) from red to violet, comprises an extremely wide bandwidth. An effective video recording system would have to be capable of recording a frequency spectrum of at least four million cycles per second. In comparison, audio bandwidths extend from twenty to twenty thousand cycles per second.

The Ampex Corporation introduced the first professional broadcast-quality monochrome video recorder in 1957. Although the machine was cumbersome (approximately the size of a washer and a dryer), and very expensive, it was in extreme demand from the moment it became available. The main clients for the videotape machine were television broadcast stations on the West Coast. Up until this time, all production carried out locally had to be done live or had to be captured on film.

As late as the 1960s many television news operations continued to rely upon 16mm film production. The major detriment to the use of film was that it had to be developed. When news of a breaking story occurred, it was common to hear the announcer give some details and close with a statement such as "film at eleven." The reason no pictures of the news event were immediately available was because they had been captured on film and the film was being developed for showing on the local news program. Videotape did not have to be developed and it offered an immediacy of production capabilities never before obtainable. Another advantage to production on videotape was that it bypassed a necessary transformation (and possible degradation) for broadcast through the telecine process.

Yet another advantage for the use of video tape on television was that a videotape machine could record the television signal with no intermediate processing steps. This would prove useful for time delay of programs broadcast "live" across the United States. Shows that originated in New York at 8:00 P.M. could be broadcast live in Los Angeles, but the time would be three hours earlier, or 5:00 P.M. To maintain program scheduling, a process known as kinescoping was used, which made a film of the television signal. This film could be played back later to maintain the program schedule, but the quality of the program suffered somewhat from the generation loss. Videotape proved to be a better solution to time delay program feeds. In retrospect, it is fortunate that kinescopes were made of some of these live television broadcast shows for they now serve, in some cases, as the only remaining reference for early broadcast television. Eventually, other important factors would emerge with the development of videotape—the processes of electronic editing and electronic field production (EFP).

Visual Motion and Meaning

The combination of camera angle and lens produces the structure of the shot. A variety of terms are used to express how the camera shot is to be made and a cursory look at a screenplay will indicate the variety of shots at the disposal of the producer—all of which contribute meaning to the finished product.

The shot is named by what is in the camera's viewfinder or the shot frame that is referred to as "framing." A two-shot, for example, is of two people.

A close-up (CU) will place the object fully inside the viewfinder. An extreme close-up (ECU) may fill the viewfinder with a very small section of the object or person.

Medium shots (MS) and long shots (LS) place the focal part of the image farther and farther away from the viewer and communicate distance and separation. Headroom indicates how much space is above the actor or talent's head. If effective headroom is not maintained in shooting, the results can range from an amateur look in the finished project to a purposeful communication of insignificance.

Nose room or "lead room" is the composition of the shot with regard to the profile, or side view, of the actor. If the nose of the actor is facing the right, it is best to maintain some space in the image from the tip of the nose to the right edge of the screen. The brain attempts to fill out the image beyond the boundaries of the television set or screen. If lead room is not maintained in the shot the viewer can become disoriented, or worse, may assume inappropriately that some other action is occurring off-screen.

The sequence of camera shots, when edited together, can contribute volumes to visual communication. Although there are no specific rules to determine how camera shots should be arranged, there are practices used to avoid confusing the viewer.

For example, suppose action is established with two subjects in a long shot. This long shot allows the viewer to determine the location environment and the placement of the subjects in their environment. Then, in order to communicate additional information about the plot, it is desirable to move closer to the subject—perhaps one of the subjects is arguing with the other. The medium shot will more clearly show the body language of the two. A close-up might follow to show one of the subjects reaching into a pocket to pull out a knife. An extreme close-up following might show just the facial expression of the other. In this case, the shot order was performed consecutively from farthest to closest. It would be possible to mix up these shots while editing, but the message would not be communicated as well. For example, say the ECU shot was displayed first followed by the LS, then the MS, and finally the CU. The action did not change, but the message is harder to understand. The natural progression of LS to CU or ECU is more closely parallel to the way our brains comprehend both sight and language.

The way a camera is used can also communicate a first-person point of view (POV) shot. This is especially true now with the number of lightweight cameras available. A POV shot is commonly used in suspense movies. If the director wants the viewer to identify more strongly with the character on the screen, the camera can be utilized to substitute for the eyes of the character. The camera is talking in the first person and the viewers become the character. The viewer sees a long shot of woman getting off a bus. The camera tracks towards the woman, then cuts to the bus as it leaves the stop, panning with the bus as it goes down the street. In order to place the shot in the first person, an edit will have to take place. A new shot will have to establish that we are looking down a deserted, dimly lit street. A noise behind us causes the camera to spin toward the source. We are the camera. We are the woman. The camera does a swish pan back to the front, imitating a sudden move of the head back to see where we are going, and we, the viewers, are all dreading what made that noise. Point of view is powerful when used judiciously, but it can become tedious when overused—then it only calls attention to itself.

Lighting for film and video is an art and can be used to communicate a wealth of information. Indeed, lighting can make or break a production. Many of us are not immediately sensitive to the power of lighting, but we are probably aware of the quality expressed in lighting the set when we watch TV or movies. Lighting adds dimension and separation to shots. It can be used to hide elements, to soften rough edges, or to expose the smallest detail. It can communicate warmth or coolness. Lighting can be used to create atmospheres that are happy or sinister. It would not be overstatement to say that, in capturing visual motion, the most important elements for communication of messages are the subject in the picture and the way the subject is lit.

The way visual motion is put together, or edited, is also significant to communicating a message. Editing allows the production to speak in a narrative format. We are familiar with the basic reasons for editing—to shorten scenes, to insert other scenes, or to remove errors. But the edit is much more important than simply inserting or removing material. It is the way in which the production can communicate nonverbally to the viewer. Scenes can be cut to communicate rhythm, or a pacing. They can be cut to compress or expand time. Editing also allows the viewer to see the scene from a variety of viewpoints to more accurately calculate intention or significance. The edit can also be used to create parallel storylines so that two, or more sets of action can be taking place simultaneously. Editing can also be used to create montages, which may be short segments designed to illustrate the passage of time or other kinds of information. Editing to portray a continuous flow of events in a realistic manner is termed "continuity editing." If, on the other hand, the edited flow is designed to fragment the action or to go back and forth in time it is termed "dynamic editing."

Cameras

Of course, film or video would not be possible without the device that converts the play of shadow and light into a tangible, moving image—the camera. The camera is a transducer that can convert visible images into other formats for storage on film, magnetic tape, or digital media. The conversion is the result of interaction between available light and the sensitivity of the media to changes in that light. These conversions may rely upon changes in chemical structure, as in film, upon magnetic level, as in videotape, or upon binary representation, as in digital video.

The first television studio cameras were extremely bulky and relied upon tubes to generate the picture information. The electronics tended to drift over time and the camera needed to be constantly realigned. To realign the camera's electronics and to make checks on the entire video signal path, two specialized oscilloscopes, called the waveform monitor and the vectorscope, are used. The waveform monitor is used to check for strength of video signal, and the vectorscope is used to calibrate the color information in the video signal.

Video cameras also need to be calibrated for white level. This white balance procedure establishes a correct color balance for the camera in different lighting situations. To accomplish correct color shading, the camera is trained on a white card in the same lighting situation to be used in the shot. In most cases a white balance can be performed automatically at the camera, though some cameras require the adjustment of remote electronics. This procedure is sometimes referred to as "shading" the camera.

It was not until the mid-1980s that semiconductor technology was reliably employed in video camera design. In 1986, the charge coupled device chip (CCD) began to replace the tube for generation of color signal in the video camera. The CCD chip has made remarkable improvements to the video signal and has contributed to the development of much smaller and lighter-weight cameras. The explosion of popularity of personal camcorders in both VHS and Hi8 (8mm) formats has been made possible by CCD technology. Although the CCD chips are stabler than their tube counterparts, they still require monitoring for video alignment and require white balancing for correct color level.

A studio camera mounted on a movable pedestal dolly is typically capable of a number of moves and should be able to make these moves in a very fluid manner. Depending upon the shot intended, the camera person should be able to pan left or right, zoom in or out (if the lens in use is of variable focal length), pedestal up or down, dolly in or out, truck left or right, and tilt up or down.

Along with the improvements in camera technology, there have been improvements in the ways cameras may be used in shots. The Steadicam is a device that allows the camera person to perform a fluid shot while in motion and from a variety of positions—even hanging off a helicopter. Robot-controlled cameras have been improved as well, allowing photography of images in hazardous conditions, or allowing precise animation and models to be systematically shot for incorporation into feature films.

Of course, the most revolutionary improvement in camera technology is the conversion to digital formats. Personal camcorders developed by Sony and other manufacturers now allow several features previously impossible. These include the capability to videotape at or near broadcast quality with improved specifications for the number of lines of resolution and color detailing. Digital processing also allows for error correction so that any data that might be corrupted during the videotaping

Lightweight television cameras allow live transmission of events far from the studio.

Christopher R. Harris

or later playback can be correctly played. Another exciting possibility afforded by digital cameras is the potential for interface with the personal computer for desktop-based editing of the video data. Finally, digital camera technology also allows for unprecedented video shooting regardless of the light source. Some personal camcorders are even equipped with infrared emitters to allow recording in the dark.

The Camera Lens

The lens is also crucial to the communication of visual messages. Coupled with the camera, it determines the depth of field seen in the image. Like the human eye, the lens will lend focus to the intended subject, though a camera's lens is not as variable. Therefore the proper selection and use of a lens are of utmost importance in visual communication.

The two major factors affecting lens use are focal length and f-stop. Focal length is the distance, measured in millimeters, from the light-sensitive part of the camera (chip or tube) to the center of the curved glass that makes up the lens optics. The f-stop is the variable aperture that increases or decreases the amount of light allowed into the camera. Thus, the behavior of a lens f-stop control is similar to that of the human pupil. The longer the lens, the narrower the image area; the shorter the lens, the wider acceptable image area. The wider the aperture, the lower the f-stop number (1, 1.4)—therefore allowing more light into the camera. Higher numbered f-stops (16, 22) close down the aperture, allowing only a small amount of light into the camera.

The range of focus in an image is referred to as depth of field. Both the length of the lens and the f-stop control the available depth of field. Once a shot has been composed as long, medium, wide, and so on, the lens selection or zoom is used to focus on the subject. This will determine initial depth of field. Additional control over depth of field is obtained with the f-stop control. If it is desirable to keep the background behind the subject out of focus, thereby decreasing the perceived depth of field, it will be necessary to increase available light by increasing the f-stop aperture. If, on the other hand, it is desirable to increase the depth of field—to have as deep a focus as possible, it is necessary to decrease, or stop the aperture down. This will also typically mean that available light on the set (or on location) will have to be increased to compensate.

The most common lens on video cameras today is a zoom lens that allows adjustment from the wide angle (short) to telephoto (long). In overall focal length, a wide-angle lens is typically 25mm. Telephoto lenses vary, but a common zoom length will be in the area of 200mm. Zoom lenses are generally remotely controlled by the camera operator to provide a smooth adjustment in focal length.

Lighting

The visual journalist must be familiar with basic lighting concepts when attempting to capture images on film or video. As mentioned earlier, lighting can make or break a production and lighting is in itself an art form. However, for our purposes, it will suffice to discuss some basic concepts and to describe some of the basic instruments and techniques used to light sets or supplement location lighting.

The existence of light gives us a ratio of contrast. When working with light, we are working with both the direct, or incident, light coming directly from sources of illumination as well as the reflected, or ambient, light present as a result of the incident light. The human eye can experience a great deal of contrast ratio—perhaps as great as 100 to 1. The use of film, depending on the type of stock used, can begin to approximate human capabilities. In analog video technology, however—even with the newer CCD devices—ratios of only up to about 40 to 1 are possible.

A light meter, which measures light in foot-candles, is an excellent aid to help determine the contrast ratio of direct and reflected light on the set. The foot-candle is the measure of light produced by a candle flame at a distance of one foot. Typical lighting instruments can produce 600 foot-candles or more. What will be important to determine is the ratio of lighting in the intended shot, from the directly lit subject to the reflected contrast. Comparing the readings taken on the light meter can serve as a guide of acceptability.

In addition to contrast ratio, light also introduces a basic color of its own, measured in degrees Kelvin. Different types of lights generate different color temperatures, according to the way they function. To some extent, humans can perceive these differences, but video cameras are much more sensitive to changes in color temperature and require the use of lighting instruments calibrated to produce a lighting temperature of approximately 3200 °Kelvin. When shooting in bright sun where Kelvin temperatures may exceed 10,000 degrees, color filters may be used to maintain a consistent color temperature for video work.

Of the many types of lighting instruments available to the visual journalist, each might be classified as one of two types—spotlight and floodlight. The spotlight controls the beam of light leaving the instrument. The floodlight, on the other hand, creates a more diffuse light source. The most common spotlight instrument used in moving image production is the Fresnel spot, which uses a specially designed lens at the front of the light canister that allows the light to be accurately focused without heat buildup in the instrument. Additionally, the bulb can be moved back and forth in the canister to vary the width and intensity of the light beam. The most common floodlight instrument is called a "scoop," a large dome-shaped housing designed to create a diffuse light pattern.

To illustrate common uses of lighting, a brief discussion of a three-point lighting scheme might be appropriate. Three-point lighting uses three light sources on the subject in the frame—key light, fill light, and back light. As its name implies, the key light is the primary light on the subject. It commonly comes from a spotlight placed above and forward of the subject. In some situations calling for dramatic lighting a low key light may be used to illuminate the subject from below. The back light, also generally a spotlight, is designed to remove the subject from the background to give it some space. The fill light, placed to the side of the subject, is generally a floodlight and is used to give the subject some depth.

Lighting designers use many accessories to control the action of light. To further focus light on a subject and to remove shadow, barn doors may be mounted on lighting instruments. To change the color and tint of lighting, gels may be used. Floodlights can be made more diffuse by using scrims made of wire mesh or by using opaque fiberglass filters. Foil reflectors can enhance natural light. (Still photography uses similar lighting techniques; see Chapter 4 for additional information about lighting.)

Switchers

A switcher routes video signals from cameras, videotape machines, or other video storage devices. The switcher uses a system of video buses, similar to an audio mixing console, so that signals may be combined or controlled for special effects. Like the video camera and all other aspects of the video system, a professional switcher must be synchronized to prevent timing errors. Sources on the switcher will include not only videotape signals, but also other signals such as a source of video black, used for fades. The rate of the fade to black or fade up from black will be determined by a fader control. To fade, the video engineer must select a black source on the secondary bus while the primary bus is displaying current picture information. The fade from primary to secondary bus will produce a fade to black. A fade from secondary to primary bus will produce a fade up from black.

The switcher can also be used to create editing effects such as cuts, dissolves, wipes, and superimpositions. On the switcher a cut is simply a take. When directed, selecting an alternate source without the fader will cut or "jump" to the other visual message. The dissolve places visual information on both buses. The fader then can be slowly moved from one picture bus to the other to produce the dissolve. Wipes will also use two channels of visual message, but typically push the video image left to right or right to left. Superimpositions, or "supers," allow the video engineer to place an active video image in its own window on top of another active video image. Many of these effects are seen daily in television news and sports programs.

Another important source on the switcher is the character generator. The character generator is used to place text on the video screen and is commonly placed as a super.

With the development of digital electronics for use in video production, many other special effects are possible as well. Switchers that can produce special video effects are typically referred to as special effects generators (SEG). The SEG digital signal processing effects may include flips, rotations, or other visual message convolutions.

Editors

Videotape editing began in a method similar to that of film editing—mechanically with a razor blade. Unlike film, however, the videotape engineer cannot see the image while performing the cut. The problem is that in order to record sufficient bandwidth videotape is recorded by a helical scanning method. The videotape head meets the tape at an angle to the direction of tape travel. If a vertical cut were made on a videotape, it would cut across the scan lines recorded by the head, rendering a flaw in the edit. Timing information would be lost, causing a jump or flip in the picture. Initially, videotape engineers used magnetic developing "ink" so that the lines of magnetic flux produced by the videotape head could be seen with a microscope. Then, the engineer could perform the edit by cutting between the diagonal flux lines. Obviously this method of editing was tedious. For this reason, as videotape machines improved in quality, newer methods of electronic editing were also developed.

Electronic editing involves dubbing material from one machine to another by two means: assembly editing and insert editing. Assembly editing arranges edited events in a linear fashion, from start to end. Insert editing allows new material to be recorded in between other recorded events or recorded over previously recorded events. Electronic editing requires at least two machines: a playback machine and a record machine. For the edit to be performed properly, the machines must both run at the same speed and their transports must be electronically synchronized. If synchronization is not established between the playback and record machines, the edit will "crash," causing picture distortions due to improper timing. One method of forcing the machines to synchronize was to use a control track, a pulse occurring at the frame rate of the video signal. Control track is used by the video tape recorder to determine how a tape should be played back, rather like electronic sprocket holes. The control track is recorded as a signal on a dedicated track of the videotape. Using this method, edits could take place under proper synchronization, but they could not be precisely controlled or repeated. An alternative was developed in

Christopher R. Harris

Editing videotape for use on news Web site.

the late 1960s that allowed the recording of a time code on a track of the machine. This time code is calibrated in hours, minutes, seconds, and frames. Each unique frame had its own "address," and editing thus became much more reliable. The Society of Motion Picture and Television Engineers (SMPTE) has incorporated and oversees the use of this time code.

Synchronization of machines implies a master/slave relationship. Only one machine or one source can be the master in a synchronized system. Since most production facilities use more than one machine for editing and other production, a method of solving the master/slave conflict is to synchronize all machines, switchers, and cameras to a single accurate clock. This system of synchronization is known as "house sync" and the synchronization source is typically a single source of video black.

Since the development of SMPTE time code, it has also been possible to prepare the visual productions sometimes requiring hundreds if not thousands of complicated edits using what is known as an edit decision list (EDL). The EDL may be prepared by viewing copies of the working production tapes. These copies will use a process known as a "window burn" to insert a viewable version of the time code on the tape in its own visual window. The director and editors may work together previewing these tapes and preparing the EDL based on the time code numbers. Since the early 1970s, it has been possible to store data versions of these EDLs on disk so that the edit can take place under computer control. The earliest form of computerized EDL event editing was developed by CBS and Memorex and was called the CMX system. Companies such as Grass Valley and Ampex have developed other digital EDL protocols. Obviously, a multi-machine edit taking place under computer control is a fairly expensive proposal. Therefore it is important to work the edit out as much as possible beforehand, off-line. Today, using desktop computer video systems to preview the edit or to actually conform the edited master can reduce many of these expenses.

Professional-quality video recorders or cameras afford many standard video editing possibilities. To perform an assembly edit, new material is added to the end of previously recorded material by using the machine's or camera's internal sync. In other words, every time the record button is hit, the record machine will record video, audio, and control track. An insert edit, on the other hand, would record only new video or new audio over existing control track, without erasing other material. An insert edit preserves the original timing on the videotape.

The simplest of editing procedures involving two machines is referred to as "cuts only." This is a simple machine-to-machine edit, usually assembly style. If a switcher is used, material from two machines (A and B) may be edited in sequence (assembled) or inserted to a third record machine. The advantage of A/B roll editing is the flexibility of shot selection and effects between shots made possible by the use of the switcher.

CONCLUSION

This chapter has served as a basic introduction to the techniques and tools available to the visual journalist endeavoring to capture visual motion. Increases in technology over the last century have brought about numerous advantages to the communication of messages by this medium. Cameras have become lighter, smaller, and more accurate. Digital technology is revolutionizing the capabilities of the video camera. Lighting equipment and lenses have improved as well. The increasingly portable equipment for capturing visual motion has stimulated growth in areas such as electronic news gathering (ENG) and electronic field production (EFP). The influx into the consumer market of products designed to capture visual motion has also increased the potential for the communication of messages through alternative media such as multimedia and the World Wide Web.

And while technology has improved, there has also been a tendency to communicate a defiance of technological improvements, evidenced by a variety of comedy shows and music videos, with "anti-technology" shooting maneuvers like the "shaky cam" handheld camera shots, use of high-contrast, grainy film, purposeful streaking and tearing of screen images, and so forth. The message may be twofold: on the one hand, an expression of opposition to volumes of slickly produced, yet

A modern TV control room.

Tom Jimison

meaningless material; on the other, an indication of a populist approach to visual communication. Video production is much less expensive now than it ever was before and more people than ever before are experimenting with the medium and its possibilities.

Although the history of visual motion capture technology is entering its second century, the widespread availability of visual motion capturing tools to the consumer market is just entering its second decade. It will be interesting to observe the changes and the benefits to the communication of visual messages that occur over the next decade.

IDEAS FOR FURTHER STUDY

- With editing equipment and software, see if you can condense a five-minute video news report to three minutes. Does the story still make sense?

- Find a previously produced video clip or tape a story from a television set. What would you have to do to edit the story for different audiences—a young MTV-watching crowd or an older clientele?

- Write a paper that explains the differences and similarities in presentation and techniques between a motion picture and a television program.

VISUAL PERSPECTIVES

Fake Videotape

by Larry L. Burriss

Now you see it; now you don't. That's what a lot of people are saying about revelations that what we were seeing during CBS's New Year's Eve coverage wasn't what it was all cracked up to be.

It seems that while Dan Rather was on the air, behind him, in Times Square, was an NBC logo. Except that what we saw at home was a CBS logo electronically inserted into the picture.

Actually this sort of thing is nothing new. During sporting events like baseball and football, advertisements are often electronically inserted into blank spaces around the field. And we've seen the same kind of thing in entertainment programs as various products and logos are electronically inserted into scenes where they don't really exist.

Product placement is, of course, nothing new. Soft drinks, candy bars, cars, airplanes, and almost everything else imaginable are used in movies and television programs as advertisements. So it's only natural that instead of real products, fake, electronic images should be used.

The problem, however, comes when news images start to be manipulated. Now, it's absolutely true that news we read in the papers or see on television isn't exactly reality. Photographers decide what pictures to take, reporters decide which part of an event to cover, and editors decide what part of a story to print

or broadcast. But what is generally considered beyond the pale is for news organizations to actually alter a scene. And that's just what CBS did.

Now, some people have said that the CBS program coverage of Times Square on New Year's Eve wasn't really news but was, instead, something known as "infotainment." But if it wasn't news coverage, then Dan Rather, a newsman, shouldn't have been the anchor.

Following the 1938 Halloween broadcast of *War of the Worlds,* which used fake newscasts as part of the adventure, broadcasters pretty much agreed not to use newscast formats in entertainment programs if they could be mistaken for the real thing.

Now broadcasters need to do the same kind of thing in reverse: They need to agree not to manipulate the video if the fake could be mistaken for the real thing.

A few years ago, ABC news got into trouble when it staged pictures of a spy without telling the news audience the scenes weren't real. And NBC news was rightly pilloried for enhancing the explosion of a truck in a story about vehicle safety.

News is one of the last bastions of reality in our all too media-saturated world. And the people who create news programs should make every effort to make sure that what we are seeing is reality, not something enhanced at the whim of an overeager producer. ■

Originally aired over WMOT-FM on Jan. 29, 2000.

CHAPTER 13

Audio and Motion

by Douglas Mitchell
Middle Tennessee State University

Combining sound with moving images is an extremely powerful way to communicate messages. Imagine that you are watching television or are at the movies and suddenly the sound accompanying the picture is gone. You may still make sense of the image due to an actor's expressions or the camera shots and edits, but much of the impact of the presentation is gone. We can easily observe that communication can take place with the dialogue accompanying a moving image, but there are other ways in which audio can be used as a communication tool. Background music and the use of sound effects also impart meaning to video and film productions.

Quite often when we are watching moving image presentations, we are not (or should not be) conscious of the sound accompanying the picture. The sound designer is a specialized visual journalist who works with sound to communicate aural messages accompanying film or video productions. The art of the sound designer in film and video production is to place sound where it belongs in the mix—not to call attention to itself. When viewers become conscious of the sound track, their attention is removed from the image on the screen. You've noticed this when dialogue is out of synchronization, when the lips are not moving with the recorded words. This aural error has caused you to pay more attention to the fact that the dialogue was poorly dubbed or re-synchronized than to the story unfolding on the screen.

The objective of the "sound designer"—a term coined by Oscar-winning film and sound editor Walter Murch, responsible for the incredibly dense and wonderful soundtrack for *Apocalypse Now*—is to help tell the story and amplify it by creative use of sound. The sound designer works as a team member with the video or film producer and the editors to create visual communication. There are many tools in the sound designer's kit.

Sound and Meaning

Unlike the visual picture, sound is ephemeral. It stretches beyond the screen to touch the very fiber of our being. The sense of hearing communicates at both the conscious and subconscious levels. Hearing is strongly linked with the human capacity for self-preservation—a kind of built-in alarm system that functions regardless of the conscious state.

*Electronic composition
for the film industry.*

Tom Jimison

Sound can be used as a way to communicate things not expressed on the screen. Since sight in visual communication is limited by the frame of the picture, sound may be used to tell the viewer something about the off-screen environment. Sound may also be used as a metaphor for something not displayed visually. Although the picture may be exhibiting scenes that are happy, the simultaneous sound can be used to communicate a sense of foreboding or danger.

Sound may also be used to help create meaning by reinforcing what is seen in the picture. In this way, sound may be used to create literal meaning. Sight tends to be an extremely literal perception, and the use of sound accompanying the picture may augment the visual message. The heightened use of natural sound can more effectively place the viewer in a particular environment and lend an overall ambiance conducive to imparting visual meaning.

This chapter will examine some of the ways in which sound is used to accompany moving images and it will introduce the reader to some of the practices of sound production used by the visual journalist.

History of Sound with Picture

Today we take sound accompanying video or film for granted. But the practice of placing a soundtrack directly on the film was not an easy accomplishment, and it did not take place until the 1920s.

Shortly after the development of celluloid flexible film by George Eastman in 1889, Thomas Alva Edison and his staff were already hard at work on film media. One of Edison's staff, William Kennedy Laurie Dickson, produced the Kinetoscope. Edison linked Dickson's Kinetoscope with his own phonograph to come up with a device they called the Kinetophone. The synchronization between flexible film and the cylinder phonograph proved to be very crude.

In the early 1900s Frenchman Eugene Lauste was able to record sound onto a piece of photographic film by varying the amount of exposure on the film with an audio signal. However, later developments for sound in film media would concentrate on better synchronization of sound-with-film—as in the Warner Brothers Vitaphone system, used to give a voice to Al Jolson in the 1927 film, *The Jazz Singer*. Popularized as the first "talkie," *The Jazz Singer* was a sound-with-film production—the sound was on synchronized 16-inch transcription disks. Although *The Jazz Singer* was not actually the first "talkie," it was the first movie to feature both synchronized dialogue and singing throughout the picture.

Following the development of the Audion tube by Lee DeForest in 1914, it was possible to amplify a sound track so that it could be heard easily by all in a large hall by means of a loudspeaker. In 1927, the Fox Movie Corporation, in a joint venture with Western Electric, promoted a sound-on-film approach. The result was called the Movietone News. The sound was recorded optically on the film with a variable density sound track. Fox used this system to produce newsreels that would play before feature films in theatres. Some of the first big publicity coups for the Movietone News were the interviews with Charles Lindbergh before and after his flight across the Atlantic.

Optical variable density sound tracks continued to be popular until the mid-1930s, when variable area sound tracks were perfected with the use of limiting amplifiers. The benefit of variable area to variable density sound tracks is that they are more easily copied, with less noise, and with less signal degradation. All optical film tracks today are of the variable area format.

Magnetic Recording

Although the original patent for a magnetic recording device was issued in 1896 to Valdemar Poulsen, a Danish inventor, methods for magnetic recording in film were not employed until the late 1940s. Magnetic recording techniques suffered initially from several technical problems that prevented the recordings from having any degree of high fidelity. It was during World War II, however, that magnetic recording systems and technology were improved and developed on both sides of the Atlantic. By 1950, magnetic film stock (mag) was being substituted in the production process of film making. Magnetic tape did not have to be developed, could be made more portable than optical could, and was better in overall sound quality. By the late 1950s, the process of recording the visual message and the sound to magnetic tape had been perfected as well. Videotape recording offered an unprecedented opportunity for production possibilities including electronic field production (EFP), electronic news gathering (ENG), and editing.

Synchronization

Synchronization is the process of interlocking separate film or tape machines so that picture and sound elements can occur simultaneously. Since the earliest days of film, there have been numerous methods for synchronizing the various elements required to produce visual communication.

Synchronization in film is rather mechanical. In order to fool the eye, there are twenty-four separate frames projected each second. For each frame there are four sprocket holes that serve not only to pull the film through the camera and projector assemblies, but also serve to synchronize separate pieces of film or film and sound when editing. Since the distance between each sprocket hole is identical, the separate pieces can remain in sync as long as a common motor shaft rotates the sprocket assemblies. When synchronization of non-sprocket elements is attempted, as with videotape or magnetic sound tape, the process is not so easy.

One method used for synchronization of magnetic sound tape with the sprocket film is to use a sync pulse—usually a pulse tone at sixty cycles per second. This sync tone, sometimes referred to as pilot tone, is generated at the camera and is recorded by means of a cable on a track of the magnetic sound recorder. The sync tone generator controls the speed of the camera so that when it comes time to synchronize the film and the sound track, all that is needed is to resolve the playback of the sound tape according to the sync pulse recorded on it. Any speed deviations on the part of the camera will be correspondingly recorded on the track of the tape machine. To begin this synchronization process, a clapper board is used. The clapper board displays the take number and other relevant data. When the scene is to begin, the top half of the clapper board is banged together with the bottom half producing a clap sound that is used to synchronize the beginning of the reel.

The problem with sync tone is that there is no way to identify specific points within the reel for editing purposes. For this reason, and to improve the synchronization process for videotape and sound to videotape, a time code system (which had been developed in part by NASA for telemetry purposes) was incorporated. The Society of Motion Picture and Television Engineers (SMPTE) now standardizes this time code system for use. The SMPTE Time Code is a digital representation of hours, minutes, seconds, and frames. Each frame, therefore, has a unique address and may be located on the tape at any time. This system has vastly improved the possibilities for videotape editing and has made the process of synchronizing audio tape to film or videotape much easier.

Depending upon what medium is being used, the time code frame count will vary. It is important to know, before editing or attempting to synchronize sound and picture, what time code format is being used. For film, the frame rate is 24fps. For European television and videotape, the rate is 25fps. For North American and Japanese black and white television and video the original frame rate was 30fps. The introduction of color to the NTSC television system forces the actual frame rate to 29.97fps. In order to compensate for number variances over time, the frame numbers may shift to reflect actual time when 29.97fps is used. This form of time code, known as drop frame, drops 108 frames over the course of an hour.

When working on a project, the producers, directors, and editors will most likely have a large number of shots to choose from. In order to determine the final

Synchronization

edit, decisions must be made about which shots to use, which angles, whether to use the close-up or the long shot, and so forth. Obviously these decisions can eat up a lot of time and should not be made in an expensive editing suite. Therefore, with the development of time code a practice of off-line editing has become more predominant. After all of the shooting has taken place, the producer will order transfers made of all the film and/or video and have time code placed in the picture during the transfer. This is generally called a window burn and can be used to prepare an off-line edit decision list by viewing the tapes on any videotape machine.

Time code has also made possible the practice of synchronizing multiple tape machines and other audio sources to picture with extreme accuracy. Edit decision lists based upon time code locations prepared for visual editing may also be used to determine where sounds will occur in the picture.

Microphones

The microphone is the heart of the sound recording process. It is with the microphone that sound recording begins by converting acoustical sound wave energy into signal voltage energy. Depending upon what needs to be recorded, the sound designer may choose microphones that vary by operational principle, pickup pattern, and special purposes.

Operational Principle of Microphones

Inside the microphone is a transducer that converts forms of energy. In a dynamic moving coil microphone, acoustic sound pressure waves hit the diaphragm of the transducer that moves in relationship to a magnetic field. Around the magnetic structure of the microphone is wrapped a coil of wire. This coil behaves like an electromagnet in reverse. When the diaphragm moves in relationship to the fixed magnetic structure of the transducer, current flows down the wires of the coil in direct relationship to the acoustic wave hitting the diaphragm. Moving coil microphones are known for their ruggedness and ability to work even after being roughed up in the field.

Ribbon microphones are constructed in a similar manner, but substitute a thin metal ribbon for the diaphragm in the transducer. As is easily imaginable, a ribbon microphone is much more delicate than a moving coil microphone. Ribbon microphones, therefore, would not be a good choice for use on location but might be suitable for recording voice or instruments in the studio.

The capacitor, or condenser (as it is referred to in the United States), microphone substitutes one of the plates of a capacitor for the diaphragm in its trans-

Tom Jimison

Sound recording at a well-equipped modern studio.

ducer design. The back plate of the capacitor is charged with external power either through a battery in the microphone or via a remote, phantom power source. A universal phantom power supply (usually +48 volts DC for professional condenser microphones) is often built into recording consoles or may even be available on remote mixers and cameras. When the diaphragm, or front plate, of the capacitor moves in relationship to the charged back plate in the condenser microphone, current analogous to the acoustic waveform is produced.

Condenser microphones are known for having very good frequency response and quite often produce higher output levels than moving coil microphones. Many professional studio- and field-grade microphones are of the condenser variety.

Pickup Patterns

Unlike our sense of hearing, which can be very selective, microphones will respond to all signals within their area of pickup. A microphone's pickup pattern, or polarity response, will demonstrate its ability to react to acoustic sound pressure waves. The design principle of the microphone will determine how it will respond to sound sources. Most microphones are designed to respond with only one response pattern. However, some special purpose condenser microphones may be designed to respond with several different patterns of response.

An omnidirectional response pattern will indicate that the microphone responds to signals all around it. A bidirectional, or figure eight, pattern indicates that the microphone picks up only to the front and the rear. A more selective pattern of response is the unidirectional, or cardioid (heart-shaped), response pattern. There are several specialized types of unidirectional response patterns. Each becomes narrower in its response to the front and is designated as supercardioid, hypercardioid, and ultracardioid. Each of these patterns results from increased cancellation of sound arriving at the sides and/or rear of the microphone. In order to become extremely selective to sound directly in front, the microphone will employ additional rear or side entrance ports to increase sound rejection to the sides.

Special Purpose Microphones

Perhaps one of the most common microphones is the hand-held microphone. As signified by its name, this microphone is designed to be held by the user or can be mounted in a special clip on a stand. Most microphones used by vocalists in live musical performances are of this variety. The hand-held microphone is designed so that the inner transducer is shock-mounted to prevent undue handling noise. Most hand-held microphones are moving coil designs.

In many cases, however, it is not appropriate for a microphone to be seen on the set—whether hand-held or not. In some cases a microphone may be concealed on the user. One small type of microphone especially suited for this purpose is the lavalier microphone. The lavalier is a miniature microphone design. Most lavaliers use miniaturized condenser transducers usually of the electric variety, that is, a permanently charged capacitor design. Some lavaliers may require external power, either through a concealed battery pack or through phantom power.

A "shotgun" microphone may be used to selectively capture the dialogue of actors on a set. A shotgun microphone utilizes a hyper- or ultracardioid response pattern to give it a tighter pickup. They are often used on sets with special microphone dollies that allow the microphones to be swung out of the camera shot and to be aimed directly at the intended sound source. In the field, shotgun microphones are often used as well, but may be used with lightweight boom arms or pistol grips. Wind is a considerable problem with shotgun microphones, so it is common to see them in use with a specialized wind screen, sometimes called a zeppelin.

Another special purpose microphone ideally suited for use in video and film production is a boundary microphone. The boundary microphone is placed on a reflective surface, say, for example, a stage floor, and will respond to acoustical sound pressure in the hemisphere above the reflective surface. The boundary microphone places a small transducer element a short distance above and facing the reflective surface. The benefit of using this boundary area—one manufacturer of microphones refers to it as a pressure zone—is that the small pickup area under the transducer prevents pickup of out-of-phase sound.

Virtually any microphone can be used in a wireless configuration. All that is required is a transmitter and a receiver. For video and film work wireless microphones are handy, freeing the set of wires that might get in the shot. For scenes where disguising the microphone is extremely important, use of a wireless lavalier microphone is quite common. In these cases, the microphone can be hidden under clothing, in the brim of a hat, or somewhere on the set itself. The most important requirement with the use of wireless microphones is that the frequency the transmitter and receiver operate on be free of external interference from other wireless broadcasting sources such as public service bands, citizens band, and local television stations.

Mixers and Consoles

The mixing console is used to bring together all of the sounds to be used in a production and balance them before sending them off to their final mixing destination—either a film, video, or audio-only master. By balancing, or mixing, the sound designer attempts to recreate an aural reality that will match and support the picture on the screen. There are several specialized film and audio post-mixing console designs whose functions are determined largely by the status of the production: production, post-production, dubbing/re-recording, playback/transfer.

A production console may often be as simple as a portable field mixer. The main responsibility of this mixer is to bring microphone levels up to acceptable levels for recording on magnetic tape. Even when the intention is to replace dialogue in post-production, it is still necessary to get a clean recording of the dialogue on-set in order to provide the editor with a good cue track for writing dialogue replacement scripts and the actor with audible cues for looping in post-production.

The console used for looping, or dialogue replacement, sessions may also be fairly simple in terms of its electronics. Its main purpose is to provide the audio engineer with a means to bring microphone levels up to satisfactory recording levels. However, there are generally some additional remote switches that will give the audio engineer control over the machine to be recorded onto—whether it is an audio magnetic tape machine, a digital audio workstation, or a magnetic film dubbing machine.

When using a film dubber (a specialized film projector outfitted for playback of magnetic audio tracks), the engineer will typically roll the film back and forth over the area to be dubbed. A line on the film will indicate where the actor is to begin speaking. This method is often referred to as the "rock and roll" method. Otherwise, the engineer may simply let a magnetic loop of film roll in synchronization with a loop of edited film. Each new pass of dialogue recorded in this "looping" method will take place on a new track of magnetic film stock cut to the same length as the film loop.

With improvements in tape machine synchronization systems, much dialogue replacement is taking place on multitrack tape machines, of both the analog and digital varieties. Dialogue replacement may also be performed on a computerized digital audio workstation system. Whatever the media used for recording, it is still important for the engineer to get the best sound quality from the actor being recorded in order to ensure that the dialogue mix is not compromised.

Sound effect work done in post-production may require additional mixing console features. The process of adding sound effects to a film may be done in part by Foley artists. Foley artists, named after Jack Foley, the man who established the possibilities for replacing sound effects in motion pictures, can replicate many of the organic sounds captured on the edited film or video. These may be the sounds of people walking on different surfaces, punches and hits, clothes rustling, and so on. Foley artists watch the onscreen performance and replicate the audible sounds of the action onscreen. This activity is recorded to tape and later edited and re-synchronized to the picture. A prime consideration in a Foley session is that there be easy access to controls for video playback and that there be good communication between the session producer and the Foley artist.

Other sound work, called "sweetening," requires the ability to alter sounds: to boost them up or brighten them, add reverb, or artificial ambience, to them, perhaps add effects to them, and so forth. This type of work requires a console with a fair degree of flexibility in signal routing. No one signal processing device may be used to perform all of these sound manipulations, and so the engineer must be able to route signals to a variety of devices to obtain the required sweetened sound the producer and sound designer are listening for. Today, many of the signal processing functions used in sound sweetening for video and film productions may occur on digital audio workstations.

The most comprehensive of mixing consoles for audio post-production work is the dubbing or re-recording console. This console must be able to accept the inputs from all of the sources being used to create the final mix of sound to picture. In film productions, the mix of all of these elements will take place in a "re-recording stage," designed to imitate the listening environment of a movie theatre—even down to the seats, screen, curtains, and lighting. This gives the sound engineers the best approximation of how the general public will perceive the mix of sound with picture.

Multichannel Sound Tracks

Another important aspect of the final mix is the format of the mix itself and the way the film or video will be monitored while mixing. Since *Fantasia* was released in 1940, filmmakers have been interested in the possibilities afforded by extending the sound dimension within the theatre. *Fantasia* was originally produced with a multichannel soundtrack called, appropriately enough, Fantasound. Fantasound was made possible by running two projectors in sync with one another—one with the picture, the other with three channels of sound and a control track. The control track was used to control the level of each of the channels of sound as it played. The original Fantasound track played in only four theatres. The equipment used to produce the soundtrack included racks of equipment thirty-five feet wide and used four hundred vacuum tubes. Until recently re-released on video with a Dolby Pro-Logic sound track, *Fantasia* was relegated to mono optical playback.

Following World War II, there were advancements in film technology, both for projected image size as well as for presentation and number of sound channels, that included the development of CinemaScope, Panascope, VistaVision, Superscope, and Technorama. Sound for all of these formats typically used at least three channels for the front and may have added an "effects" channel for playing material from hall or surround speakers located on the walls of the theatre.

The Todd-AO 70mm process debuted in 1955 with the release of *Oklahoma!* This format used up to six audio channels, but because of the size of the film and the electronics required to accurately reproduce the accompanying audio, Todd-AO films could be seen only in adequately equipped theatres.

In the 1970s, Dolby Laboratories introduced the Dolby Stereo Variable Area soundtrack for 35mm film. The process, also known as Dolby Stereo, produced a discrete left and right channel audio signal optically on the film in the space where mono optical soundtracks had been located. The process also allowed for center channel information and surround, ambient, channel effects as well. The first release in Dolby Stereo was *A Star Is Born* (with Kris Kristofferson and Barbra Streisand) followed shortly by George Lucas's *Star Wars*. A similar process is used today for Dolby Pro-Logic soundtracks on VHS tape and laser disc.

Various refinements of multiple channel soundtracks have been in development in the twenty years following the development of Dolby Stereo. THX, named for Thomlinson Holman Experiment, advanced the capabilities of Dolby Stereo releases and prescribed minimum requirements for sound capabilities of THX cinemas. Thomlinson Holman served as the sound advisor to George Lucas's Skywalker Ranch film post-production studios. The success of THX releases in theatres also prompted development of THX components for home theatre as well.

Since Dolby Stereo and THX, there have been further developments to the addition of channels with the capabilities of digital audio for film sound. These have included the Dolby Digital system, Sony Dynamic Digital Sound (SDDS) and Digital Theatre Systems (DTS) Coherent Acoustics Digital Surround. For theatre and home presentation, both Dolby Digital and DTS use a 5.1 channel approach. The five digital audio main channels are front left, front center, front right, rear left, and rear right. The .1 channel is referred to as a low-frequency effects (LFE) channel reserved for use with a subwoofer. The Sony SDDS system uses eight channels: five behind the screen, discrete left and right surrounds, and an LFE channel.

Depending upon the final release format, the sound engineers must mix the separate music, effects, and dialogue tracks so that they correspond with the correct number of channels and the way in which they are positioned throughout the theatre or other listening environment. Additionally, it is extremely important to be aware of alternate mix possibilities and to monitor the mix for these as well. For example, the theatrical release of a motion picture may be in DTS format, but the consumer VHS tape of the project would likely be released for Dolby Pro-Logic surround playback. In this case, it would have to be ascertained at the time of the mix how much information will be lost in the transfer and if that loss is acceptable. Alternative mixes of film and video product may also include M&E mixes (mixes with music and effects only). These are mixes for foreign markets where the dialogue is to be re-dubbed.

Recording Technology

Today there are two predominant methods of storing sound recorded either by analog or digital recording systems. However, with the infusion of computer-based technology, digital systems are rapidly outpacing analog systems. Analog recording methods use a transducer—the record head—to convert incoming signal energy into lines of magnetic flux that may be stored on magnetic tape. The play head of an analog tape recording machine also acts as a transducer, converting changes in magnetic flux back into signal energy that can be amplified and played through loudspeakers. Digital recording methods do not store analogous changes in signal energy as lines of magnetic flux on tape. Instead, they convert incoming signal energy into a set of binary representations of the signal, which can then be stored magnetically on tape or may be stored in other computer-based media such as a disk drive or even random-access memory (RAM). Permanently stored binary instructions that may not be overwritten are stored to read-only memory (ROM).

To record signals on either a digital or analog recording system, it is important to consider the level at which these signals will be recorded. The range over which signals may be recorded on either system is termed *dynamic range.* This range extends from the base level of the system—usually termed *noise floor*—to the highest level of recording before saturation and distortion, otherwise known as *clipping.* Analog recording systems use a metering system that will indicate the recording level. In the United States the volume unit (VU) meter is common. This meter displays an optimal signal level at "0" on the meter. The "0" indicates the reference level of the recording device. The area above "0" and before clipping is termed *headroom.* The range between the reference level and the noise floor is the signal-to-noise ratio of the device. On analog recording systems it is important to record signals at a level around the "0" indicator. Too high above "0" will yield distortion. Recording at too low a level below "0" will cause the recording to be marred by system noise. Unlike analog recording systems, digital signal reference places the "0" at the very top of the meter. There is no headroom in a digital system, thus no margin for error. Signals that attempt to go above "0" on the meter are said to be an "over," and they produce extremely harsh digital distortion.

The primary difference between analog and digital recording systems is that while there is some inherent noise in the analog recording process (which we perceive as tape hiss) there is no added hiss in the process of digital audio recording. But there are also drawbacks to the digital recording process. The number of values that may be stored in an analog medium are infinite within the system limitations (noise floor to clipping), while the number of values that may be stored in a digital system is limited to the number of operational bits in the digital word structure. Therefore, analog recording systems are still very popular because they maintain better signal resolution in the recording process.

Tape Recorders

A variety of machines may be used to record the audio that will be synchronized to picture. In the analog domain, there are high-quality portable reel-to-reel machines. The Nagra company makes a professional-quality portable reel-to-reel recorder that is popular for field work. It uses a synchronization tone system so that the audio recorded on the reel may later be synchronized with the film or video. Lately, the portable reel-to-reel machines have been supplanted by newer digital versions. Also popular now are DAT (Digital Audio Tape) machines. Some portable DAT machines even allow the use of time codes for synchronization of recorded audio to picture.

Audio can also be recorded on the audio tracks of the tape in the camera. Professional- and consumer-grade VHS, Hi-8, and Beta SP video cameras allow for audio recording from either a microphone or line level input on the camera itself. Depending upon the type of camera being utilized on the shoot, the audio may be recorded in analog format to linear or hi-fi frequency-modulated (FM) tracks or may be recorded digitally to the videotape.

For film sound mixing, specialized film projectors called dubbers are often used. These projectors use the same system of sprockets for transport in the projector, but use film stock coated with magnetic oxide. Unlike a regular projector, there are no optical lamps on these projectors—they are only used to synchronize the playback of magnetic audio tracks to the edited picture track.

The digital audio workstations used so often in producing the sound tracks for video and film today use the power of the computer and specialized software to handle digital audio. Many of these workstations are used in a manner similar to word processors for audio. They may be used to cut and paste audio where desired and in many cases may be used to create reverb and other audio effects in the digital domain.

One of the benefits to the use of digital audio workstations is the random access capability of the computer system. Once synchronized to picture by using time codes, the digital audio workstation may be used to call up any of the sounds it has stored to digital memory. The random access nature of digital audio workstations also enhances the editing of sounds stored in the memory because many sounds from disk drives can be retrieved simultaneously.

On-Location Sound Recording

In film and video on-location recording, there are two different styles of recording sound to accompany the picture. In many low-budget recording situations, sound is recorded directly to the film or video as it is being shot. This type of recording, termed the single-system recording technique, normally works fine—especially with the improved audio recording possibilities of present-day cameras. But it is not always possible to get the best quality sound when recording the audio directly with the video shot.

Many aspects of the visual element do not necessarily lend themselves well to recording good audio simultaneously. For example, in order to create the illusion of mystery, the video producer may wish to use a fogger or smoke machine. Quite often these machines make a substantial amount of noise that can be picked up by microphones on the camera. Another problem typically encountered is the incidental noise of traffic or airplanes on the set. If the shot to be used in a production is intended to portray a time before these everyday sounds were a reality (say, turn of the century) then the audio picked up on location will give the viewer a false cue about the setting.

When sound first was added to pictures, early Hollywood producers had to come up with ways to prevent the mechanical sound of the film camera from leaking into open microphones. Covering up the camera in thick blankets or pads, called *blimping,* was one method used.

A major benefit to single-system sound is that the audio recorded is always in sync with the recorded video. No matter what edits take place for the finished production, the audio recorded along with the video remains in the same location with regard to picture.

But, obviously, when the video producer is relying entirely upon the sound picked up by the microphone on the camera, single-system audio can be problematic.

The other method of recording sound in the field—called double-system recording—offers more control over the final product. In double-system recording, a separate audio recorder (or recorders) is used to record audio separate from the video or film. This method allows the sound engineer more control over what is being recorded live, on location, or on-set.

The obvious major drawback to double-system recording is that at some point the audio recorded will have to be re-synchronized to the picture. The final, and most critical, mix of audio and picture will not have to take place, however, until post-production—after all of the edit decisions have been made. Until then, synchronization of sound and picture will only have to take place in a "rough" format. This may occur if the producer wishes to determine how well the dialogue was recorded on location in order to decide if additional recording of elements must be scheduled. These rough mixes, called *dailies* or *rushes,* of picture and audio are a normal part of large film productions. Not only are dailies a good method of checking for quality of the sound recorded on the set or on location, they also provide the director with feedback for the emotion captured in the shot and provide assistant directors and editors with visual cues for continuity.

Recording Technology

Post-Production

The post-production stage of film and video production takes place after all of the principal footage has been shot. Post-production processes include editing the footage and the addition of visual effects, along with the processes used to add sound to the finished project. Up to this point, the only sound included in the production will have been some of the onscreen dialogue recorded on the set or on location and some of the natural sound, or "ambiance," also recorded at the time of filming.

In film and video sound track production, there are three main sets of tracks: music, effects, and dialogue. While the dialogue may be the most effective at direct communication, the music and effects, tracks are also extremely important in communicating messages to the viewer. The mixing process for major motion pictures has become so specialized that there are three separate sections of the mixing console and three separate sound engineers during the mix for music, effects, and dialogue. Video production is generally not this specialized—nor as expensive to produce.

Most motion pictures today rely upon post-production of dialogue, which involves lip-synching the original lines of the film in order to get better quality audio than what was recorded during filming. In some cases, a voice other than the actor's may be used. This is the process used to dub foreign language versions of a film. As may be quite obvious, dialogue is most important in the communication of the message in film and video. Before sound films, subtitles were used where language was necessary. Foreign films without translated dialogue may use subtitles as well. But not all of the communication may take place onscreen. Off-screen narration is often used to add more detail and is recorded in a post-production manner.

Finished music tracks are added to the project in post-production. However, music may have been used in the production stage in order to allow filmed action to occur in time with the music, either for rhythmic pacing or for scenes that require action related to music, such as dance numbers. Music videos are a good example of this type of production.

Effects tracks will generally include natural, or "nat," sound, recorded on location to help add sonic realism to the production. Since so much is often going on while the action of filming is taking place, there is usually little that can be done with the original natural sound picked up while the cameras roll. Some directors will go to extremes to try to obtain as natural a sound as possible by using only the original nat sound, but this approach will often get in the way of the rest of the activity taking place on the set. Therefore, just before or after filming is complete on the set, the sound recordist will probably record several minutes of sound on the location. Since this recording has no actual relation to the original action, it is often referred to as "wild" sound. These recordings may later be assembled as loops, either on digital audio workstations or on mag stock for film dubbers. Care must be taken so that the loop of sound does not exhibit a noticeable beginning and end; otherwise the loop will be evident.

Other effects to be added to the project are the traditional sound effects produced by Foley artists, wild sound recording, or come from sound effect libraries on compact disc. The captured sound of a gun firing on the set, for example, will sound fairly weak. Adding an effect to the sound track will enhance the sound of the gun. This practice of sweetening sound effects has been used to such an extent, it has been reported, that when people hear real gunfire they are not as alarmed as they should be, since they have been conditioned by the movies to expect guns to sound "bigger."

Some sounds do not exist in any format and must be created—for example, the sounds of extinct creatures or the sounds of aliens and fictitious environments. The sound designer must be creative with the sound, both to conjure up new sounds from old and to create something believable to the ear.

CONCLUSION

The use of sound affords many possibilities for the visual journalist. This chapter should give you some insight into the importance of the use of sound in visual journalism.

Remember, there are many tools at your disposal, but always trust your brain to attempt to create something that will add meaning to your message.

IDEAS FOR FURTHER STUDY

- Watch a motion picture or a television news report without the sound. What do you miss? What do you gain?
- Watch a silent movie from the early history of motion pictures. How did the producers include the hint of audio even though their presentations were completely visual?
- More and more Web site producers are making presentations that are sensitive to the needs of the deaf community and other individuals with accessibility concerns. Can you think how you could create presentations so that a deaf person would be able to use and enjoy your video and other Web site work?

Sound Advice: Creating Great Audio—on a Budget

by Lisa Horan, Freelance Writer specializing in
the television, film, and video industries

It can elicit bursts of laughter, cause that stinging lump of sadness in your throat, or make the hairs on the back of your neck rise as danger looms. Audio: it is that all-powerful element that professionals often obsess over, for even the lay audience can detect poor sound. And, despite the amount of eye candy offered throughout the program, if it's out of sync, it's over.

"Sound is like a back door to emotional responses that video does not otherwise have," says Kennedy Wright, a master sound designer and the owner of Kennedy Sound. According to Wright, even more so than a visual image, sound can create different moods—whether tense, nostalgic, or mysterious—and serve as a short path to emotional response.

But does perfect audio come with a price? Although many editors may think that achieving awesome audio is out of their grasp, there are some secrets to creating great sound on a small budget. Several Avid editors and audio professionals shed some light on simple, cost-saving techniques to streamline the audio process and meet tight budget restrictions without sacrificing sound quality.

Sounding It Out: Preparing a Piece for an Audio Mixer

Generally speaking, it's more costly for a project to be sent to an outside audio facility for sound design and mixing than it is for an editor to complete the piece himself. Often, however, the intricacies of a piece require the expertise of an audio professional. In this case, there are several steps the Avid editor can take to prepare a piece for the most economical use of an outside audio facility. Perhaps the most important step is also the simplest: planning.

"One of the first things I do if a piece I'm working on will ultimately go to another environment for final audio is to call the mixer who will be finishing it," says Martin Nelson, an Emmy Award–winning freelance Avid editor. Nelson says he asks questions like, "What elements would you like me to include?" "What can I do to facilitate the process for you?" and "How would you like the sound configured?" By asking these types of questions, says Nelson, "not only do I look good in the eyes of the producer and audio technician, but I can save a lot of time—not to mention headaches—in the long run."

This article originally appeared on the AvidProNet.com(TM) Web site. To access the article online, visit http://www.avidpronet.com/zine/stories/200009_soundadvice/index.html.

Sal Chandon, an audio mixer and the general manager of Phoenix, Maryland–based Sheffield Audio, echoes Nelson's emphasis on planning. He says it's wise to establish beforehand what parts of the project the editor and sound technician will be responsible for, and to plan the steps to complete the process accordingly.

Among the most important reasons for planning is that every audio professional is going to have a different setup and require a different set of criteria. One criterion that should be considered early on is the audio sample rate the audio facility is working in. For instance, if the facility is designed to accept 48 kHz and a piece of audio is submitted in 44.1 kHz, the picture and audio will most likely be out of sync. "Although there are conversion processes available, they can be a huge hassle, so I always find out which format the sound person is working with and make sure to export the sample audio at the proper rate," says writer/producer/director and Avid editor Matt Borten. He also recommends doing a test with the facility to make sure they can read the audio output correctly.

Another time-saving tip is to recommend that producers allow time in the schedule for the editor to complete some of the track work. In so doing, the final audio session is more likely to go smoother and faster. "It's good policy to split out the tracks so the sound technician will have an easier time working with a piece," says Nelson. "For example, I'll put narration on channel 1, voiceovers on 2, ambient sound on 3, sound effects on 4, and so on, so the tracks will be very clean and there will be

less of a chance for surprises." This step can shave hours, hence dollars, off the time the audio professional will have to spend on the project.

According to both editors and audio professionals, a number of features built into Avid® editing systems can also expedite the process. Avid-developed Open Media Framework Interchange®, often abbreviated as OMF® or OMFI, is one example. Karl Kalbaugh, a veteran sound designer and audio mixer currently with Washington, D.C.–based audio post house Park Group, says OMF Interchange is the "single biggest time saver in the audio mixing process."

"Most current digital audio workstations accept OMFI. And for larger projects, like documentaries, it can save as much as a day or two in auto conforming audio sources," Kalbaugh says. In fact, Nelson considers it a job requirement to set up OMF Interchange properly so that the next person in the process can handle the audio he's laid down. As a backup to OMF Interchange, Kalbaugh suggests editors also supply edit decision lists (EDLs) on both disk and paper. "EDLs can be the saving grace," if a problem should arise, he says. Resolving time code issues before sending a piece to another environment for audio post is another crucial step. "While it is not going to be a factor in every scenario, if you're dealing with soundtracks that need to be sweetened, synchronization issues are going to become real," says Sheffield Audio's Chandon. For that reason, "It's crucial that the editor pay attention to detail in terms of the time code used in these situations to eliminate as much guesswork and confusion as possible on the part of the sound technician." While the Avid Media Composer® system has a built-in feature called Sync Break that alerts the editor to how far the audio and video are out of sync, sync issues are sometimes irreparable. "If a piece is film-originated and synchronization is not perfectly achieved during the transfer to tape process, once the tape has been digitized into the Avid in low resolution, it is difficult—sometimes impossible—for the editor to detect, since the image is soft," explains Nelson.

Another surprising economical solution for some situations is to send the audio to an audio facility early in the process. For example, Borten annually produces a group of separate video productions for Discovery Communications (owner and operator of the Discovery Channel) that are all presented on the same day at a high-profile, live event. Once he's got the time line locked on each of the programs, he sends the audio to an outside facility for final mixing, while he adds effects, layers, and other elements to the video. "These programs often take an audio facility a few days to complete, especially if there's an elaborate mix involved. So by the time the final mix is complete, I'm finished tweaking the picture and I can either take the finished audio, put it back into the Avid, marry everything, and pump it out or send the finished video output to the audio facility for them to marry everything there," explains Borten. This is a great way to work if you know you're not changing your time line, Borten says, because it lets you maximize your productivity. "It's just another example of how Avid expedites the whole postproduction process."

No matter which approach you take, you should keep in mind that "once two elements are mixed together—like music and voice—they're married forever," warns Chandon. The Park Group's Kalbaugh, who generally works with editors who work on Avid Media Composer 9000s, cautions editors and producers against assuming that everything can be fixed in post. He says that "fixing it in the mix" really means one of three things: replacing it, augmenting it, or covering it up. "Getting it right on location is far less expensive than 'fixing it in post,'" says Kalbaugh.

Hitting Your Own High Note: Tips for Avid-Generated Sound

In many cases, the Avid editor is solely responsible for sweetening and completing the final mix for a project. Whether a result of budget restrictions or a personal choice (Borten says as many as half of all video projects can effectively use audio from the Avid), editors are at an advantage right from the start. "Because of our close interaction with a project, the editor is arguably the person who knows a show best in its final stages," contends Nelson. That being said, the average editor is usually not primarily a sound designer or mixer. This fact has not been overlooked by Avid, as is evidenced by the various built-in features geared to help editors accomplish sound design and the final mix on the editing side.

Avid's waveform display in the time line, for instance, provides a graphical depiction of the sound, which allows editors to see peaks and valleys in the recordings. In a recent audio session recorded on DAT via an ISDN feed from New York, Borten used the "best" audio takes and used the waveform display to visually track the sound. "The wave table allowed me to find the exact point the narrator's sentence ended so I could remove pops, breaths, et cetera," explains Borten. "By doing this, I was able to create a very clean track that is similar to what would be created if the piece had gone to an audio suite, but for a lot less cost."

Editors also have the ability to equalize tracks using Avid software. "The software allows me to make sure the levels are nice and crisp when I take it back to tape," says Borten, who sometimes does the EQ entirely in the Avid editing system as opposed to an external mixing board. Avid plug-ins, like Digidesign® AudioSuite™ software, are also useful. Nelson says he uses the technology in instances where it is necessary to speed up or slow narration.

Another tool Avid editors have at their fingertips when working in Media Composer or Symphony™ systems is what is referred to as rubber-banding. "I can look at the time line for a piece on the Media Composer and see where the narration comes in and the background audio needs to dip down, and then come back up when the narration is through," explains Nelson. "The rubber-banding tool allows me to expand the portion of the time line that shows me the audio I want to dip down and allows me to put marks where I want it to start to dip, start to climb back up, and be all the way up—much like tugging on a rubber band." The tool is simple for editors to use, and it provides for smooth, elegant audio shifts.

When it comes to the incorporation of music, audio scrubbing is a useful technique that allows the editor to go frame by frame and hear exactly what each frame represents. "I can listen for exactly when the drum beat is coming in, which helps me figure out how to loop the music or a good place to create a natural cut," explains Nelson. In addition, the Media Composer series contains locators, which are beneficial in pieces that are particularly cut to music in that they allow an editor to mark out the beats as they listen. "One of the great aspects about locators is that they let me map out a piece of music on the fly—every time I hear a beat, I can tap a key, which creates a dot on my time line, and then I can go to each of those locators and put in my next edit of picture," says Nelson.

Speaking of Music

Music often serves as a final touch, but incorporating music can also be an expensive proposition. Library music, usually less costly than original music, is often the solution, though some believe it can compromise the originality of a piece. Choosing from a large library is one way to get around this. According to Nelson, one of the benefits of library music is that it is usually composed in such a way that it can be manipulated and adjusted to fit the piece of video. For instance, it may contain several repetitive bars that can be made shorter or longer depending on the situation.

Kalbaugh's take on stock music is slightly different. He says scoring a one-hour show from a music library can easily add days to the sound design process. "One of the first concerns with library music is finding a cut of music that has the right tone and flavor for a given scene. The second concern is editing the music to time and picture," explains Kalbaugh. These factors, coupled with the average cost of a "laser drop" (single use of any cut) of library music can add up quickly—in many cases to anywhere between $6,000 and $10,000. Kalbaugh points out that this figure excludes costs associated with selection and editing time for a one-hour show.

If you're editing a piece that will serve as a promotion for a program already produced, you may be able to bypass both avenues altogether. Borten says he was able to save nearly $1,000 by regenerating music and sound effects from a Discovery Channel documentary to create two promotional pieces for a travel-ing museum exhibit based on the program. "In addition to capturing natural sound during a live shoot, I was able to take the split tracks of sound effects and music from the DA88 audio master of the original two-hour program, which had separate audio elements on individual tracks, then edit those tracks appropriately."

Whether you're preparing a piece for an outside audio facility to complete or are doing the sound design and final mix yourself, there is one general rule of thumb: The caliber of the final audio is a product of the quality of the audio that was originally recorded. Sometimes even the most gifted editor can't change that. ■

CHAPTER 14

Interactive Multimedia

by Marc J. Barr
Middle Tennessee State University

Increasingly, the visual journalist will be required to produce data, both still and moving images, to be used in an interactive environment. Instead of being viewed on paper in a traditional newspaper or magazine, these presentations are viewed on a monitor and delivered by way of the Internet or disk-based materials.

Three examples of the uses of these materials are CNN (www.cnn.com), which has in addition to its cable TV networks its Web site CNN Interactive. Another is the joint venture between Microsoft and NBC, MSNBC (www.msnbc.com), which delivers its materials also both by cable and the Internet. The third example is the Weather Channel (www.weather.com), which also maintains an extensive Web site. All of their Web sites have available text, still images, audio, and video clips.

Other examples that have developed from traditional print formats are *The San Jose Mercury*, the *New York Times*, the *Chicago Tribune*, and many Knight Ridder and Gannett Publications.

If you were to ask a dozen people what the term "interactive multimedia" means, you would probably get a dozen different answers. Although currently associated with the computer, the term has much deeper roots. The merger of images, text, and sound has occurred in many different forms over many years. In this chapter, we will consider what a visual journalist needs to know in order to produce moving images with audio for television and interactive multimedia, whether stand-alone or networked.

Traditional methods of communicating pictures, words, and sounds have always been one-way, from the message to the viewer. The challenge for visual journalists is to create an environment that is conducive to two-way communication that allows the user to interact with the message.

There are many aspects to consider when planning to develop this type of product. For example:

- What is the nature of the information that you wish to present?
- What will the presentation be used for—news, training for industry, or self-paced education?
- Which qualities of the experience (information, impressions, and so on) would the audience gain immediately, and which do they take away with them?
- Is this for public or private purposes?

Project Creation and Development

Depending on the level and type of interactivity the visual journalist may want the user to experience, visual message can be developed in a number of ways. There are many products that, using a card or page metaphor, enable the user to look at images, video, text, and hear sounds with the click of a mouse. The data for these products could reside on a disk drive or on a CD. Another means is through links on a Web page where the data would reside on a Web server.

Design, Delivery, and Display Parameters

What type of computer are they going to present it on? Although the ability to create products that run successfully on multiple platforms is improving, there are still differences in operating systems and a vast range of configurations.

Christopher R. Harris

Collaboration on multimedia projects often leads to better problem solving.

Tools for Multimedia

How mature is your audience and what level of knowledge do they have, either regarding your content, or the method of interaction? The design of the product, its interface and what it contains can be different.

A person who is preparing visual materials must take into consideration what the final size of the image will be. Anyone who has viewed a movie in the theatre and then watched it again on his or her home television knows that the size format can make a tremendous difference in the impact that image makes.

Tools for Multimedia

The visual information that you are presenting can be developed from mathematical data or from images. For image capture, the visual journalist can choose between traditional film, videotape, or digital means to record, store, and play back images. Multimedia presentations may contain single or combinations of visual information. The reporter will decide what would be appropriate for each situation.

There are many differences in the qualities of visual information delivered on paper and on a monitor. Some of these are the difference in the size of the image, the range in the number of colors visible, and the resolution of the viewing screen.

Image quality is subjective. This aspect is particularly frustrating when you are trying to decide how to balance image quality requirements with storage needs and delivery. Some types of picture compression methods have difficulty handling lots of fast motion with detailed backgrounds, areas of highly contrasting light intensity, and two-dimensional animation sequences. Fortunately, various types of digital filtering techniques can be employed to hide these problems.

Image composition requires planning for the smaller viewing area of a Web page or other type of desktop presentation.

The type of camera, film, tape, or digital equipment selected will make a difference to the final product. Although there has been rapid advancement in the types and quality of digital camera equipment available, images shot on film or videotape will generally be of a higher quality than those shot with the current range of digital cameras. However, film and video pictures must be digitized in order to be used with a computer. It is also very important to realize that the scanners and digitizers used vary greatly in their quality.

Photography, with a film-based camera, provides far greater resolution possibilities than today's digital cameras. If you use a film-based camera you must decide the degree of resolution of the scanned image. The greater resolution you select, the

Multimedia classes often use multiple software programs to meet their needs.

Christopher R. Harris

larger the file size, which proportionately increases storage, downloading time, and the viewing machine RAM requirements.

Videographic techniques must also be adapted for these new methods of delivery. Compared to other types of data files, digitized video files are enormous. Digitized movies of the two-hour variety, for example, even in highly compressed form, still require a billion or more bytes of data each. In noncompressed form these files are impractical to store and time consuming to transfer.

One popular format for compressed video is MPEG. MPEG is an acronym for Moving Picture Experts Group, which commonly refers to the international standard for digital video and audio compression. MPEG is a collection of tools for compressing audio and video.

There are two types of MPEG files, MPEG-1 and MPEG-2. They are not competitors to one another, and MPEG-2 is not an improved version of MPEG-1. MPEG-1 was designed for delivering video from a single-speed CD-ROM drive.

MPEG-2 is a completely different standard from MPEG-1 and is designed for different purposes. MPEG-2 is specifically targeted at digital transmission or broadcast of video signals and supports a much wider range of resolutions and bit rates than the MPEG-1 standard. MPEG-2 has been chosen as the standard on which high-definition TV (HDTV) systems will be based.

When planning to capture images that will be compressed digitally, it is wise to anticipate some of the potential problems that can lead to degraded image quality and delivery problems.

Video of fast-moving highly detailed sequences, and sequences with high contrasts in lighting, can result in a type of blockiness in the final images. Diagonal lines can display jagged edges called "aliasing." Images may appear as though your monitor is dirty, with little gray or white flecks that intrude randomly throughout the picture. Low-quality video or bad digitizing can result in poor image quality. The outlines of moving objects may appear to have a halo or other area of distortion.

Video should be captured in a component format if possible. Converting video to or from a composite format at any time during production or post-production will have an irreversible quality loss and can introduce image artifacts. High-quality video is often less "noisy." Compressors such as MPEG cannot distinguish between moving video and "noise," so it will attempt to encode the noise, taking bits and quality away from your moving video.

When combining words with images, small serif family typefaces should be avoided because they are hard to read on most screens. Try to use sans serif family typefaces as large as possible. (See Chapter 9 for a more detailed discussion of typefaces).

Christopher R. Harris

Digital animation programs allow the user to construct images for use in multimedia projects.

Animation should have a medium amount of detail and lines that are several pixels thick. Computer-rendered animation with extremely fine lines (less than three pixels) and extremely fine details tend to "disappear" due to MPEG's lower resolutions.

Use tightly focused close-ups and avoid using fast-moving video where background and foreground are both highly detailed and in focus. When the background and foreground are both in focus, this technique can lead to blockiness or "pixelization."

Do not use close-up shots of talking heads that are too small. When people talk on the screen the viewer's focus is drawn to the mouth. If the mouth is too small, it will not be clear and will not look correct.

Use computer or hand-drawn animation, but do not use computer or hand-drawn animation with sharp diagonal or vertical lines. This technique can lead to aliasing, which makes smooth lines look like stairsteps.

Use scene changes and relatively quick cuts, but do not use extremely fast scene changes that take less than two frames or rapidly blinking or flashing areas. Rapidly blinking screens and rapid scene changes are difficult for MPEG encoders to handle. Encoders need to work over multiple frames in order to achieve optimal compression.

Tools for Multimedia

Use video with contrast but do not use very high contrasts in luminance, as this can lead to blockiness. Use video with lots of colors and avoid using monochrome scenes.

Depending on the types of materials that you wish to include in your production, various types of files will need to be created. Images that began with a camera will then be manipulated using techniques that emulate traditional darkroom methods. Video images and sound also are edited digitally in a manner that also emulates traditional methods.

Interactive Multimedia Programs

Interactive multimedia programs for meeting interactive challenges a visual journalist may face can be divided into two broad categories: function-based and picture-based software solutions. Function-based software includes, for example, the presentation programs PowerPoint and Persuasion, the interactive programs HyperCard and Director, and the networked interactive multimedia products using the HTML (Hypertext Markup Language) convention. Picture-based interactive multimedia programs are designed for the user to be able to interact with still and moving images. These programs include QuickTime VR, IPIX (formerly known as Photobubbles), Surround Video, Digital Photogrammetry, and VRML. As a visual journalist responsible for the production of an interactive multimedia production, you must decide on the best software solutions for your particular communications assignment.

Function-Based Programs

PowerPoint and Persuasion are popular presentation graphics programs that can be used on stand-alone (not networked) computers to aid users during a speech or to learn about a particular product or service. As more people become aware of what the computer can accomplish, it is expected that the colored markers and poster boards used for traditional presentations will give way to portable computers linked to an overhead projection system. Whether for business summaries or classroom discussion, presentation graphics is an extremely fast-growing field for visual journalists.

HyperCard and Macromedia Director are two popular sophisticated software programs that can be used to create elaborate interactive materials—from motion pictures to CD books and mystery games. One of the most popular CD games,

Myst, was created using the Director program. Presentations created with these programs can be saved on magnetic disk or CD laser discs if the number of images (both still and moving) and audio clips is extensive. Users move their mouse to look at additional information by clicking buttons or hypertext (the term for underlined or colored words that indicate links to other parts of the program).

When interactive multimedia programs are presented on computer networks using the World Wide Web, users have a great deal of individual flexibility to seek as much information about a topic as they want. Several years ago writers using word processing programs needed to know the commands for changing the size or attribute of a typeface. Today, authors can easily highlight text and click on a button to make changes. Likewise, in the early days (1996) of networked interactive multimedia production visual journalists needed to know the commands necessary to create homepages and other files for the World Wide Web (see Chapter 16 for an example). Today there are several software products that make homepage creation as simple as word processing. Some of the more popular programs are DreamWeaver, HotDog, FrontPage, and PageMill. In addition, the word processing programs of WordPerfect and Microsoft Word contain format options that allow homepage creation. Unlike word processing programs, however, a visual journalist serious about the graphic look of her homepage file must still be familiar with HTML programming in order to customize a homepage to a specific communications need.

Picture-Based Programs

Some developing methods of creating and delivering interactive visual information are through the use of QuickTime VR (Virtual Reality), IPIX, Surround Video, Digital Photogrammetry, and VRML (Virtual Reality Modeling Language).

Virtual Reality (VR) describes a range of experiences that enable a person to interact in the illusion of a three-dimensional environment through a computer. These environments can be developed with images from film or tape, and from simple or complex computer models. VR applications usually require specialized hardware or accessories, such as high-end graphics workstations, stereo displays, 3-D goggles, or gloves.

QuickTime VR

QuickTime VR is system software that allows users to experience these kinds of spatial interactions using only a personal computer, without any of the specialized equipment commonly used. Through the use of 360-degree panoramic photography, it enables these interactions using film and video images, along with computer simulations. They can be viewed on any computer capable of supporting the Apple QuickTime standard.

For the recording of scenes, QuickTime VR uses 360-degree panoramic photography. For rendered scene representations, standard commercial packages for 2D and 3D graphics and animation can be used.

The panoramic photograph represents the view one would see by standing in a single spot and turning full circle. The QuickTime VR authoring tools allow the scene to be captured using a standard camera to take a series of adjacent photographs. The use of readily available cameras allows for complete exposure control over the 360-degree view. The ability to use standard cameras also enables the photographer to use any available lenses, filters, and many other traditional photographic accessories. The number of panoramic photographs taken for a particular scene will depend on the type of experience the content developer wants to provide to the end-user. A larger number of images within a space will result in smoother transitions within that space but the tradeoff will occur in a larger number of files.

These images are brought into software that "stitches" them together into a single panoramic view. There are painting and rendering packages that can also create images representing a panoramic view or a series of images that together create the overall view. For the representation of computer-generated objects, images of the object must be rendered from all the points of view that you want to enable the end-user to experience.

As the user changes his point of view of a scene in real time, correct perspective is always maintained, creating the effect of actually looking around.

IPIX

IPIX images are spherical photographs that capture the entire contents of any location in 180- or 360-degree images that can be reproduced for viewing on a computer or TV display. This technique allows the user to be immersed inside a 360-degree digital image representing anything that can be photographed. The user is able to navigate in any desired direction in the photograph, magnifying or moving to any part of the image.

These images can be taken with a standard 35mm camera attached to a fisheye lens. The film is processed traditionally and electronically scanned to create a digital file. The digitized images are then processed to remove distortion and correct the perspective for viewing. A single fisheye shot can capture a hemisphere (180 degrees) or a sphere (360 degrees) can be created from two opposing shots.

Differences Between QuickTimeVR and IPIX Images

There are some similarities to the Apple product in that both use photographs and computers in the creation of an interactive environment. The main differences are found in the manner in which the data are captured and displayed. A QuickTime VR scene requires between eight and twenty-four photographs that must be captured and stitched together. The IPIX image can be created from one shot to provide 180- or 220-degree viewing or two shots captured in opposite directions to generate a 360-degree view. The data that are captured in the QuickTime VR scene are cylindrically shaped in form, having no "top" or "bottom," with vertical boundaries to the scene. The IPIX image is captured in its entirety, with the resulting image having no boundaries. With both products, the user has interactive control over the part of the picture to be viewed.

Surround Video

Surround Video is a collection of tools that developers can use to add 360-degree panoramic images to an application as well as Internet control to allow the use of Surround Video images in HTML documents or Web pages. It supports the use of progressive rendering, image Hotspots with URL links, and development of Internet and native multimedia titles.

Central to Surround Video technology is its ability to manage 360-degree photographic images, typically photographed with a panoramic camera. Panoramic images have a drawback in that they show the proper perspective only when viewed as a cylinder. When flattened out, features that would normally be seen as straight lines become warped. The development software corrects the problem of image distortion when it is projected onto a flat surface. The effect to the user is similar to panning through a camera's viewfinder.

Surround Video images are taken with a 360-degree, or panoramic, camera. The geometry of a panoramic camera is significantly different than a normal camera in that all points along the length of the film are equidistant from the camera's focal point at the time of exposure. This, in effect, creates a cylindrical image that only appears correct when viewed from the exact center of the cylinder. When the film is "unrolled" onto a flat surface, such as a monitor, the image shows very noticeable distortion. Surround Video compensates for this by mathematically projecting a portion of the cylindrical image (typically, about 70 degrees) onto a flat surface. The resulting image is the same as if it were taken with a normal camera.

The Surround Video Editor (SVEdit) is used to create Surround Video images, which usually start off as elongated graphic files that are the result of scanning a panoramic photograph. The SVEdit is used first to crop the left and right edges of the photograph to produce a seamless image. The horizontal center of the image is then established. The final image is then saved in a compressed format, to produce the completed Surround Video image.

The resultant Surround Video image consists of a series of vertical stripes that make up the complete image. Any stripe can be loaded independently, so only the visible portion of the image needs to be furnished before the current view is rendered.

Digital Photogrammetry

Photogrammetry has long been used to map the surface of the earth from aircraft and, more recently, from satellites. Since the early 1970s the cameras and mathematics have been adapted to perform close-range or industrial photogrammetry. Virtually everything visible on the photographic image can be measured and modeled in a 3-D CAD file.

Photogrammetry and remote sensing are the art, science, and technology of obtaining reliable information from noncontact imaging and other sensor systems around the earth, the environment, and other physical objects and processes through recording, measuring, analyzing, and representation.

The term *photogrammetry* was first used in 1867 when photography was still in its infancy. Over the last 80 years the principal application of photogrammetry has been the compilation of maps from aerial photographs. During the most recent decade, photogrammetry and remote sensing have provided the primary source data for geographic information systems. There has been in addition a continuing development of applications of photogrammetric techniques to many fields—engineering, architecture, archeology, medicine, industrial quality control, and robotics.

Photos may be taken with a digital camera or with a conventional film camera and then scanned into digital form by a high-resolution digital scanner. Images are brought up on a computer screen and a 3-D CAD model can be constructed directly onto the digital image.

The process is quick and the models produced can be exported in DXF format for input into most CAD, animation, and rendering programs. This method can be used by animators, archeologists, architects, and engineers to produce models of terrain, structures, human anatomy, and machines.

VRML

VRML is an acronym for Virtual Reality Modeling Language. Early in its history, the M stood for "Markup," as with HTML (HyperText Markup Language), used for Web page production. There are two versions of VRML 1.0 and 2.0, and each is defined by a specification. A VRML file resides on a Web site just like an HTML file. It is currently also a plain or compressed text file, and its name generally ends in ".wrl," "wrl.gz," or ".wrz." The contents of this file (plus whatever files it might load in via "inline" statements) are called a "world." The standards to which these files are created are platform independent—that is, they can be used on any type of computer.

These worlds can be designed to contain the 3-D representations of any type of object. They appear with material surfaces and are lighted. A user can navigate her way through the world through an interface resembling the dashboard of a car.

In order to view these files you can use software like Netscape 4.X, which has a VRML browser (Live3D) built in and pre-installed, or there are a number of stand-alone VRML browsers, VRML browser helper applications, or VRML plug-ins.

Although a text editor alone is all that is necessary for creating VRML files, the use of a modeler will make the process easier by using a 3-D visual interface instead of typing commands and numbers. These worlds are then integrated into the design of a Web site by embedding, either in a frame or in a Web page.

Although VRML is not commonly used as part of the news-gathering and presentation process, it is being used in a variety of scientific and mathematical visualization applications. The current exception to this is in the area of weather forecasting.

It is also used in several related areas:

- Architecture and engineering for interactive models of projects.
- Many online magazines include articles and embedded examples on VRML.
- Forensic investigators in court accident defense and prosecution regularly use 3-D graphics to explain actions. VRML is a logical extension of this use.
- Many television news departments now use 3-D terrains to show weather activity.
- Any numerical data, such as voting results or market reports, may also be displayed in a similar manner.

In many situations VRML can be used to visually communicate information that is beyond the capabilities of traditional methods. Using satellite data to create

DEM's (Digital Elevation Maps), three-dimensional surface maps can then be created to illustrate the landform, movements of persons, or objects such as military vehicles.

Doing these complex simulations of events is labor- and computationally intensive. In its current level of development, it is unlikely that more complicated worlds can be created within the short deadlines needed for timely news production.

Publications with longer production cycles, such as online magazines and books, and traditional publications with supplemental disks and CDs are using complex 3-D visualizations and simulations for illustrations. Physics, science, and engineering areas are using interactive materials to explain concepts, principles, and phenomena. Historians can use animation to show the movement of troops, armament, and refugees. The use of a 3-D terrain in such a simulation will help to illustrate how an event develops and can give users a greater sense of context and involvement.

CONCLUSION

The end-user will no longer be limited to a particular view or perspective but will be able to move from a global to a local view and be at any location throughout the entire world. With such programming options, combined with still and moving images and with text and audio, a visual journalist can create messages that make the world an interactive place for users.

IDEAS FOR FURTHER STUDY

- What are some of the aspects to consider when planning to develop visual content?
- What are some of the aspects to consider regarding the design, delivery, and display of multimedia content?
- What are some of the differences and similarities between the various graphics file formats?
- What are some of the ways video can be delivered over the Internet?
- What are some of the considerations necessary to consider when preparing video content for the Internet?

Interactive Multimedia Turn Readers, Viewers, and Users into Learners

by Paul Martin Lester

As part of a sabbatical leave from my university, I made a month-long, 4,500-mile drive that took me north to San Francisco, northeast to a visual literacy conference in Cheyenne, Wyoming, northwest to Montana, west to Seattle, and back home again.

There are many words to say and pictures to describe this trip, but I wanted to share three stories that have demonstrated to me that we all need to think more carefully about how we create and use interactive multimedia on the World Wide Web.

Colonel "Buffalo Bill" Cody helped found the town named in his honor at the foothills of Yellowstone National Park. After I checked into his hotel named "The Irma" after his daughter and built in 1902, I sat around the little bar that faces the main street in town. It was Sunday and the Indianapolis Colts were winning on TV.

To my right was a rancher and to my left was an older man who worked for the state. Next to him was a jeweler who worked exclusively in gold. I imagined that such professional demographics, along with a schoolteacher from California, would have easily been common in this bar at the turn of the last century.

"Are you a hunter?" one asked. "Sort of," I replied vaguely. When I told them who I was and what I did, I happened to mention a topic that stopped all conversation at the bar. Their

eyes got wide. They turned down the TV set. They all wanted to know everything I knew about this subject.

In this smoky little bar in this isolated little town, we were planning how my students in Fullerton could set up interactive Web pages for these guys in Wyoming.

Another stop along my sabbatical route was to be a guest of Microsoft's MSNBC.com online news network and to have long conversations with Brian Storm. No need to explain interactive multimedia to Brian, since he's the director of multimedia, responsible for audio, video, and photography. Brian introduced me to multimedia (not picture) editor Robert Hood. The workstation looked like any picture desk in any newspaper.

Robert's main job was to find pictures for stories from a variety of sources and crop and fit them into pages. Only these pages were online frames and sometimes the images came from moving video and included audio. Storm, an online news zealot in the best possible sense of the word, explained how still photographers need to learn moving image production and editing. Multimedia editors need to look at moving image coverage that tells stories, doesn't shake, and includes clear, crisp audio. From that stock, a still picture will be selected to stand with the story.

And for me, that was a key—the single, still moment is by far the best way for a reader, viewer, or user to be introduced to an online news story. But it made me a little uneasy that this new, so-called revolutionary medium looked so much like a printed newspaper with occasional attributes from television.

I took that queasiness with me to a brown bag meeting of graduate students and faculty members at the School of Journalism at the University of Oregon. Our hour-long discussion quickly focused on one question: How can the interactive multimedia on the World Wide Web be truly revolutionary when we use the same terms to describe newspapers and television?

One answer, I think, is that other media have a longer history that gives us time to analyze their social importance. Although newspapers have been around since the late sixteenth century and television has been with us for about three generations, we're still arguing about their social impact. The Web came to the average user in 1994—not even a hint of a blink of the eye. No wonder we are still dazzled and a little fearful of the medium's sleight-of-hand tricks.

Another answer is that it is enormously difficult to create a brand new way of presenting words and pictures that doesn't use the lessons learned from past media and that readers or viewers are comfortable with using.

But on this trip around a little corner of the world, I learned that such creativity is vital simply because with all the opportunities on the Web using interactive multimedia, and all the competition, there is no way any single online newspaper will be successful.

With so many international sources available to Web users for news, for example, why would anyone go to one particular site? I can read about a California earthquake from an online version of the *Los Angeles Times*, the Dallas Cowboys from the *Dallas Morning News* online, and the troubles in Northern Ireland from the online version of the *Belfast Telegraph*. Wouldn't the local perspective give me much more information than a generalized compilation of sources? Yes, most of the time.

It used to be thought that interactive multimedia would turn passive readers and couch-potato viewers into active users. And that is true. But more importantly for the future growth of this new medium, we must think of those who use the Web as learners. We must somehow come up with ways to present news stories with words—both written and heard—and with pictures—both still and moving—that help learning. A compelling, thought-provoking, and mind-expanding display of information will be entertaining and educational to online learners and will assure that they return to your Web site for more.

If we create new ways to tell old stories with interactive multimedia, cowboys in a Cody bar will already be on the Web, the MSNBC.com news service will be the most popular source of information in the world, and theories and analysis of the new medium will come from graduate students and faculty members. With such synergy, we will begin to use new terms and ideas that will help shape the future of communication for all of us. ■

Using Computers

The two chapters in this section explain how you can use a computer for researching and processing. Chapter 15 describes how to link with databases around the world to find information in the library and through various online services, including Lexis/Nexis, e-mail, and the World Wide Web. This skill is useful for researching story ideas and procedures used by visual journalists to complete those stories. Chapter 16 describes basic computer operations handy for visual journalists to know and explains the use, meaning, and production of computer-based images for print and screen media. Chapter 16 also outlines the workstation and software requirements of today's visual journalism.

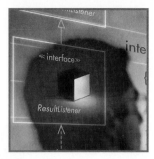

CHAPTER 15

Internet Research

by Robert Spires
Middle Tennessee State University

The existence of the Internet in its current configuration gives visual journalists access to a research resource unprecedented in the history of journalism. The Internet bridges the distances of geography, politics, economics, interpersonal communication, and business and government functions by linking reporters to sources of data and information, enabling them to achieve higher levels of reportage with more accuracy and depth and with increased timeliness and less expense than has heretofore been possible.

Empowerment and access come with a caveat, however: There are a growing number of examples that illustrate that not all this universe of content, so easily accessed with a few mouse clicks or keystrokes, is what it appears to be. Empowerment is a two-edged sword. The same power is given those who would deceive, by manipulating and distorting content, as it is to those who would post legitimate sources of honest and accurate information. All facts and images on the Internet may appear at first blush to be honest, reliable, and accurate. But everything may not be as it seems. As the history of

One of the stumbling blocks to successful Internet research is finding where something you are looking for is stored.

Will Crocker

Internet fraud, misinformation, and deception continues to be written, reporters who do not follow long-established tenets of news gathering and fact checking can easily find themselves victims of content that appears legitimate, but is in reality far removed from the principles of balance, objectivity, and fairness.

This chapter discusses the Internet as a research tool for visual journalists. The discussion is based on the assumption that research and the gathering of information, whether in images or words, follow identical and time-tested methodologies. Although a new medium, the principles behind gathering useful, accurate, and reliable information are the same throughout the modern history of journalism. Following the discussion, two case studies illustrate the process of using the Internet as a research tool for visual journalists.

A Brief History of the Internet

The roots of today's Internet are buried in the soil of the Cold War. The former Soviet Union's launch of Sputnik caused the U.S. military establishment to reexamine many of its strategic plans and capabilities. The Department of Defense created the "Advanced Research Projects Agency" (ARPA) in 1957 to reestablish the United States as the leader in military science and technology. In searching for ways to share the computing power of various universities and agencies, the theoretical and practical aspects of computer networking were studied and subsequently created. The ARPANET, forerunner of the Internet, grew from this work and was first demonstrated in 1969. Interest in this new form of communication was tremendous, and the technological improvements to make the ARPANET transmit more information faster and with greater reliability were developed and implemented almost monthly. The international computing community also became interested and involved in network communication technology, and the first international consortium, the International Network Working Group, was formed in 1972.

Throughout the 1970s more countries, agencies, and universities began to use computer networks for nonmilitary uses, such as the sharing of traditional academic research and information, and by the early 1980s file transfers and e-mail were common practices among these users. Closely coinciding with the increasing popularity of the home computer, the public's awareness of the Internet began to grow in the mid- to late 1980s. Many processes and procedures now taken for granted were developed and implemented during these formative years. By today's standards they were cumbersome to the average computer user. With the development of more user-friendly tools and services such as BITNET (Because It's Time NETwork), TELNET, and USENET, accessing data sites and the transfer of information between these sites were simplified for both home and business users.

The number of host sites reached 1,000 in 1984, and the Domain Name System (DNS) was introduced. By 1989, the number of hosts reached 100,000. The ARPANET celebrated its twentieth birthday in 1989, and went out of existence the following year. In 1992, with the development of the World Wide Web (WWW) and even more user-friendly "browsers" such as MOSAIC, the Internet's usage among the public exploded, proliferating at an estimated 300,000 percent growth rate during the early 1990s.

"Surfing the Internet," a term coined in 1992 by Jean Armour Polly, became a pop cultural buzzword practically overnight. Along with this explosion of users came an ever-increasing number of hosts and Web sites that could be accessed.

The U.S. government recognized the growing importance of the Internet as a commercial and communication tool with the passage of the National Information Infrastructure Act of 1993. Society came to the realization that the Internet could be an empowering form of communication, and that any entity or person with something to say and the money to make that statement available on a data server could become a sender of messages, a Web site. This phenomenon caused fundamental changes in the ways both interpersonal and mediated communication is studied and practiced in this society.

The Internet also proved to be a convenient conveyer of images of all types. Scanned images and digital camera images (both still and video) included on Web pages enabled users to see and experience visual messages previously unavailable. Microsoft began a move to store all the great works of art in digitized form to be made available online. Live Webcams gave people ways to see cities, tops of mountains, even into people's bedrooms around the world, demonstrating the power of the Internet to make the world a smaller—and less private—place.

Role of Search Engines

Without the development of browsers and search engines to ease the search process, the user would be forced to remember long strings of address numbers and esoteric computer operating languages rather than the actual names of Web sites or the ability to search using words. These tools allow the user to search the Internet using language rather than numbers. Uniform Resource Locators (URLs) and Hypertext Transfer Protocols (https) are methods agreed upon by the organizations that regulate access to the Internet. What the user enters as words, the browser and search engine convert to numbers and symbols invisible to the user, but essential in the world of computers and networks that make up the World Wide Web.

The growth and increasing popularity of the Internet also signaled the potential for profits and the rise of e-commerce. The sales of software, advertising space on browser sites, and products and services by e-commerce by Internet Service Providers (ISPs) such as CompuServe and America Online also attracted the attention of traditional media conglomerates like Time-Warner and the American Broadcasting Company.

The possibility of the merger of the Internet with traditional media forms is met with concern by social scientists and media observers because of the dissimilarities between the two media. For example, editors manage messages sent to the public from traditional media during a "gatekeeping" process. That is, they have been systematically gathered, fact-checked, pored over by libel attorneys, and packaged into familiar forms (for example, a reporter's stand-up from the White House lawn). By contrast, the Internet is a free marketplace of ideas. Anyone with a little knowledge and access to a computer can put up a message or an image practically free from any constraints of time, form, or gatekeeping, and as long as they are willing to accept legal challenges that may arise from its presence.

It is this "free speech" nature of the Internet that makes it so valuable to reportage because the lack of message control by a media organization means that content can be put up on a Web site presumably free of corporate pressure. Persons who support and encourage such freedom worry when an entity like the American Broadcasting Company buys the GO! Netsite or when Time-Warner and AOL merge, because they fear the traditional model of information management will be applied to the GO! or AOL site and their free spirit will be more tightly controlled.

Why Use the Internet as a Research Tool?

With the passage of the National Information Infrastructure Act, in which the federal government acknowledged the importance of the Internet and of guaranteeing access to all U.S. citizens, three levels of Internet content were defined:

1. *Data.* This category of content exists in huge chunks in a myriad of databases and Web sites accessible for free or for some fee-based system. It can be words or images and may have little or no newsworthiness on its own, but possesses value to a reporter as reference material or in support of research. For example: Satellite images of most of the United States and the world are available for downloading at several Internet sites. Obviously these images were not gathered in support of reportage and exist as a file of images for the public's consumption. In general, little or no interpretation or value judgments are placed on data, which exist as facts. Government (and other) databases around the world are invaluable sources for tremendous amounts of data.

2. *Information.* This content category comprises data that have some value judgment or interpretation placed upon them. A bon afide news Web site with reportage and gatekeeping mechanisms would be one such example. A site that tracks motion picture attendance over time and compares present trends to past is another example (www.endata.com). Information can be valuable to reporters because there is an effort to make the data useful. Information is also a potential minefield because the entities that provide this information may not always be objective, balanced, or fair in the interpretations they provide. Most likely, these sites forward only information useful to their purposes.

3. *Knowledge.* This last content category is the end product of using both data and information. It is also the leap from the content on the Internet into the mind of the reporter and eventually to the receiver of the reporter's message. Knowledge implies that some conscious change has taken place from the data and information accessed on the Internet, and that all users of those data and information are beneficiaries of that change. A reporter's use of the data and information gained from Internet searches leads to her knowledge of the subject being reported and makes her a better and more accurate communicator. This is the Internet's greatest potential as a research and communication tool.

Cultural Differences in Approaches to Searching

Searching the Internet for information is a combination of language, ethnocentrism, technology, and interpretation. As word usage varies by culture, a reporter's understanding of the culture in which the search is launched and the culture into which the search may lead influences the search process. For example, the word "provost" in the United States usually means the chief academic officer of a university. In the United Kingdom, "provost" is sometimes used to describe a municipal official, somewhat equivalent to the mayor of a U.S. city. A reporter searching for information about municipal officials in the United Kingdom might be frustrated by having thousands of references to university officials in the United States returned as the result of a word search using the word "provost."

You also need to know the capability and limitations of the computer you are using to search and the type of access that computer has to the Internet. Processor power, modem/network card speed, and browser software versions are all possible impediments to a useful search. An older computer with less processing power, a slow modem, and dated versions of browser software may not be able to display all the information contained at a Web site. For example, "frames" versus "non-frames" browsing is related to the computer and its software's ability to handle the images and animations that may be included in a Web site.

Obviously, the usefulness of a site for visual journalism is diminished if the search computer cannot display the content a site contains. For that reason, you should always try to search with the newest technology and browser version or resign yourself to a less-than-complete search experience. Additionally, if you encounter a site with an unusual file format, the latest browser versions will automatically detect the needed software "plug-ins" to fully utilize a site and may even find, download, and install them while you wait so that you may view all site data and information.

The physical connection to the Internet used by the computer you use for searching will also determine the speed at which data and information flow from a site back to you. It may be useful to imagine these connections as analogous to water lines—the larger the line, the faster and greater the volume of water that flows through it. There are four possible connections available as of this writing:

- modem,
- ethernet,
- cable modem, and
- Wireless Application Protocol (WAP).

A "modem" (*mo*dulator/*dem*odulator) is a device inside your computer that connects you by a telephone line to a portal (entrance) to the Internet. Modems are classified by the speed at which they transfer data. For example, a modem with a 56,000 baud per second data transfer rate will theoretically communicate twice as fast as a modem with a 28,000 BPS transfer rate. Web sites with heavy graphics, animation, high-resolution images, and so on will be transferred at an agonizingly slow rate over a slow modem. Integrated Services Data Network (ISDN) and Asynchronous Data Transfer (ASDT) are efforts to make standard telephone connections work at higher transfer rates, but they add significantly to phone line charges. In any event, the term *modem* refers to a telephone connection to your computer.

An ethernet connection puts your computer into a network of users and transfers data at a much higher rate. Ethernet connections are not by telephone cable, but by cables and computer networking cards shared by all users of the network. Generally, unless network traffic is high, data and information will be returned to your computer quickly, sometimes instantaneously, by way of an ethernet connection. Most home users do not have ethernet connections.

A cable modem is a variation of an ethernet connection available to home users which uses the coaxial cable from a local cable television provider to boost home browsing to even greater speeds than those of standard ethernet connections. While the service is generally expensive, cable modems are gaining in popularity because the speed at which they operate is superior to even the fastest telephone line modem transfer rate.

The final connection method, Wireless Application Protocol (WAP), is at the cutting edge of Internet access and involves data and information being delivered to cellular phones and personal computing devices without any physical connection. Still in its infancy at this writing, WAP promises to make Internet access available anywhere, another invaluable tool for reporting research because reporters are no longer restricted by the physical connection to the Internet.

Dissolving Geographic and Political Boundaries

In traditional journalistic research, boundaries of time, space, technology, and economics can dictate how much information a reporter might acquire. If important facts were stored in a remote location, or a reporter's travel documents were not in order, or if the political climate did not allow a reporter access to information sites, the information was inaccessible. Geographic, technological, and political boundaries have always been a frustrating reality of reporter's lives. Using the Internet as a research tool can easily conquer many (but not all) of those boundaries. Even data/information judged unsuitable for access by one country's political system may be accessed by the Internet's ability to link to a site in another country where such information is available. For example, in Germany it is illegal to sell copies of Hitler's *Mein Kampf*. But a reporter living in Germany may buy a copy of this book from Barnes and Noble's Web site in the United States. As another example, during the struggle in Kosovo when official information trickling to the outside world was scarce, Web users around the world could access the Internet radio broadcasts from Kosovo for daily updates, including news of the temporary arrest of the station manager of Radio Kosovo by the military.

As for bridging economic distance, the Internet allows a freelance reporter or a reporter for a small news organization with limited resources to access much of the identical data and information available to those larger news organizations that can afford to invest in research. This is another example of the way the Internet empowers a reporter and helps to level the playing field by helping reduce the limitations of economics in data and information gathering.

Searching the Internet

Searching begins with some creative thinking about how the data and information sought might be organized and categorized at the myriad of locations at which it might exist. A useful technique is to make a list (mental or physical) of terms and phrases by which the subject sought might be stored. For example, if you want to learn something about newspaper circulation, you might organize a search list as follows:

> Newspaper circulation statistics
> Top newspapers by circulation
> Newspaper publishing statistics
> Newspaper publishing organizations
> Newspaper circulation
> Publishing statistics
> Circulation statistics
> Newspapers
> and so on

Obviously, the more variations you make to this list, the more likely you are to find the data or information you're seeking. You should also remember the "Boolean" technique (if your search engine does not automatically do this for you) of adding "and" between words or phrases to help connect two disparate topics related to your search (for example, newspapers *and* circulation will narrow the search, limit the number of returns, and perhaps add more potential sites to access).

There may also be parameters unique to the operating system or search engine you're using. Case sensitive versus non-case sensitive, mixture of upper- and lowercase characters, and word syntax are the most common variations across operating systems and/or browsers.

Where to Search

The next step is to perform the search using your list of terms. Your browser (Netscape or Internet Explorer) and its included search function is the most obvious starting place. You also have a variety of other searching methods available to you, and these will be described throughout this section. The fastest and most efficient method is to connect to those sites known as search engines. You can usually do this at no charge to you. Search engines exist to sort through Web sites and URLs based on searches of keywords or phrases at those sites. "Yahoo!," "Infoseek," and "Excite" are some of the more popular of this type of search engine, although Internet surfers have their own favorites. These sites consolidate and display results by category and usually provide a link to each result. Some search engines are now referred to as "metasearchers" because their purpose is to search a number of other search engines and systematically display the results each of those individual engines would have returned about a search topic. "Dogpile" and "Mamma" are two examples of these metasearch engines. By summarizing the results of many search engines, they save the time and effort required to methodically go to each search engine's individual Web site to perform the search.

The results returned by any of these search engines will be located in a variety of forms at a variety of sites. Some will be provided at no charge (public records, for example) and some will ask for payment (Lexus/Nexis, Medicis, the General Records of Scotland Web sites, for example), either before the search begins, when an order for information is placed, or as a subscription fee for usage of the site and the information stored there. As a rule, the more exclusive, extensive, and specialized the information, or the more interpretation or value judgment provided by the host, the more likely the researcher will encounter a site where information is available for a fee. For example, a freelance photographer's Web site might provide a page of "thumbnails" and descriptions of the person's work with a restriction that this work is the property of the person and cannot legally be captured or reproduced from the Web site. Silver or digital prints of that work could then be ordered for a fee.

Government databases may be local, state, or national, depending on the domain and the level of data or information sought. At the national level, ".gov" is the most likely domain name (for example, the U.S. Census Bureau's available data and information can be found at www.census.gov). At the state level, the domain is commonly the state abbreviation in which the database is located followed by the abbreviation for the United States (for example, a search string for the data and information available from the state of Tennessee government directory would be www.state.tn.us). At the local level, the domain may depend on the location of the server in which the data reside. For example, Nashville and Davidson County, Tennessee, has a consolidated government. The Web site for this government is www.nashville.org.

Domain designations like .com, .edu, .org, .gov are clues to the host of the data and information. Commercial sites have the ".com" or ".net" designations, education institutions have the ".edu" designation, noncommercial entities have the ".org" designation, and any federal government sites have the ".gov" designation.

The number of sources of data and information is staggering and practically unlimited. If your search is for information about a person by surname, your browser may point you to a religious organization's site (www.familysearch.com, for instance, is the Church of Latter Day Saints' genealogy databases) or to the private Web site photo collection of an aficionado of Abraham Lincoln (www.lincolnportrait.com). As with any data or information gained in reporting, the proper attribution, releases and clearances, and appropriate legalities are the responsibility of the user. Web sites usually include usage rules, copyright information, or an e-mail address to which user questions may be sent. The mere existence of data, information, or photographs on Web sites does not imply they may be freely used, copied, or reproduced.

The "Joy of Hyperlinks"

Nowhere is the power and nature of the Internet more visible than in the process of linking. The results returned by your search string will be a list of links to possible Web site locations containing the information you are seeking. A simple click on one of those links connects you to the server containing that data and information. A listing of links can and inevitably will lead you along many branches as you follow the possibilities presented to you. A Yahoo search for flood pictures, for example, will return to you several pages of possibilities, each storing and describing their store in a different way. As you choose a link, that site may provide links to a dozen others, and so on. By the end of two minutes, you may be twenty sites away from the original search results through this linking, discarding unneeded sites, and jumping as new keywords or site descriptions catch your attention. The nonlinear approach and capability are valuable beyond description, and they can enrich your research in ways you could not have imagined before the search began. By using your browser's history file, you can always go back to the original search returns. By using the "bookmark" function you can store potentially important sites in your browser's memory and return to them later by scanning your bookmarks and re-linking to those you have saved.

Without the Internet and the linking process, gaining access to such a variety of data and information might consume weeks of painstaking and time-consuming legwork, including combing through library card catalogs, government documents, and probably expensive travel to the physical location of the sites of information. In addition, the corroboration of facts and images so critical to accuracy, balance, objectivity and fairness can be obtained by using the links to discover if other sites confirm the data or information gained from a site.

CONCLUSION

The Internet's potential as a research tool for reporters is only beginning to be realized. The empowerment that comes from that connection, be it physical or wireless, slow or speedy, splashed with color and images or plain vanilla, should provide the visual journalist with a sense of exhilaration and expertise never before possible to achieve.

To the organization, the economics of storytelling become obvious. Savings in travel and time alone should justify the fastest, affordable connection to the Internet.

To the individual visual journalist, surfing the Internet in the interest of accuracy, exhaustive information, and corroboration of fact should be embraced, not avoided. Images and bodies of text are like interviews conducted in the field or dusty volumes sorted through in scattered libraries and newspaper morgues. The hyperlinking experience in all its twists and turns, dead-end links, and permutations can only lead to more professional visual journalism for the good reporter and the organization or media outlet publishing the work, and toward the ultimate goal sought by those who created the Internet—knowledge.

IDEAS FOR FURTHER STUDY

- Write a paper that describes your personal use of the World Wide Web.
- What is your favorite Web site, and what is the worst one you have encountered?
- Write a paper about the future of all other media given the quick growth of the World Wide Web.
- Discuss the dangers and potential pitfalls of information that appears in visual and/or text form on Web sites.
- Discuss the social and cultural factors that might inadvertently limit a search for information or images on the Web.

Notes about Metasearchers

by Robert Spires

In the quest to mine nuggets of knowledge from the vast amount of information on the Internet, the "metasearch" engine or "metacrawler" was created in the mid-90s. As researchers need to sift through more material faster and more comprehensively, affinities not unlike those attached to operating systems and software arise. If I go to a metacrawler, say "Google," and it meets my needs, chances are I'll go back to it until it is no longer useful.

Why do we need them? In 1999, *PC Magazine* reported that the top eleven search engines (Yahoo!, Infoseek, and so on) actually searched only 16 percent of the Web's content. Relying on one or two of this type of search engine is artificially limiting your research, damaging its reliability and credibility.

New metacrawlers regularly appear on the Web, each claiming to offer new and advantageous search methods and results. These are growing so numerous that at least one site has been created to review and assess them. The Web site at searchenginewatch.com currently lists the major metacrawlers with a short review of each.

A thorough online search should use several metacrawlers, taking advantage of the features of each. This can be analogous to a traditional search through a library, with the researcher using many guides to printed reference materials to narrow and insure the thoroughness of the search.

The argument over which of the metacrawlers is "better" is therefore moot. Only when an exhaustive search using as many of these metasearch engines as possible is completed can a researcher truly say the Web's possibilities have been explored.

Two case studies may help your understanding of searching the Web.

Case Study #1—Researching Tennessee Williams

As a picture editor for a local entertainment magazine, you want to find images for a picture page on Tennessee Williams's impact as a contemporary playwright to celebrate an upcoming production of one of his plays in your city. In your preliminary thoughts about this picture package, you obviously want to include images of the man that show him out and about city streets rather than head-shot portraiture. You've created the following list of keywords and phrases from which to begin your search:

Tennessee Williams
American playwrights
Contemporary playwrights
Impact of Tennessee Williams
Photographs of Tennessee Williams
Biographies Tennessee Williams

For this search, let's search for "photographs of Tennessee Williams." We'll use a metasearch engine. At www.dogpile.com, we type in the search phrase (see Figure 1). Dogpile searched the following search engines and

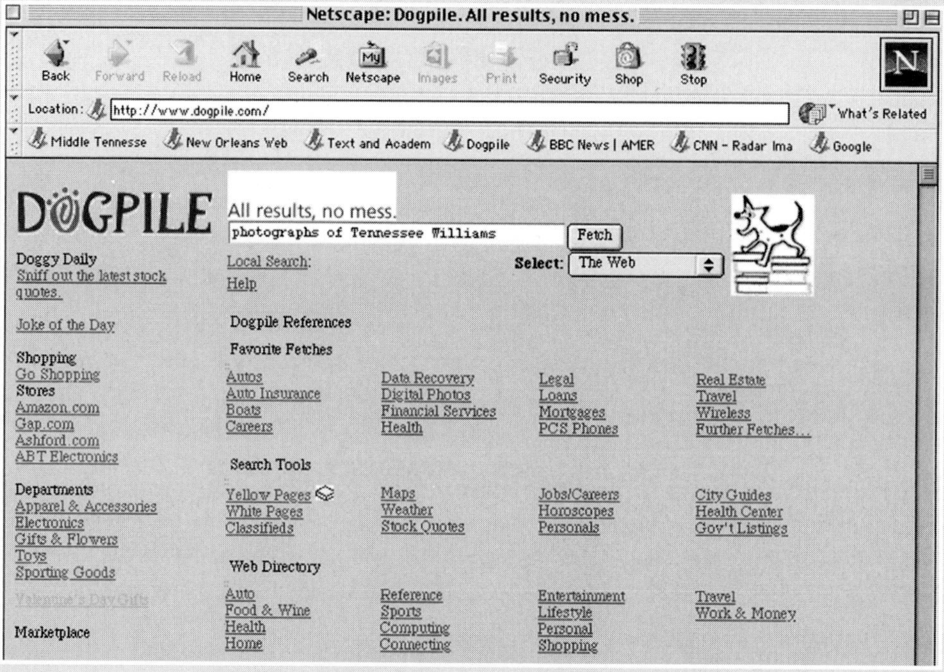

Figure 1 *A screen shot of a Dogpile search.*

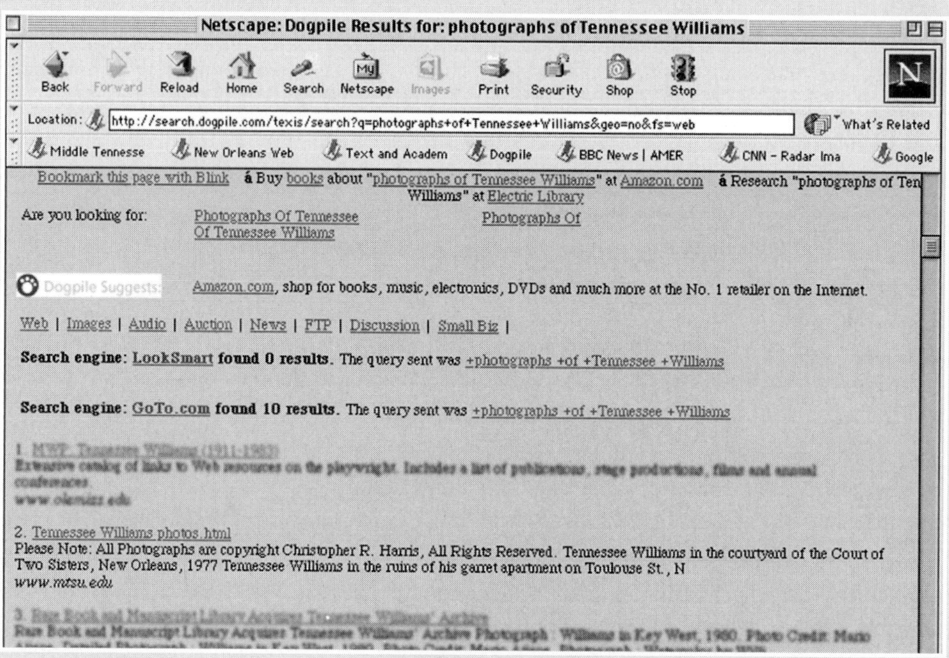

Figure 2 *A screen shot of the first results from the search for "Tennessee Williams Photographs."*

found these results using some or all of the search phrase (see Figure 2):

GoTo: 10 results
Dogpile Web Catalog: 124 results
Dogpile Open Directory: 0
Google: 5,779
About.com: 27,664
Infoseek: 0
Direct Hit: 16
Lycos: 10
RealNames: 10
Yahoo: 0

The most obvious place to start is to scan each search engine looking for returns using as much of the exact phrase as possible. In this case, "GoTo.com" found a site titled "Tennessee Williams photo.html." Clicking on the link to that site finds photos of Williams shot in and around the city of New Orleans. The photos are owned by Christopher R. Harris (also one of the authors of this text) and information and rules about the use of those photos are contained on the site (see Figure 3). This example also illustrates the scope of information available and the precision of language required to narrow the search. At Dogpile's Web Catalog search site, for example, the link to Popo Media (www.popomedia.com) will eventually lead you to a one-sentence quote attributed to Williams at www.popomedia.com/artists/john folsom.html beneath a photograph by John Folsom.

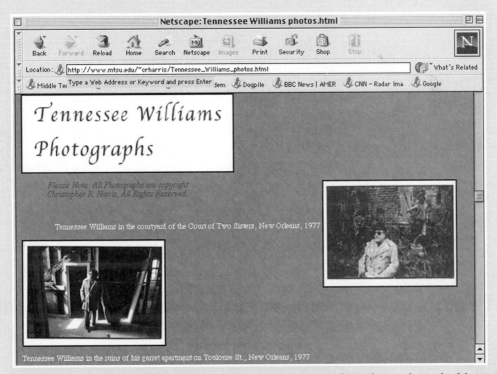

Figure 3 *A screen shot of the link to the Tennessee Williams photographic Web page, the result of the Dogpile metasearch.*

Another Dogpile search using the string "contemporary American playwrights" returned the following:

Looksmart found 0 results using any or all of the search terms
Dogpile Web Catalog found 187 results
GoTo.com found 10 or more results
Dogpile open directory found 0 results
About.com found 44,349 results
Google found 7,532 results
DirectHit found 10 results
Infoseek found 10 or more
Lycos found 10 or more
RealNames found 10 or more
Yahoo found 0
AltaVista found 0

Choosing one of the Infoseek links entitled "Contemporary American Authors W-Z" takes you to a site entitled "authors.miningco.com/arts/authors/msub01usw.htm" where you will find, in alphabetical order, three links to sites about Tennessee Williams, including two biographical sites and one academic treatise on "Love and Death" in his works.

From this search, a reporter can reconstruct the life and times of Tennessee Williams, examine documents describing his influence on contemporary American plays and play writing, purchase photos for inclusion in the article, and so forth. All this can be done without the expense of time and travel previously required for such research. With these data and information, you have the basic research for the picture spread and can expand or expound as you see fit.

Case Study #2—The Zapatistas

As a freelancer in the Southwest, you have been commissioned to photograph a documentary piece on the Zapatistas, a revolutionary group working for a cause within Mexico. Knowing little about the group or its activities, you begin with a single search word:

Zapatistas

This time you use the metasearch engine "Mamma.com." "Mamma" returns 44 links to the search word, including a link to the Zapatista homepage (www.zapatista.org) that contains histories, photos, meeting summaries, and so on. As you browse through the pages, you also find a link to the Irish Mexico Group, based in Dublin. Following that link out of curiosity, you find a link to pages containing the history of labor struggles in Ireland and its claim to commonality with the Zapatista movement. From one simple search word comes a wealth of internationally based information sites about a group you previously knew little about. Once again, time, distance, and economic barriers have been dissolved. You have a wealth of background information from which to begin your picture story. ■

CHAPTER 16

Computer Applications

by Larry Burriss
Middle Tennessee State University

Visual journalists have a long history of being comfortable with the latest tools to accomplish their work. Whether it's a new lens to get a certain photographic shot or a software filter to produce a desired effect on the computer, visual journalists have never shied away from new technology. That's one reason why they are often asked to advise other reporters and their management on computer equipment and software.

Visual journalists understand more than most that a computer is simply a device or tool for accomplishing work—it is not an end in itself. They know that the key to being productive is to be an effective software user, not simply a computer user. But even an experienced visual journalist needs to review some computer basics to be able to use a computer to more effectively produce messages audiences want to see and read.

Some Computer Basics

Fortunately, knowing how a computer works is not essential to using one. Few understand the mechanics of an internal combustion engine or the fluid mechanics involved when a brake pedal is pushed, although most people understand how to use the brakes. But if a driver knows a little about how a car works, that person will be a better driver and if something goes wrong, perhaps the problem can be easily fixed.

No matter what platform (PC or Macintosh) is in use, there are a few components common to all: the central processing unit (CPU), disk drives, keyboard, mouse, and monitor. Most of these pieces of hardware are self-explanatory. But it is the CPU that causes the most confusion.

At one level, the CPU is the box that is talked about when someone refers to a computer. For others, the term *computer* means the box and all of the other associated hardware (keyboard, monitor, and so on).

At another level, however, the CPU refers to a chip located inside the box. This chip contains the basic instructions that drive the computer. When you see an ad that says "Intel Inside," this is the chip being talked about. What is important to understand at this point, and what is discussed in some detail a little later, is that the chip, by itself, is worthless for accomplishing anything. Without an operating system and application software, the instructions on the chip can't do anything.

An operating system is the software that allows the CPU and the application software (word processor, desktop publishing program, and so on) to communi-

The "guts" of a computer: a circuit board.

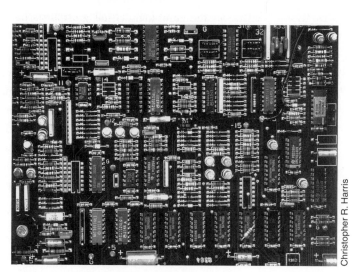

Christopher R. Harris

cate with each other. The genealogical line of PC operating systems usually goes from CP/M (control processor/microcomputer) to DOS (disk operating system) to Windows. The Macintosh uses a completely different operating system, which is incompatible with PC operating systems (which is why it is difficult to run PC programs on a Mac), although there are computers that can run both.

Another important aspect of the CPU is its speed. Generally speaking, the faster the chip, the more information it can pass to other components of the machine. Speed is thus an essential factor for visual journalists working with large picture files. In order to use pictures, they must be moved from a storage medium (floppy, hard drive, CD, zip drive, and so on) into RAM (random access memory). Once in RAM, the picture (or text file or layout) is instantly available. But how quickly such tasks happen depends on the speed of the chip. The faster the speed, the faster the machine can carry out its instructions. When personal computers first became popular back in the early 1980s, most had a clock speed of eight megahertz. Today's processors have speeds of more than 1,000 megahertz.

Another factor that defines the kind of computer a visual journalist should use is the memory capacity of the system. Read-only memory (ROM) is built into the CPU and makes the computer operate. When a computer is turned on, ROM is activated and begins a series of tests to make sure everything works properly, the so-called POST—power-on self-test. ROM then waits for information from the operating system.

The other kind of memory is usually called random access memory, or RAM. And like most everything else, a higher number indicates a higher-quality computer.

Most files (application and data) reside on another component in the computer, the hard drive. But in order for a person to use them they must be moved from the drive and into RAM. Logically, if more of the file can be moved into RAM, the faster the program will run. For example, if a computer has only one megabyte of RAM, but a file is 16MB in size, in order to work with the file, the computer can only load less than 1MB at a time. Consequently, a computer will spend a lot of time moving chunks of the file back and forth from the hard drive and memory.

On the other hand, if a computer has 128MB of RAM, it can load an entire file into RAM where it is instantly accessible for processing. All this is to say that a visual journalist should have as much RAM within a computer as can be afforded. More RAM means the computer works faster and a hard drive is saved much wear and tear.

To make matters more complicated, there are different kinds of RAM. DRAM (dynamic random access memory) has traditionally been the most common type of memory. The memory is really a charge stored in a capacitor, which has to be refreshed every thousandth of a second.

Today, most machines use EDO RAM (extended data out random access memory). EDO RAM chips can both send and receive data at the same time, thus making them faster than DRAM. A still better kind of RAM (and, of course, more expensive) is called SRAM (static random access memory). These chips do not need to be refreshed, so they are faster than DRAM.

The final kind of memory is VRAM, or video RAM. This kind of memory is made specifically for video adapters and does two things at once: It refreshes the monitor while also receiving data. Thus, generally speaking, the more VRAM, the better your monitor's picture will look. For many visual journalists, VRAM is the preferred type of RAM.

The other big number that needs attention is the size of the hard drive. The hard drive is where the operating system, application software, and most of the work files are located. The hard drive is essentially a stack of platters coated with a magnetic medium. Just like magnetic tape, data are stored on the drive in the form of magnetic pulses that are either on or off, just like the data stored in RAM. Obviously, the larger the hard drive (not larger in the physical sense because they are all about the same size, but larger in terms of storage capacity), the more data, programs, projects, and so on can be stored.

For visual journalists, the most memory-intensive element involved with production is the image. Pictures on a computer screen are composed of a series of red, green, and blue picture elements (pixels), each usually 1/72-inch square, and arranged much like tiles on the floor. Manipulating the image is thus little more than recoloring the pixels. For example, if a picture is nothing more than a red square, and it should be blue, then a program simply recolors the pixels.

There is also a distinction between monitor pixels and printed (output) dots per inch. Obviously, the more output pixels there are per inch, the more realistic a picture will look. Unfortunately, the file also grows accordingly. A picture with a specification of 72 pixels per inch will look fine on a computer screen, where the resolution of the screen itself is fairly low. However, for magazine reproduction, 300 pixels (technically, dots per inch, or dpi) are necessary. In terms of file size, a picture one-inch square, at 72 pixels per inch, will contain a little over 5,000 pixels. But a picture at 300 pixels per inch will contain 90,000 pixels, resulting in a much higher resolution. Therefore if you increase the resolution of the printed image (more dots per inch), you are going to dramatically increase the file size.

Although the concept of pixels is straightforward, how the software uses those pixels is another matter. Fortunately, there are only two basic picture element display systems: bitmap and vector images.

Bitmap images treat each pixel in the graphic as a single dot. Thus, if you draw a circle, the graphic file will save every point on that circle. This procedure can result in tremendously large files, although the result can be near-photographic quality. But remember, the higher the quality (that is, the more pixels per inch), the larger the file size. There are several hundred different graphical formats that use bitmap images. Some of the more common file formats and their extensions are discussed below.

BMP (Bitmap)

Although bitmaps and vectors refer to categories, they also refer to a specific kind of graphic format. Bitmap images are something of a default picture format because images can be opened in Microsoft Paint, a program that comes with Windows. And because Paint comes with Windows, it may be the only graphics program a person has on his home computer. Paint is thus used mostly for e-mail attachments because almost all e-mail programs are compatible with Windows.

Paint, however, is not the most user-friendly program, and is really not suitable for anything beyond the most basic graphics applications. In fact, about the only real reason for creating your own bitmap image is to produce your own computer wallpaper.

In addition to its limited functionality, the file size of a bitmap image is huge. A screen print saved as a bitmap will be in the neighborhood of 2 or 3 megabytes; the same image, saved in GIF format, will be about 40 kilobytes.

GIF (Graphic Interchange Format)

The GIF (pronounced, "Jiff") format was developed in the late 1980s as a way to exchange files over CompuServe. An image saved in GIF format can have 256 colors and compresses an image at a 4:1 ratio. If you have an image with only a few colors, GIF works particularly well because the compression algorithm seems to favor large pixel areas that are the same color.

GIF also allows transparency saves and animation, two elements particularly useful for Web publication. A transparent image (the name is something of a misnomer, because it is not the image that is transparent, but the background) seems to float on the Web page. Suppose you have an image that is on a red background, and you want to put it onto a blue Web page. Using your graphics or presentation software you change the background color of the image to the color of the Web page. The original background (red) is still there, but it is now the same color as the Web background (remember our discussion just a few paragraphs earlier: When you change the colors in an image, you are merely changing the colors of the pixels).

Note that there is something of a danger in trying to create transparencies: If the image you want to save contains the same color as the background you are trying to make transparent, then those colors will also become transparent. Suppose you have a picture of a face that has blue eyes, and the face is on a blue background. Further, suppose you want to put the image onto a white Web page. If the eye color matches the background color, and you change the background to white in order to match the Web page, then the eye color will also become white. This can, however, result in some interesting effects if used with color clip art.

Animation for Web pages is really nothing more than a series of slightly different images saved in one file. When the file loads, each of the images appears successively, thus giving the appearance of movement. Obviously, the more individual images that are in the file, the more realistic the movement will be. But, at the same time, the file will be larger.

You need to be aware of some aspects of Web animation that can cause problems:

- If the images are viewed on a browser that does not support animation, then only the first image in the set will be displayed.
- If you do not set the animation to "loop" (that is, play indefinitely), then the last image in the set will be the one that stays on the screen.

You can create an image set that appears on the screen after a few seconds by inserting an empty frame at the beginning of the set. However, a browser that does not support animation will only show an empty frame because, as just noted, only the first frame is displayed.

When should you use GIFs? GIFs work best if:

- You are using a simple drawing with only a few colors.
- You are placing an image on a Web page.
- You want to animate the Web image.
- You need a transparent image

JPEG (Joint Photographic Experts Group)

JPEG (pronounced, "jay-peg") is one of two formats (the other is TIFF) considered de facto standards for printed (as opposed to Web) graphic design work. They both have excellent compression and are supported by most graphics applications.

JPEG is particularly useful if you are using full-color or grayscale images (photographs). JPEG is able to reproduce 24-bit images (16.7 million colors) and has a compression ratio as high as 100:1. Because of its compression algorithm, JPEG is not as suited for high-contrast images like line drawings and screen shots.

Another word of warning: Each time programs such as Adobe PhotoShop open and then close a JPEG image, it loses a slight amount of data. Thus you should apply JPEG only after you have finished working on an image.

You should use JPEG when:

- You want to use a smaller file.
- You are working with continuous tone images (i.e., photographs).
- Your image has more than 256 colors.
- You want to control the compression ratio. Because all compression schemes result in some loss of picture quality, JPEG allows you to trade file size for quality.

TIFF (Tagged Image File Format)

The other well-supported image format is TIFF, which was originally developed as a cross-platform program for both Macs and PCs. In fact, TIFF's major advantage is that the image you are working on can be saved in either PC or Mac formats. As a general rule, you should work on your images in TIFF format, then save them as JPEGs.

By the way, you may become tempted to use a program such as PKZIP or WinZIP to compress JPEG or TIFF files. Don't bother. When the files are saved, both JPEG and TIFF automatically compress them using the same algorithm as PKZIP and WinZIP.

Finally, note that Web browsers do not support TIFF images.

EPS (Encapsulated PostScript)

EPS (pronounced "E-P-S") is a page-description language used by laser printers, image setters, and other high-end printers. Whereas formats such as GIF and TIFF save images only, EPS saves everything the printer can print. Thus EPS files tend to be huge (up to three times as much space as the same image stored in TIFF).

CMYK (Color Separations)

CMYK (cyan, magenta, yellow, black) isn't so much a format as a way of producing high-quality color. All of the formats mentioned so far produce a composite image. That is, all of the colors are combined on a single page. Unfortunately, color quality suffers, and printing out more than fifty or so copies on your color printer can be an expensive proposition.

BMP (Bitmap)

With color separations you use your graphic image design program to produce four pages, one for each of the primary colors. When you print this separation, you get four pages that look something like a standard black-and-white image. For example, suppose you have a page divided into quadrants. Each quadrant is a single color: cyan, magenta, yellow, or black. When you print this out in CMYK, you will have four pages, and each page will have a black square corresponding to the appropriate primary color. These pages would then be used by your printer (person, not machine) to run off color copies.

There are literally thousands of other image formats, and just about every piece of design software has its own native version. Your best bet is to use the format that offers you the most choices for controlling your image, and then transfer it to the Web, print shop, or even a friend with a compatible format.

Vector Images

Unlike bitmap graphics, vector graphics treat lines, circles, and solids as mathematical formulas. Thus, a vector graphic of a line will simply record the starting and stopping point of the line, and let the software fill in the rest, resulting in a much smaller file.

Until recently there were serious problems with vector images. For example, because each element is represented by a mathematical formula, images were limited to fairly simple shapes. Complex shapes usually ended up with jagged edges. New programs, however, allow vector images with smoother edges.

On the other hand, because the images are not representations of the actual pixels, they can be scaled to large sizes without any increase in file size. If, however, you enlarge a bitmap, you suffer either a loss in resolution (because you now have fewer pixels per inch), or an increase in file size as the program adds pixels to fill in the now empty space.

With vector images, a major concern is the enormous amount of computer power necessary to render the graphics. Because the computer has to mathematically compute the image, the result is a significantly slower load time.

The Digital Darkroom

Perhaps nowhere is the digital revolution so evident as in the darkroom—or actually the lack of a darkroom. The days of wet processing using chemicals are rapidly coming to an end as more and more visual artists convert to digital. But for many visual projects, the first step in the production chain is still taking a picture, and more and more often with a digital camera.

As we discussed earlier, digital images are composed of pixels. The more pixels there are per inch, the higher the quality of the picture. Juggling pixels and quality involves a trade-off between having a picture that has smooth, apparently continuous lines (lots of pixels), or an image that has jagged lines (fewer pixels, but a smaller file). Here's a good rule of thumb: If your image is only going to be viewed on a monitor (that is, as a Web page), then 100 pixels per inch is more than adequate. (Because the screen resolution on most monitors is only 72 pixels per inch, some experts say you can go as low as 72 pixels per inch.) If, on the other hand, you are going to print your image, then 300 pixels is the absolute minimum.

The number of pixels in the image output by a digital camera is dependent on the CCD (charge coupled device) or CMOS (complementary metal-oxide semiconductor) chip in the camera. Some camera CCDs go as low as 340×220 pixels (that's 340 pixels across and 220 pixels down) to a high of 2048×1536 pixels. So, if you are using a camera that is 340×220, it means your useful printed image size is only about one inch square (remember, the lowest usable resolution for printed output is 300 dots per inch)! Even a 1280×1024 camera will yield a useful print size of only about 4.2 inches wide, the size of a standard postcard picture (divide 1280×300—the minimal resolution for a print—and you get 4.27). A camera that shoots at 2048×1536 pixels can comfortably give you an 8×10-inch print, but the file size is going to be 3.34 megapixels, far more than the standard floppy can hold. Obviously, a digital camera is not useful for making those 10×12-inch blowups.

But again, a little arithmetic will show us that we can take an image made with a 1024×768 camera and blow it up to 10×14 for a computer monitor without any apparent loss of detail. (Divide the 1024 and 768×72—the minimum resolution for a computer monitor—and you will get 14.2×10.6.)

Another advantage to a digital camera is in the tremendous reduction in the recurring costs of film and chemicals. With a digital camera you can see the picture immediately after you take it, so you can take as many as you need until you get it right, without wasting film. This savings alone can be tremendous. Some photographers estimate they shoot at a 10:1 ratio—ten frames will yield one usable print.

Newspapers can get away with using a 300 dots per inch (newspaper personnel usually talk in terms of dots per inch, rather than pixels per inch) image because the quality of the paper is not all that good, and the pictures, usually in black-and-white, don't need to be all that sharp. For magazines and other products printed on good-quality paper, however, 300 is the absolute minimum.

The Digital Darkroom

Once the picture is taken, there are two primary storage methods. Some cameras use a standard 3.5-inch floppy. Since this floppy has 1.44MB of storage, you can put forty 640 × 480 pictures on it after they are compressed (see the above section on compression methods).

Other cameras use Flash memory, which in most digital cameras is a nonremovable chip. When this 2MB chip is full, the images must be downloaded to your computer unless the camera comes with a removable PC card.

Another way of getting images to your computer is by way of a scanner. In fact, many visual artists take a photograph with a regular camera, and then begin the actual digital editing and manipulation process with a scanner. Scanners are usually more affordable than digital cameras, and a flatbed scanner will have a resolution of 1200 pixels per inch.

Manipulating Your Work

Before you can send your work off to the Web or a printer, you will, in all probability, have to do at least some minimal digital manipulation. Maybe you just need to resize an image, or perhaps you need to do more complex manipulation such as cropping an image, changing colors, or preparing a four-color separation. In any case, you will need to have access to two basic kinds of software: an image manipulation program and a publishing program. As the names imply, an image manipulation program lets you make numerous changes to a graphic image (line art, photograph, and so on). The publishing program then allows you to take all of the various graphic elements (which may include both text and images) and then lay them out in a publication (print or Web).

Most visual design professionals use Adobe Photoshop, a program that lets you both create original designs, or edit preexisting designs (photographs you load into the program, clip art from various sources, and so on). Remember: These are bitmapped graphics that you edit pixel by pixel.

Another program that has a large number of supporters is the CorelDraw suite, which is really composed of two packages: Photo-Paint and CorelDraw. A third package is Macromedia Freehand.

For vector graphics (both original creations and modification of existing vector graphics) Adobe Illustrator and Macromedia Freehand are the programs of choice. Remember: Vector graphics use mathematical algorithms to render lines, curves, and other shapes, so the resultant file sizes of the images can be smaller, but greater computer power is needed to compute the images.

Once all of the images are created, they are then moved into a desktop or Web page publishing program. In the print arena, Adobe PageMaker and QuarkXPress are the two major competing systems.

Although the software described above can be used for Web productions, the visual artist must remember that these products were originally intended for print applications, and thus may not be entirely suitable for use on the World Wide Web or in presentations intended to be displayed on a computer (for example, in a kiosk in a presentation). A new product, Fireworks, from Macromedia, is designed as a graphic design package optimized for the Web. To be most effective, Fireworks should be used in conjunction with Macromedia's Dreamweaver, a page design program that allows the creation of sites in either HTML, or the newer VTML.

Finally, at the highest end of the visual design spectrum are animation and 3-D effects. Here Alias|Wavefront pretty much has the market to itself with its Maya software. Note, however, that Maya is generally used for the final output, and numerous programs are available for generating animation effects, textures, wire frames, and so on.

When working with print or the Web, the designer must keep in mind that print products are static, while Web products are dynamic: Once a page is printed out, it is somewhat difficult, if not impossible, to go back and change elements (once your story and infographics are printed in a national publication, you can't get them back). Web pages, however, can be manipulated in real time. Thus products that are specifically designed for Web applications can help remove some of the tedium associated with coding pages and allow the designer more time for creative activities.

Outputting Work

There are two types of presentations available to visual journalists—print and screen. But because of media convergence and new technology, the lines between print and screen presentations are becoming blurred. Generally speaking, print presentations refer to photographs, informational graphics, and graphic layouts. Screen presentations include video productions, Web homepages, and digital multimedia work that include products such as PowerPoint and Harvard Graphics.

Good design principles apply to both online and printed media forms. However, there is one important aspect that can save you a lot of time and trouble, and that is to remember that screen resolutions and print resolutions are different.

For a screen presentation (for example, Web pages), monitor resolution is the determining factor in terms of picture quality. As we discussed before, since most screen resolutions are either 72 dpi (Mac) or 96 dpi (PC), it makes no sense to store a screen image at a higher resolution. Thus you can save a lot of file space and download time by saving your screen work at 96 dpi. Higher picture resolution will not result in any improvement in the on-screen image. In addition, higher resolutions result in larger file sizes, which in turn means longer download times.

Although we normally think of the Web when discussing digital output, the visual artist must also remember that digital may include presentations. This is where programs such as PowerPoint, Harvard Graphics, and Lotus Freehand come into play. Many people think of these packages as only being used in presentations where there are a speaker and an audience. But all of their presentations can be adapted for the Web, and all can be converted to print output.

As with each kind of software described in this chapter, there is a tendency for the beginner, for some reason, to forget all of the rules of good design when using these products. They all allow you to create professional-looking products, but they all also allow you to go overboard with dozens, if not hundreds, of fonts, graphic elements, and animation. So, a few rules for digital presentations are in order here:

- Use animation sparingly, if at all. There is almost never a need to animate text.
- If the graphic image doesn't directly add anything to the presentation, don't use it. Your audience is attending your presentation to get information, not "ooh" and "ahh" over your graphics.
- Use your slides for bullet points, not complete text. Research has shown that if your presentation contains your complete text, and you prepare handouts, the audience will read your text, rather than listen to you.
- Make sure all of the equipment works. Remember, if the data projector bulb burns out when you get to slide number two, you won't be able to change it. What is your backup plan?
- The less strain you put on your computer, the better. Everything you have running during the presentation (remote control, multimedia, Internet connection) increases the probability the machine will crash during the presentation. What is your backup plan?

Print Output

Despite the convergence of new technologies, most print presentations need an output device to view the work. The term *output device* is merely a fancy name for printer, although there are a number of other kinds of output devices. In terms of quality (and price), output devices include laser printers, color printers, image setters, and film recorders.

Laser printers are glorified photocopiers, and work on the same principle. An electrostatic charge is applied to the drum inside the printer, which attracts the superfine oil-based particles called toner. As the paper moves through the printer, the particles are transferred from the drum to the paper where they are fused or fixed to the paper by a heating element. Most laser printers have a resolution of 300 dots per inch, with new models having a resolution of 600, 1200, or more.

Color printers fall into three groups: ink-jet, thermal-wax, and dye-sublimation. Ink-jet printers literally squirt dots of colored ink (cyan, magenta, yellow, and black) onto the paper. Thermal-wax printers apply wax-based pigments to the page. At the high end, dye-sublimation printers use ink that literally dyes the paper.

Image setters print on photosensitive paper much like a photograph. The output looks like a black-and-white photograph, with resolutions from 1200 dpi and higher.

Film recorders, as the name implies, copy images to color film, usually slide film, for presentations.

Until a few years ago, there was a sharp distinction between a service bureau and a commercial print shop. A service bureau generally used laser printers and photocopiers, whereas a commercial printer used offset presses, web presses, and so on, resulting in higher quality work, with a correspondingly higher price. But with the development of high-quality printers and faster computers, shops such as Kinko's can now produce work that matches, if not exceeds, that of a commercial print shop.

And now, with high-quality printers readily available even to home users, no longer outsourcing your printing needs may make those shops obsolete. New printers costing under $200 can print at a resolution of 2400 × 1200 on plain paper, which yields a near-photo-quality look. This kind of quality is obtained by using extremely small dots of ink (seven picoliters, or seven-trillionths of a liter) and a six-color cartridge, which in some printers allows a dot that is invisible to the naked eye yet still has more than thirty color gradations per dot. But remember, a picture printed on plain paper will still look flat. For that photo look, glossy paper must still be used. But here again there are trade-offs. Copier paper costs less than a penny a sheet. Glossy paper may cost as much as a dollar a sheet.

But wait, what are the six-color cartridges just mentioned? What happened to the four-color process (CMYK) we talked about earlier? Recall that those four colors were cyan, magenta, yellow, and something called "true black." Now, a six-color process adds halftones of cyan and magenta for even more realistic color reproduction. Seven-color cartridges add "photoblack."

Note that there are also three-color printers available, which use cyan, magenta, and yellow. These printers, however, use the CMY cartridge to produce black, but more often than not the "black" turns out to be a gray-brown rather than real black.

It should also be noted that the "dot" or "no dot" argument is splitting the printing industry. The "dot" faction is represented by those who use halftones to reproduce photographs. This segment of the industry is concerned with producing the best possible screen and dot. At its extreme, the halftone camp contends that digital prints are good only for samples and proofs.

The "no dot" camp, however, contends that the halftone process is outmoded and outdated (the first halftones were created back in the 1880s, and the process has remained substantially unchanged since then) and that because digital printing can produce the same results as halftones, but a lot more cheaply and easily, that the future rests with them.

In fact, they may both be wrong, as increasingly we see the medium of choice for presentations is the Internet. The Internet has many useful components including e-mail, the World Wide Web, File Transfer Protocol (FTP), User News Groups, and Listservs.

- E-mail is a technology that allows users to communicate through asynchronous text.
- The World Wide Web connects hyperlinked resources such as text and pictures. Below is a list of Web addresses for some of the more popular graphic design and publishing software:

    Adobe Photoshop (image creation and manipulation software): dtphelp.com/adobe/index.html

    Adobe PageMaker (desktop publishing): www.adobe.com/products/pagemaker/main.html

    Alias|Wavefront (Maya 3-D computer-aided design software): www.aw.sgi.com/pages/home/

    Omnipage (OCR software): www.caere.com/

    Quark (desktop publishing): www.quark.com/indexflash.html

    Macromedia (Web design and authoring software): www.macromedia.com/software/

    Silicon Graphics (high-end animation workstations): www.sgi.com/
- File Transfer Protocol (FTP) is used to transfer files between computers.

■ Usenet news groups are discussion groups dealing with almost any subject imaginable. Usenet messages are collected by a news server and made available to anyone who wants to read them. News groups are usually sources of information provided by the general public. Consequently facts used during a discussion may be dubious. However, news groups are good sources to learn about stories that might be interesting to cover.

■ Listservs are one of the most powerful but underused parts of the Internet. They are e-mail discussion groups dealing with a particular topic. They are usually more restrained than news groups, are easier to access, and are generally controlled and maintained by professionals in various fields with credible information. If expert opinions or information is desired, a listserv is a good place to start. There are many search engines that can help find a listserv group. Here are just a few of the addresses:

www.liszt.com/   Liszt Directory of E-Mail Discussion Groups.

www.tile.net/tile/listserv/index.html   Tile.Net Mailing Lists.

www.neosoft.com/internet/paml/   Publicly Accessible Mailing Lists.

www.impulse-research.com/impulse/list.html#   Search E-Mail discussion groups and lists.

www.onelist.com/   OneList clickable directory of nearly 300,000 lists.

CONCLUSION

As might be expected, there are hundreds of terms, techniques, tips, and tricks available to visual journalists. But here is the best tip of all: Learn by doing. Get on the computer and play with the software. Read the manuals that come with the hardware and software, consider buying a couple of other manuals and guides, and keep practicing and improving.

IDEAS FOR FURTHER STUDY

■ Describe your favorite computer graphic effect in motion pictures, television, or on computers.

■ Lead a discussion about the future of computers.

■ Write a paper that discusses the ethical concerns with computer interactive programs with particular emphasis on the portrayal of sex and violence.

VISUAL PERSPECTIVES

A Brief History of the Computer

by Larry Burriss

People have always had a need to manipulate numbers, to try to make sense of the world around them, and to create stories and images. What is amazing, however, is that all three of these tasks are related, and they are perfectly suited to computer manipulation.

More than four thousand years ago, merchants developed elaborate notation systems for tracking grain shipments and sales. At the same time, astronomers began using number systems to try to match crop growth and star movements. And itinerant storytellers, in an attempt to explain the world around them, took those same stars and constructed elaborate fables and myths about them.

Although everyone uses numbers, manipulating them can be tedious, tiresome, and prone to error. Thus developed the need for some kind of mechanical device that would make using numbers easier. This need was met about fifteen hundred years ago with the development of the first computer—the abacus, an arrangement of rods and beads on which the beads on the rods represented what today are tens, hundreds, and so on. Although few people today still use the abacus, its effect on number manipulation was so profound that it was unchallenged as a computational tool until the early 1600s when John Napier of Scotland discovered the computational power of logarithms. Then, in the 1620s William Oughtred and others put a logarithmic scale on a couple of thin strips of wood and developed the slide rule.

The next leap forward in the development of the computer was carried out by Blaise Pascal, who, in 1642, began construction of a crude adding machine that used an interlocking series of wheels to carry out calculations. Although using the machine was cumbersome at best, the principle of interlocking wheels remained basically unchanged in adding machines for more than three hundred years, until the development of electronic computers and calculators.

The computer programming language bearing his name still used today recognizes Pascal's high place in the history of computer development.

Throughout the seventeenth and eighteenth centuries most precursors to today's computers were in the realm of numbers. But in 1804, Joseph Marie Jacquard developed a loom that created designs through the use of punched cards. The cards were, in essence, a "program" that controlled the functions of the loom, and Jacquard was able to create incredibly complex designs by simply inserting a different set of cards.

Of all those involved in the development of better computing machines, none came so close, and was perhaps so frustrated, as Charles Babbage. Although Babbage was able to develop the *idea* of a computer, that is, a machine that could both be programmed and carry out a fixed set of numerical operations, the technology of the 1800s was woefully lacking for its actual construction, since the final product would have been a series of interlocking clock-type mechanisms, all carefully weighted and balanced, driven by steam.

Babbage designed what he termed an "Analytical Engine" that would store one hundred 40-digit numbers in what we now call "memory." A "mill" would manipulate the numbers, then move the results back into the "store." But because of its complexity (it would have required some twenty-five thousand finely machined parts), all Babbage was able to actually build was a small portion of the mill and a printer. The remainder of the machine exists today only as plans and drawings.

Assisting Babbage with his Analytical Engine was Augusta Ada Byron, the Countess of Lovelace. The countess is considered by many to be the first computer programmer, and today's Ada computer language is named for her.

The final link in the chain from counting by fingers to counting by computers was forged when Herman Hollerith used punched cards to help tabulate the 1890 census. Hollerith linked a card reader with a numerical tabulator and a series of analog display dials to complete the 1890 census in six weeks. It is a feat that had taken seven years when the 1880 census data were gathered.

As a result of his invention, Hollerith formed the Tabulating Machine Company. After a series of mergers and name changes, the final company, International Business Machine, emerged in 1924.

From this point on, a plethora of innovations, devices, hardware, and software has flooded the computer world, making it diffi-cult to track computer development in a straight line. Herewith is just a sampling of a computer time line from the last century:

1938—In Germany, Konrad Zuse builds the first binary calculator.
1945—The chairman of IBM says there will never be a need for more than five computers in the world.
1946—ENIAC, the first electronic digital computer. The machine can be reprogrammed, but only by rewiring it using dozens of patch cords.
1947—Transistor developed.
1956—The first operating system, GM-NAA I/O, developed.
1957—FORTRAN developed by IBM. This is the first computer language designed for non-computer scientists.
1959—The integrated circuit developed by Jack Kilby and Robert Noyce. Kilby will win the 2000 Nobel Prize in physics for his microchip work.
1960—COBOL developed.
1963—ASCII developed.
1964—BASIC (Beginners All-purpose Symbolic Instruction Code) created.
1964—SABRE developed with a 500 megabyte memory.
1964—DAC-1 (Design Augmented by Computers) developed by General Motors and IBM.
1965—DEC introduced the first desktop minicomputer. It cost $18,000.
1965—Advanced Research Projects Agency begins work on what is now the Internet.
1967—IBM introduces the floppy disk.

Visual Perspectives

The first of the modern-day computers: the ENIAC.

1968—Intel founded.

1968—First public demonstration of hypertext.

1969—UNIX developed.

1969—Computers at four universities and research institutions are interconnected in what will become the Internet.

The Day the Entire Internet Crashed

Everyone remembers what happened when Thomas Edison said, "Watson, come here, I want you." And we all recall the occasion when Samuel F.B. Morse telegraphed, "What hath God wrought?" And you know what's even more interesting? We remember the who, what, when, where, why, and how of these communication events even though they were more than one hundred years ago.

Now, let's test your knowledge of another communications breakthrough: What was the first message sent over the Internet? Who sent it? From where to where? When? You don't know? Ask your friends. See if they know. After all, we're talking about an event that occurred in 1969, only about thirty years ago, well within the memory of hundreds of thousands of people. But strange as it may sound, the beginning of the computer information age was not accompanied by popping flash bulbs and little cries of joy. Merely the soft tapping of a keyboard, with no one to really record the event.

On the Saturday before Labor Day, 1969, a device too large to fit into the elevator arrived at Boelter Hall, U.C.L.A. The machine was an Interface Message Processor, IMP, based on a Honeywell DDP-516 computer. The device was put in Room 3400 under the watchful eye of Leonard Kleinrock, already a legend among those who delved into the arcane world of something called "queuing theory."

On Tuesday, September 2, computers in the lab were coaxed into communicating with each other over a distance of twenty feet. In attendance were representatives of AT&T long-distance service and GTE (providing the phone lines), Scientific Data Systems (manufacturers of the U.C.L.A. host computer), Honeywell (maker of the IMP), ARPA (providing the money), U.C.L.A., and representatives of Bolt, Beranek and Newman (BBN), working under contract with the Defense Department's Advanced Research Projects Agency to provide the communications "backbone," and the company that had modified the Honeywell computer.

The real achievement was not that the computers communicated successfully; Claude Shannon and Warren Weaver had described that process years earlier. The success was in the fact that the Honeywell and SDS computers used completely different protocols within themselves. The router, using what we call "packet switching," was able to work around those differences and still successfully process messages.

On October 29 (or perhaps it was October 20, no one seems to be sure of the date), 1969, a U.C.L.A. graduate student, Charlie Klein, using the refrigerator-sized device we now call a "router," sent the letters "l" and "o" to a computer three hundred miles away at the Stanford Research Institute. When Klein sent the letter "g," the SRI computer was supposed to complete the command and transmit "login." However, the third letter caused a memory buffer overflow, and the entire Internet (all two computers!) crashed. Bill Duvall, at the SRI terminus, did some minor adjusting, and the test was successfully completed. And as in the previous test at U.C.L.A., the success was not in getting two computers to "talk" with each other. Rather, the event marked the first time two IMP's (routers) successfully broke a message into packets, sent the packets across phone lines, and then reassembled them into a coherent whole.

And the speed of the lines supplied by AT&T? A whopping 50 kilobytes per second! Today's high-speed lines operate at gigabytes-per-second levels.

That historic router, by the way, is tucked away in a corner of the computer science library, gathering dust, barely noticed.

In November an IMP node was added at the University of California, Santa Barbara, and in December the Internet made its way to the University of Utah. Soon the entire nation was covered, after a fashion, when BBN in Cambridge, Massachusetts, was hooked up. BBN, it seems, was the prime contractor in a Defense Department project designed to test the feasibility of linking independent computers into a network that could both share information among devices and survive a nuclear attack. The government agency running the project was something called the Advanced Research Projects Agency, and its creation was known as ARPANET.

1970—Programming language Pascal introduced.

1971—The first Automated Teller Machine (ATM) opens for business in Valdosta, Georgia.

1971—The Intel 4004 chip developed. The chip performs 60,000 operations per second.

1972—Smalltalk, a precursor to the Windows graphical display, introduced.

1972—The first mass market computer game, Pong, introduced.

1972—The "C" programming language developed.

1973—IBM develops the 30-megabyte Winchester disk.

1973—Ethernet developed by Xerox.

1974—Hewlett-Packard introduces the HP-65 programmable calculator. The pocket calculator sold for $795.

1975—Microsoft founded.

1975—IBM introduces the first commercially available laser printer.

1975—Telnet begun.

1976—The first word processor for personal computers, Electric Pencil, developed.

1976—The CP/M operating system developed.

1977—The home computer market is opened up by Apple Computer (Apple II), Tandy-Radio Shack (TRS-80), and Commodore (PET).

1978—The 5.25-inch floppy disk developed.

1978—Speak-and-Spell (Texas Instruments), the first speech synthesis toy, introduced.

1979—CompuServe and The Source go online.

1979—WordStar, the first successful word processing package, introduced.

1979—VisiCalc introduced.

1980—In what may be history's all-time great deal, Bill Gates pays Seattle Computer Products $75,000 for a computer operating system.

1981—Osbourne Computers introduces the first portable computer, a 25-pound machine.

1981—IBM develops the PC, based on an Intel chip and Microsoft's Basic and Disk Operating System (DOS).

1981—Dbase II introduced.

1982—TCP/IP (Transfer Control Protocol/Internet Protocol) established as the standard for the ARPANET.

1982—Lotus 1-2-3 introduced.

1983—Apple introduces the Lisa personal computer. Its $10,000 price tag doomed the machine.

1984—The Apple Macintosh introduced.

1984—The word "cyberspace" is introduced by William Gibson in his novel *Neuromancer.*

1984—The 3.5-inch diskette developed by Sony.

1984—IBM introduces the PC-AT. It featured a 20-megabyte hard drive.

1985—CD-ROM disks become available.

1985—Aldus PageMaker introduced.

1990—Microsoft releases Windows 3.0, establishing Windows as the primary working environment for PCs.

1991—A computer beats Russian chess champion Anatoly Karpov.

1991—Computer craftsmen finally build Babbage's Difference Engine No. 2.

1993—Intel introduces the Pentium chip, which contains 3.1 million transistors and is twice as fast as its closest competitor.

1993—Mosaic introduced by the University of Illinois. This is the first graphical interface for use on the World Wide Web.

1993—There are an estimated 130 Web sites around the world.

1993—Microsoft announces the Plug and Play standard for adding peripheral devices.

1995—The first Internet wiretap. The Secret Service and Drug Enforcement Administration arrest three people who are illegally manufacturing cell phone equipment.

1995—Microsoft introduces Windows 95.

1998—Apple Computer introduces the iMac.

1999—*Star Wars Episode One* contains 66 digital characters in live motion.

1999—Y2K worldwide panic in which billions of dollars were spent correcting the computer problem.

2000—Y2K computer problem turned out not to be such a problem.

2000—The "I Love You" e-mail virus infected millions of computers worldwide.

2001—The Code Red virus scares more people than are actually affected by the spread of the virus. ■

Visual Perspectives

Visual Journalism Awaits You

The importance of good visual journalism was proved many times over both during and after the tragic events of September 11, 2001. Starting with the first reports of an explosion and fire at New York's World Trade Center, visual information undergirded the reporting of the attacks and their outcomes. Still and video photography, live television, and charts, maps, and other infographics showed what was happening—sometimes even while it was happening, such as the collapse of the towers at the World Trade Center. Many old-line media newspapers updated their Web sites as the events unfolded—something that would have been impossible a few short years ago. People around the world obtained up-to-date visual information from the airwaves, print media, and the Internet. And new-media visual journalists provided much of that valuable information.

Christopher R. Harris

Now that you have finished this textbook on visual journalism, you are aware of basic techniques that you will need to become a successful visual reporter. With a little more preparation, you will be ready to enter the mainstream of visual journalism. With a broad base of knowledge in graphic design, photojournalism, multimedia, and technology, you will have what it takes to get that first job as a visual reporter.

A student working on a still digital imaging project using Photoshop® software.

321

A prospective employer will be happy to hear you talk about your abilities and experiences, but the real measure of your talent will be revealed in your work samples. Assembling a professional portfolio is essential to obtaining good work. Most likely you have produced portfolio-quality work during your college career. Take stock of what you have produced, and what you still need to produce, for your portfolio. Seek advice from teachers or professionals as you set up your portfolio. Eliminate samples that hold emotional value for you but not much professional value. Also, a good grade on a project does not mean it belongs in your portfolio. Get rid of "cute" work and stock your portfolio with examples that display your creativity, your ability to solve problems, and the range of your talent. Portfolios should indicate the type of work you can produce as well as your technical skills.

Once you determine your portfolio's content, spend time packaging it well. Whether you use a traditional "flat art" portfolio, a web site, or a CD or DVD, a professional presentation will help make a positive impression on a prospective employer.

A creative director might also be looking for proof that you have already been hired for your expertise. Gaining a track record as a creator of finished products that met needs of the clients will help impress your prospective employer.

How do you get that experience?

Simple. Work at your school's newspaper or other media outlet. Volunteer your talents in graphic design, writing, infographics, or photography. Then get good, clean "tearsheets" of the final product. You can use them as samples in your portfolio.

Another way to get recognition for your work is to enter some of the numerous contests offered in the area of visual graphics. Student organizations of the National Press Photographers Association (NPPA), International Television Association (ITVA), or Society of Newspaper Design (SND sponsor contests for college students. Additionally, many professional graphics publications and software firms offer international contests for students. Take advantage of any means of promoting your name within the mainstream of graphics arts and journalism. Published pieces and awards will make your portfolio stand out.

Another way of obtaining good portfolio pieces, as well as insider information about the visual reporting business, is through student internships. Check with your academic advisor about internships with local firms. Such an experience will give you a taste the business side of the industry before you commit to the profession. Also, firms often hire interns once they graduate from college. It's not bad to get college credit while learning the ropes of the industry.

Once you have developed your portfolio, you need to get it to the people who need to see it—those who hire visual reporters. Portfolios can be shipped to any destination, and printed samples, such as self-promotion brochures, can be mailed. And you can also upload pages of samples to the Internet in the form of web pages. The World Wide Web is unsurpassed in its potential to promote the work of the visual journalist. Web pages can show off the work of the visual artist to anyone with computer access. Prospective clients throughout the world can quickly access a portfolio, and the artist is spared the time, energy, and money it takes to ship sample books to prospective clients or employers. By clicking a hot-link on your page, the viewer can contact you via e-mail. This modern method of self-promotion is a must for the visual journalist seeking employment, whether permanent or freelance.

After you have produced a good portfolio, promoted your work, and obtained a job, start planning for job advancement and growth. Join professional organizations in your area. Many will be branches of the professional groups that you have affiliated with as a student. Also, learn how to network. Talk with a variety of people at professional gatherings. Take advantage of any chance to show your work, and how you work, to others. A strong portfolio plus a good public persona will help creative staffs remember your name when they are hiring.

Strive to provide your best work on every assignment, and you will have an exciting and rewarding career in visual journalism. Develop your own personal style and stay true to your own beliefs.

The interesting and challenging world of the visual journalist awaits you.

Conclusion

The Web and Visual Journalism
by Tom Kennedy, The Washington Post–Newsweek Interactive Web Site

My interest in moving to the online world really began in the early 1990s. First, I began to use the Internet as a research tool to support story research while I was at the *National Geographic* as director of photography. Second, in 1993, I participated in the "Open" project, an attempt to create a print magazine, from start to finish, in an entirely digital manner.

When the Web began to emerge in 1994, I saw the immediate potential to present still photography in a more robust fashion by blending and integrating it with other forms of media such as audio, video, and text to tell a more complete story than one could do in print alone.

I moved into the digital world with great enthusiasm in early 1998, recognizing that I would have a strong uphill learning curve. Keep in mind that the digital revolution sweeping newspapers began in 1985 with the introduction of Macs into newsrooms just as I was leaving the *Philadelphia Inquirer* to go to *National Geographic*. Throughout my tenure at *National Geographic*, many of the cutting-edge advances in digital image capture, production, and outputting were largely irrelevant to our production processes. Thus, I hadn't had exposure to the tools and faced some rather formidable obstacles. Nonetheless, I believed that the lessons learned about doing quality photojournalism at the *Inquirer*, the *National Geographic*, and from other newspapers earlier in my career might also continue to apply to work on the Web. Happily, I have been proven right so far in that assumption.

I feel extremely lucky to have made this transition at this stage in my career. There is so much to figure out in this new medium that I feel I could be busy for the next thirty years and still not have experienced everything I could get from working in it.

This remains a tremendously complicated medium right now. Not only do we face the daily complexities of merging and integrating various forms of media, but we all face enormous publishing complexities due to different hardware platforms, browsers, operating systems, display devices, and connection speeds. Technology remains both a barrier and an opportunity, and it is unlikely to change within the next few years. But the simultaneous arrival of ubiquitous broadband connectivity and high-definition display devices should act as formidable spurs to further technological developments that might solve some of today's problems.

As I initially moved into the medium, I quickly came to realize that we are trading the space limitations inherent in print for time limitations related to the necessity of constantly updating our content to stay abreast of breaking news developments. In addition, most news Web sites have many fewer personnel than their print counterparts. The limitations of small staff size also impose certain natural limits on our content-creating capability.

After working in this medium for two years, I have come to profoundly appreciate the content presentation possibilities it has unleashed, and I can't imagine ever returning to print. I am driven by the endless possibilities I see for visual communication on the Web and linking it with other forms of media. I believe passionately in photojournalism's power to communicate visceral information that is at once highly specific but also revealing of underlying fundamental truths about the human condition and our relationship to the rest of the natural world. By combining and integrating still photos in certain ways, we are able to give voice to a more complete form of communication—one that can actually link subjects, photographers, and end-users in an ongoing dialogue about the meaning of a story.

In the past thirty years, I have seen a steady decline in print and broadcast media's appetite for documentary photojournalism. Instead we are treated often to the spectacle produced by the collusion of celebrity culture, fantasy, and rampant consumerism that turns commodities into everything and everyone.

This reality has left precious little room for photojournalists to tell meaningful real stories about the human condition. I see the Web as being a space where such work can find a voice and a home and an audience, and thus survive in the twenty-first century. Right now, individual practitioners have as much chance to create content and find an audience as giant media conglomerates have. This inherent leveling of the playing field appeals to my democratic instinct. I also think a multiplicity of visions, and voices, is far preferable to a homogeneous media voice that essentially has become our version of Roman "bread and circuses" designed to distract from rather than elevate public discourse.

I am heartened to see enormously creative work being undertaken by many people in this new medium, notwithstanding certain challenges and limitations. Perhaps my greatest surprise in moving into this medium has been the difficulty of blending certain kinds of multimedia, due to the primitive state of our tools and technology. I don't see this changing immediately, although there has been a steady progress in tool development over the last decade. The lack of absolute standards for many aspects of content production and delivery (browsers, modem connection speeds, hardware platforms, operating system software, differing screen sizes and resolutions, and processor speeds, for example) conspires to challenge efforts to create content that embodies the strengths of multimedia in every aspect. Overcoming these limitations still occupies a lot of our daily creative thinking. The trick is not to let the obstacles distract from the basic task of creating compelling content.

In moving from print to the Web, I have had to learn many new skills and understand more completely how to blend different forms of media for maximum impact and clarity. Much of it is trial-and-error experimentation, borrowing from the experiences of others and trying to adapt them so I can continue to communicate with my own visual sensibility.

The current limitations of screen display define some of my editing choices each day. I liken it in many respects to the time in the late 1960s when newspapers were beginning to migrate from bad letterpress to offset. Of necessity, I look for graphic, quick-reading images, cropped tightly to create interesting graphic design. Images with strong uses of light and color are preferred but I also want the storytelling content to be present in the image choices. Cropping plays a larger role than in my recent print experience and I tend to eliminate overly complicated visual constructions that simply won't read at the small sizes we currently use in our templates. I see this situation changing dramatically when we change our publishing platforms at the same time that broadband connectivity becomes ubiquitous and high-definition screen standards apply to both computer screens and televisions. I think these changes will inevitably lead to a greater role for video in the reporting of stories on the Web. However, I think the inherent power of still photography, particularly when fused with strong narrative text and ambient sound, will continue to insure a rich role for still photography. I am expecting both still photography and video to coexist and blend in interesting ways on the Web for the foreseeable future.

My role daily is to promote the use of multimedia on the site. In this activity, I work with a team of photographers, photo editors, and video editors. We shape a variety of complex multimedia packages for "CameraWorks" [washingtonpost.com/wp-dyn/photo/index.html] while also supporting editorial content on the rest of the site by placing individual photographs in various article templates. My task is to insure that we present news content in the most accurate, compelling fashion possible. I do some daily editing for specific Camera-Works photo galleries and then act as a final editorial check on the major multimedia packages that we build.

I like doing hands-on editing and occasional production so I remain conversant with the possibilities and pitfalls of our technology. But my primary role is to supply energy and vision to aid with development of storytelling techniques and content. I love the challenge of interacting with news developments and producing packages like our convention coverage in "real time."

The working collaborations necessary to support the Web actually much more closely resemble traditional broadcast models than do those on the Web. While not a surprise, given the reliance on technology to accomplish tasks, it does require some adjustments in thinking for people coming directly from print. I think most newspapers create content using a "silo situation," where the Web requires the "round barn" approach from the outset. It is important to make projects work on the basis of individually melded efforts in multimedia where often a single piece is touched by several hands from the beginning.

Production coordination is a key to doing serious work and there the broadcast or movie-making model is better.

I have been asked recently about how the need for speed and the requirements for continuous updating might affect our editorial judgment. This is a very good question and illustrates a major difference between newspapers and the Web. Most newspapers aim all activity at meeting several key deadlines for publication on a daily basis. Editors bring together the fruits of solitary activity (writing and photography, often not done simultaneously). The entire system works backward from the deadline of starting the presses.

In contrast, we are often faced with the task of immediate revision to take account of new developments and changing circumstances. The opportunities for revision offer a chance to correct mistakes, but our goal is to publish with the same accuracy and attention to detail as the *Washington Post* newspaper, each and every time. I think operating in the Web environment requires more sustained concentration and focus, as updating and revising are often technically complicated procedures. Editorial judgments must be made quickly, but not so quickly that fact-checking, proofing, and editorial ramifications are ignored.

We represent the ethics and integrity of *Post* reporting online and feel a great obligation to maintain the journalism standards of the *Post* in every circumstance. If decisions are to be made quickly, we try to make sure that all relevant concerns and facts are surfaced at the point a decision is required. ∎

BIBLIOGRAPHY

Abramson, Albert. (1987) *The History of Television, 1880 to 1941.* Jefferson, Mo.: McFarland.

Ackerman, Diane. (1990) *A Natural History of the Senses.* New York: Random House.

Adir, Karin. (1988) *The Great Clowns of American Television.* Jefferson, Mo.: McFarland.

Allen, Dianne. (July 17, 1992) "Benetton Not Sorry about AIDS Ad." *The Toronto Star,* p. G4.

Altschul, Charles. (1992) "The Center for Creative Imaging and the Influence of Technology on Creativity." In *Ethics, Copyright, and the Bottom Line.* Camden: Center for Creative Imaging, pp. 59–61.

Arnheim, Rudolf. (1974) *Art and Visual Perception.* Berkeley: University of California Press.

Augarten, Stan. (1984) *Bit by Bit: An Illustrated History of Computers.* New York: Ticknor & Fields.

Barnhurst, Kevin. (December 1991) "News as Art," *Journalism Monographs.*

Barnouw, Erik. (1974) *Documentary: A History of the Non-Fiction Film.* London: Oxford University Press.

Barthes, Roland. (1981) *Camera Lucida.* New York: Hill & Wang.

———. (1977) *Image Music Text.* New York: Hill & Wang.

Bazin, Andre. (1972) *Orson Welles: A Critical View.* New York: Harper & Row.

Begley, Sharon et al. (April 20, 1992) "Mapping the Brain," *Newsweek,* pp. 66–70.

Berelson, Bernard, and Patricia J. Salter. "Majority and Minority Americans: An Analysis of Magazine Fiction." In Cohen, Stanley, and Jock Young, eds. (1973). *The Manufacture of News.* Beverly Hills: Sage Publications, pp. 107–126.

Berger, Arthur A. (1989) *Seeing Is Believing: An Introduction to Visual Communication.* Mountain View: Mayfield Publishing.

———. (1977) *Ways of Seeing.* London: Penguin Books.

Berger, John, and Jean Mohr. (1982) *Another Way of Telling.* New York: Pantheon Books.

Berger, John. (1977) *Ways of Seeing.* London: Penguin Books.

Bernard, Bruce. (1980) *Photodiscovery.* New York: Harry N. Abrams.

Berryman, Clifford. (June 7, 1926) "Development of the Cartoon," *University of Missouri Bulletin.*

Bianki, V.L. (1988) *The Right and Left Hemispheres of the Animal Brain.* New York: Gordon and Breach.

Biederman, Irving. (1987) "Recognition-by-Components: A Theory of Human Image Understanding." *Psychological Review,* Vol. 94, no. 2, pp. 115–147.

Birren, Faber. (1961) *Color Psychology and Color Therapy.* Secaucus, N.J.: Citadel Press.

Bivins, Thomas, and William Ryan. (1991) *How to Produce Creative Publications.* Lincolnwood: NTC Business Books.

Blakeslee, Thomas. (1980) *The Right Brain A New Understanding of the Unconscious Mind and Its Creative Powers.* Garden City, N.J.: Anchor Press.

Bloomer, Carolyn M. (1990) *Principles of Visual Perception.* New York: Design Press.

Bolton, Richard, ed. (1992) *The Context of Meaning: Critical Histories of Photography.* Cambridge: MIT Press.

Bova, Ben. (1988) *The Beauty of Light.* New York: John Wiley & Sons.

Brookhiser, Richard. (March 1, 1993) "The Melting Pot Is Still Simmering." *Time,* p. 72.

Bruce, Vicki, and Patrick Green. (1985) *Visual Perception Physiology, Psychology and Ecology.* London: Lawrence Erlbaum.

Bryson, Norman, Michael Ann Holly, and Keith Moxey, eds. (1991) *Visual Theory: Painting & Interpretation.* New York: HarperCollins.

Buck, Genevieve. (August 26, 1992) "And You Thought Thought-Provoking Art Could Only Be Found in Museums." *Chicago Tribune,* p. 16.

Butler, Pierce. (1949) *The Origin of Printing in Europe.* Chicago: University of Chicago Press.

Carringer, Robert. (1985) *The Making of* Citizen Kane. Berkeley: University of California Press.

Carter, Rob. (1989) *American Typography Today.* New York: Van Nostrand Reinhold.

———, Ben Day, and Philip Meggs. (1985) *Typographical Design: Form and Communication.* New York: Van Nostrand Reinhold.

Christians, Clifford. "Reporting and the Oppressed." In Deni Elliott, ed. (1986) *Responsible Journalism.* Beverly Hills: Sage Publications, pp. 109–130.

———, Kim Rotzoll, and Mark Fackler. (1983) *Media Ethics Cases and Moral Reasoning.* New York: Longman.

Cimons, Marlene. (December 23, 1992) "Food Labels May Be More Honest, But Are the Ads?" *Los Angeles Times,* p. A5.

Coe, Brian. (1977) *The Birth of Photography.* New York: Taplinger.

Conover, Theodore E. (1985) *Graphic Communications Today.* St. Paul, Minn.: West Publishing.

Cowie, Peter. (1965) *The Cinema of Orson Welles.* London: A. Zwemmer, Ltd.

Crookall, David, and Danny Saunders, eds. (1989) *Communication and Simulation: From Two Fields to One Theme.* Clevedon: Multilingual Matters, Ltd.

Curry, Cheryl. (April 26, 1992) "The Man Who Died in an Ad for Benetton." *The Toronto Star,* p. D1.

D'Agostino, Peter, and Antonio Muntadas, eds. (1982) *The Unnecessary Image.* New York: Tanam Press.

Davies, Duncan, Diana Bathurst, and Robin Bathurst. (1990) *The Telling Image: The Changing Balance between Pictures and Words in a Technological Age.* Oxford: Clarendon Press.

Deely, John. (1990) *Basics of Semiotics.* Bloomington: Indiana University Press.

Dennis, Everette, and John Merrill. (1991) *Media Debates Issues in Mass Communication.* New York: Longman.

———, Arnold Ismach, and Donald Gillmor, eds. (1978) *Enduring Issues in Mass Communication.* St. Paul, Minn.: West Publishing.

Denton, Craig. (1992) *Graphics for Visual Communication.* Dubuque, Iowa: Wm. C. Brown.

Dickson, Thomas. (Winter 1993) "Sensitizing Students to Racism in the News," *Journalism Educator*, pp. 28–33.

Dondis, Donis A. (1973) *A Primer of Visual Literacy*. Cambridge: MIT Press.

Eder, Josef. (1972) *History of Photography*. New York: Dover Publications.

Edom, Clifton. (1980) *Photojournalism Principles and Practices*. Dubuque, Iowa: Wm. C. Brown.

Emery, Michael, and Edwin Emery. (1988) *The Press and America*. Englewood Cliffs, N.J.: Prentice Hall.

Evans, Harold. (1978) *Pictures on a Page*. New York: Holt, Rinehart & Winston.

Fell, John. (1979) *A History of Films*. New York: Holt, Rinehart & Winston.

Finberg, Howard, and Bruce Itule. (1990) *Visual Editing*. Belmont: Wadsworth.

Fineman, Mark. (1981) *The Inquisitive Eye*. New York: Oxford University Press.

Fiske, Susan T., and Shelley E. Taylor. (1984) *Social Cognition*. Menlo Park: Addison-Wesley.

Flukinger, Roy, Larry Schaaf, and Standish Meacham. (1977) *Paul Martin: Victorian Photographer*. Austin: University of Texas Press.

Ford, Colin, ed. (1976) *An Early Victorian Album*. New York: Alfred A. Knopf.

Foss, Sonja K. (1992) "Visual Imagery as Communication." *Text and Performance Quarterly*, Vol. 12, pp. 85–96.

Fox, Stephen. (1984) *The Mirror Makers*. New York: William Morrow.

Frare, Therese. (November 1990) "The End." *Life*, pp. 8–9.

Freiberger, Paul, and Michael Swaine. (1984) *Fire in the Valley: The Making of the Personal Computer*. Berkeley: Osborne/McGraw Hill.

Friedhoff, Richard Mark, and William Benzon. (1988) *The Second Computer Revolution Visualization*. New York: W. H. Freeman.

Friedman, Milton, et al. (1989) *Graphic Design in America*. New York: Harry N. Abrams.

Fuhrmann, Otto. (1937) *The 500th Anniversary of the Invention of Printing*. New York: Philip C. Duschnes.

Fulton, Marianne. (1988) *Eyes of Time: Photojournalism in America*. New York: New York Graphic Society.

Gaarder, Kenneth R. (1975) *Eye Movements, Vision and Behavior: A Hierarchical Visual Information Processing Model*. New York: John Wiley & Sons.

Garcia, Mario, and Pegie Stark. (1991) *Eyes on the News*. St. Petersburg, Fla.: The Poynter Institute for Media Studies.

Gardner, Howard. (1982) *Art, Mind, and Brain: A Cognitive Approach to Creativity*. New York: Basic Books.

Geipel, John. (1972) *The Cartoon*. South Brunswick: A.S. Barnes.

Ghiselin, Brewster. (1952) *The Creative Process*. New York: New American Library.

Gibson, James J. (1979) *The Ecological Approach to Visual Perception*. Boston: Houghton Mifflin.

Goffman, Irving. (1979) *Gender Advertisements*. New York: Harper & Row.

Goldberg, Vicki. (February 28, 1993) "Still Photos Trace the Moving Image of Blacks." *New York Times*, p. H23.

———. (May 3, 1992) "Images of Catastrophe as Corporate Ballyhoo." *New York Times*, p. 33.

———. (1991) *The Power of Photography*. New York: Abbeville Press.

Goldstein, E. Bruce. (1989) *Sensation and Perception*. Belmont, Calif.: Wadsworth.

Goodwin, H. Eugene. (1983) *Groping for Ethics in Journalism*. Ames: Iowa State University Press.

Gregory, R.L. (1970) *The Intelligent Eye*. New York: McGraw Hill.

Gross, Larry, "The Ethics of (Mis)representation." In Gross, Larry, John Stuart Katz, and Jay Ruby, eds. (1988) *Image Ethics*, pp. 188–202. New York: Oxford University Press.

Gross, Lynn. (1979) *See/Hear An Introduction to Broadcasting*. Dubuque, Iowa: Wm. C. Brown.

Hall, Jane, and John Lippman. (February 26, 1993) "Logging Story Leaves NBC Red-Faced Again." *Los Angeles Times*, pp. D1–D2.

———. (February 15, 1993) "NBC News: A Question of Standards." *Los Angeles Times*, pp. F1, F15.

Hammond, Paul. (1974) *Marvellous Méliès*. New York: St. Martin's Press.

Hardt, Hanno. (April 1991) "Words and Images in the Age of Technology." *Media Development*. Vol. 38, pp. 3–5.

Harper, Laurel, ed. (March/April, 1992) "Typography Today," in *How*.

Harris, Christopher R. (2001). "Photojournalism." In R. Campbell, *Media Culture,* 3d ed. New York: St. Martin's Press.

———. (Winter 1999). "The Illustrated American." *Visual Communication Quarterly*.

———. (1997). "A Decisive Moment in Bohemia: Photographing Tennessee Williams in New Orleans." *Tennessee Williams Literary Journal, 4*(1).

———. (1994). "Manipulation of Photographs and the Lanham Act." *Communication and the Law, 16*(1).

———. (1993). "The Halftone and American Magazine Reproduction 1880–1900." *History of Photography, 17*(1).

———. (1991). "Digitization and Manipulation of News Photographs." *Journal of Mass Media Ethics, 6*(3).

———, ed. (1991). *Protocol: A Guide to Ethical Decision Making in the Newsroom.* Durham, NC: National Press Photographers Association.

Harris, Christopher R., D. Zillman, and K. Schweitzer. (1993). "Effects of Perspective and Angle Manipulations in Portrait Photographs on the Attribution of Traits to Depicted Persons." *Medien Psychologie, 5*(2).

Harris, Christopher R, and D. Tomlinson. (1992). "Free-Lance Photojournalism in a Digital World: Copyright, Lanham Act and Droit Moral Considerations Plus a Sui Generis Solution." *Federal Communications Law Journal, 45*(1).

Hartmann, Paul, and Charles Husband. "The Mass Media and Racial Conflict." In Cohen, Stanley, and Jock Young, eds. (1973) *The Manufacture of News*, pp. 270–283. Sage Publications, Inc.

Hatcher, Evelyn P. (1974) *Visual Metaphors: A Methodological Study in Visual Communication*. Albuquerque: University of New Mexico Press.

Hawthorn, Jeremy (ed.) (1987) *Propaganda, Persuasion and Polemic*. London: Edward Arnold.

Hicks, Wilson. (1973) *Words and Pictures*. New York: Arno Press.

Hochberg, Julian. "Attention, Organization, and Consciousness," in Mostofsky, David, ed. (1970) *Attention: Contemporary Theory and Analysis*. New York: Appleton Century Crofts.

Hoffman, Howard S. (1989) *Vision and the Art of Drawing*. Englewood Cliffs: Prentice Hall.

Hoistad, Gunnar. (April 1991) "How Vulnerable Are Children to Electronic Images?" *Media Development*, Vol. 38, pp. 9–11.

Holmes, Nigel. (1985) *Designing Pictorial Symbols*. New York: Watson Guptill Publications.

Horovitz, Bruce. (March 22, 1992) "'Shock Ads': New Rage That Spawns Rage." *Los Angeles Times*, p. D1.

Hubel, David H. (1988) *Eye, Brain, and Vision*. New York: Scientific American Library.

Hunter, Jefferson. (1987) *Image and Word: The Interaction of Twentieth-Century Photographs and Texts*. Cambridge: Harvard University Press.

Huxley, Aldous. (1942) *The Art of Seeing*. New York: Harper.

Inge, M. Thomas. (1990) *Comics As Culture*. Jackson: University Press of Mississippi.

Jaubert, Alain. (1986) *Making People Disappear*. Washington: Pergamon Brassey.

Javna, John. (1985) *Cult TV*. New York: St. Martin's Press.

Jean, Georges. (1992) *Writing The Story of Alphabets and Scripts*. New York: Harry N. Abrams.

Kabrisky, Matthew. (1966) *A Proposed Model for Visual Information Processing in the Human Brain*. Urbana: University of Illinois Press.

Kalat, James W. (1992) *Biological Psychology*. Belmont, Calif.: Wadsworth.

Kepes, Gyorgy, ed. (1966) *Sign Image Symbol*. New York: George Braziller.

Kerwin, Ann Marie. (January 16, 1993) "Advertiser Pressure on Newspapers Is Common: Survey." *Editor & Publisher*, pp. 28–29, 39.

Kling, J.W., and Lorrin A. Riggs, eds. (1971) *Experimental Psychology*. New York: Holt, Rinehart & Winston.

Knightley, Phillip. (1975) *The First Casualty*. New York: Harcourt Brace Jovanovich.

Kobre, Kenneth. (1980) *Photojournalism: The Professionals' Approach*. Somerville: Curtin & London.

Koole, Wim. (April 1991) "Imagination Depends on Images." *Media Development*, Vol. 38, pp. 16–17.

Kovel, Joel. (1984) *White Racism*. New York: Columbia University Press.

Kozloff, Max. (1987) *The Privileged Eye: Essays on Photography*. Albuquerque: University of New Mexico Press.

Lambeth, Edmund. (1992) *Committed Journalism*. Bloomington: Indiana University Press.

Langer, Susanne K. (1960) *Philosophy in a New Key*. Cambridge: Harvard University Press.
———. (1953) *Feeling and Form: A Theory of Art*. New York: Charles Scribner's Sons.

Lester, Paul Martin. (2000) *Visual Communication Images with Messages*, 2d ed. Belmont, Calif.: Wadsworth.
———, ed. (1996) *Images that Injure Pictorial Stereotypes in the Media*. Westport: Praeger.
———. (1996) *Desktop Computing Workbook: A Guide for Using 15 Programs in Macintosh and Windows Formats*. Belmont, Calif.: Wadsworth.
———. (Summer 1994) "African-American Photo Coverage in Four U.S. Newspapers, 1937–1990," *Journalism Quarterly*, pp. 380–394.
———. (1991) *Photojournalism: An Ethical Approach*. Hillsdale, N.J.: Lawrence Erlbaum.
———, ed. (1990) *The Ethics of Photojournalism*. Durham: NPPA.

Lester, Paul Martin, and Ron Smith. (Spring 1990) "African American Photo Coverage in *Life, Newsweek* and *Time*, 1937–1988," *Journalism Quarterly*, pp. 128–136.

Lewis, Greg. (1991) *Photojournalism Content and Technique*. Dubuque, Iowa: Wm. C. Brown.

Lippmann, Walter. (1961) *Public Opinion*. New York: Macmillan.

Lodge, David. (1984) *Small World*. New York: Warner Books.

Lucie-Smith, Edward. (1981) *The Art of Caricature*. Ithaca: Cornell University Press.

Lyons, Nathan, ed. (1966) *Photographers on Photography*. Englewood Cliffs: Prentice Hall.

Marchand, Roland. (1985) *Advertising the American Dream*. Berkeley: University of California Press.

Margolin, Victor, ed. (1989) *Design Discourse History, Theory, Criticism*. Chicago: University of Chicago Press.

Mast, Gerald. (1981) *A Short History of the Movies*. Indianapolis: Bobbs Merrill.

Mattlin, Ben. (September 1, 1991) "Personal Perspective: An Open Letter to Jerry Lewis: The Disabled Need Dignity, Not Pity," *Los Angeles Times*, p. M3.

McBride, Stewart, ed. (1992) *Ethics, Copyright, and the Bottom Line*. Camden: Center for Creative Imaging.

McCafferty, James D. (1990) *Human and Machine Vision Computing Perceptual Organization*. New York: Ellis Horwood.

Meggs, Philip. (1983) *A History of Graphic Design*. New York: Van Nostrand Reinhold.

Moeller, Susan. (1989) *Shooting War Photography and the American Experience of Combat*. New York: Basic Books.

Monaco, James. (1977) *How to Read a Film*. New York: Oxford University Press.

Monmonier, Mark. (1989) *Maps with the News*. Chicago: University of Chicago Press.

Moog, Carol. (1990) "Are They Selling Her Lips?" *Advertising and Identity*. New York: William Morrow.

Morgan, John, and Peter Welton. (1992) *See What I Mean?* London: Edward Arnold.

Mueller, Conrad G., and Mae Rudolph. (1972) *Light and Vision*. New York: Time–Life Books.

Nelson, Roy. (1991) *Publication Design*. Dubuque, Iowa: Wm. C. Brown.

O'Connor, John, ed. (1985) *American History, American Television*. New York: Frederick Unger.

O'Neal, Hank. (1976) *A Vision Shared*. New York: St. Martin's Press.

O'Neill, Michael. (1986) *Terrorist Spectaculars: Should TV Coverage Be Curbed?* New York: Priority Press.

Ohrn, Karin. (1980) *Dorothea Lange and the Documentary Tradition*. Baton Rouge: Louisiana State University Press.

Oliphant, Dave, and Thomas Zigal, eds. (1982) *Perspectives on Photography*. Austin: Humanities Research Center.

Paivio, Allan. (1971) *Imagery and Verbal Processes*. New York: Holt, Rinehart & Winston.

Parker, D.M., and J.B. Deregowski. (1990) *Perception and Artistic Style*. Amsterdam: North–Holland.

Pearce, Frank, "How to Be Immoral and Ill, Pathetic and Dangerous, All at the Same Time: Mass Media and the Homosexual." In Cohen, Stanley, and Jock Young, eds. (1973) *The Manufacture of News*, pp. 284–301. Newbury Park, CA: Sage Publications, Inc.

Petty, Richard, and John Cacioppo. (1981) *Attitudes and Persuasion: Classic and Contemporary Approaches.* Dubuque, Iowa: Wm. C. Brown.

Phelan, John M. (April 1991) "Image Industry Erodes Political Space." *Media Development,* Vol. 38, pp. 6–8.

Pollack, Peter. (1977) *The Picture History of Photography.* New York: Harry N. Abrams.

Prichard, Peter. (1987) *The Making of McPaper.* Kansas City: Andrews & McMeel.

Prida, Dolores, and Susan Ribner. "A Feminist View of the 100 Books about Puerto Ricans." In *Racism and Sexism in Children's Books.* (1976) New York: Council on Interracial Books for Children, pp. 42–48.

Reaves, Wendy. (1990) *Oliphant's Presidents.* Kansas City: Andrews & McMeel.

Richards, Stan. (1974) *Hobo Signs.* New York: Barlenmir House.

Rickards, Maurice. (1979) *Posters of Protest and Revolution.* New York: Walker & Co.

Ritchin, Fred. (1990) *In Our Own Image: The Coming Revolution in Photography.* New York: Aperture Foundation.

———. (1992) "An Image-Based Society." In *Ethics, Copyright, and the Bottom Line.* Camden: Center for Creative Imaging, pp. 19–35.

Rivera, Carla. (February 18, 1993) "Troops, LAPD Stage Riot Exercise." *Los Angeles Times,* pp. A3, A28.

Rose, Brian, ed. (1985) *TV Genres.* Westport: Greenwood Press.

Rosen, Marvin, and David DeVries. (1993) *Photography.* Belmont, Calif.: Wadsworth.

Rosenberg, Howard. (February 15, 1993) "A Tabloid Pattern of Behavior at NBC." *Los Angeles Times,* pp. F1, F12.

Rossotti, Hazel. (1983) *Colour.* Princeton: Princeton University Press.

Rothstein, Arthur. (1965) *Photojournalism.* New York: American Photographic Book Publishing Co.

Saint-Martin, Fernande. (1990) *Semiotics of Visual Language.* Bloomington: Indiana University Press.

Schiller, Dan. (1981) *Objectivity and the News.* Philadelphia: University of Pennsylvania Press.

Schudson, Michael. (1978) *Discovering the News: A Social History of American Newspapers.* New York: Basic Books.

Schwartz, Dona. (1991) "To Tell the Truth: Codes of Objectivity in Photojournalism." *Paper presented at the 74th annual convention of the AEJMC,* August 7–10, 1991. Boston.

Sculley, John. (1992) "Computers, Communications and Content," in *Ethics, Copyright, and the Bottom Line.* Camden: Center for Creative Imaging, pp. 15–21.

Sebeok, Thomas A. (1991) *Semiotics in the United States.* Bloomington: Indiana University Press.

Shepard, Roger N. (1990) *Mind Sights, Original Visual Illusions, Ambiguities, and Other Anomalies.* New York: W.H. Freeman.

Shurkin, Joel. (1984) *Engines of the Mind: A History of the Computer.* New York: W.W. Norton.

Sontag, Susan. (1978) *On Photography.* New York: Farrar, Straus & Giroux.

Spigel, Lynn. (1992) *Make Room for TV.* Chicago: University of Chicago Press.

Sterling, Christopher, and John Kittross. (1978) *Stay Tuned: A Concise History of American Broadcasting.* Belmont, Calif.: Wadsworth.

Bibliography

Stoops, Jack, and Jerry Samuelson. (1983) *Design Dialogue*. Worcester: Davis Publications.

Stroebel, Leslie, Hollis Todd, and Richard Zakia. (1980) *Visual Concepts for Photographers*. New York: Focal Press.

Szarkowski, John. (1980) *The Photographer's Eye*. New York: Museum of Modern Art.

Thiel, Philip. (1981) *Visual Awareness and Design*. Seattle: University of Washington Press.

Thorpe, James. (1975) *The Gutenberg Bible*. San Marino, Calif.: Huntington Library.

Tuchman, Gaye. (1978) *Making News*. New York: The Free Press.

Tufte, Edward. (1990) *Envisioning Information*. Cheshire: Graphics Press.

———. (1983) *The Visual Display of Quantitative Information*. Cheshire: Graphics Press.

Tumulty, Karen. (March 2, 1993) "Clinton Bashes Lobbyists, But They Like It Just Fine." *Los Angeles Times*, p. A5.

Van Loon, Hendrik. (1937) *Observations on the Mystery of Print*. New York: Book Manufacturers' Institute.

Veneto, Ponzano. (February 17, 1993) "The True Colors of Luciano Benetton." *Washington Post*, p. B1.

Vestergaard, Torben, and Kim Schrøder. (1985) *The Language of Advertising*. Oxford: Basil Blackwell.

Wade, Nicholas. (1990) *Visual Allusions: Pictures of Perception*. London: Lawrence Erlbaum.

Weale, R.A. (1982) *Focus on Vision*. Cambridge: Harvard University Press.

Welling, William. (1978) *Photography in America: The Formative Years 1839–1900*. New York: Thomas Y. Crowell.

Wilcox, Dennis, Phillip Ault, and Warren Agee. (1992) *Public Relations Strategies and Tactics*. New York: HarperCollins.

Wilk, Max. (1976) *The Golden Age of Television*. New York: Delacorte.

Willis, Jim. (1991) *The Shadow World Life Between the News Media and Reality*. New York: Praeger.

Wisan, Joseph. (1965) *The Cuban Crisis as Reflected in the New York Press (1895–1898)*. New York: Octagon Books.

Wood, Richard, ed. (1990) *Film and Propaganda in America*. New York: Greenwood Press.

Worth, Sol. (1981) *Studying Visual Communication*. Philadelphia: University of Pennsylvania Press.

Wyver, John. (1989) *The Moving Image*. Oxford: Basil Blackwell.

Yoakam, Richard, and Charles Cremer. (1989) *ENG: Television News and the New Technology*. Carbondale: Southern Illinois University Press.

INDEX

335

Index